ACCOUNTING IN ASIA

RESEARCH IN ACCOUNTING IN EMERGING ECONOMIES

Series Editors: Mathew Tsamenyi and Shahzad Uddin

Recent Volumes:

Volume 1:	Research in Third World Accounting – Edited by R. S. Olusegun Wallace
Volume 2:	Research in Third World Accounting – Edited by R. S. Olusegun Wallace
Volume 3:	Research in Accounting in Emerging Economies – Edited by R. S. Olusegun Wallace
Supplement 1:	Accounting and Development – A Special Case for Africa – Edited by R. S. Olusegun Wallace and Shabani Nzinge (Guest Editor)
Volume 4:	Research in Accounting in Emerging Economies – Edited by R. S. Olusegun Wallace, John M. Samuels, Richard J. Briston and Shahrokh M. Saudagaran
Volume 5:	Research in Accounting in Emerging Economies – Edited by R. S. Olusegun Wallace, John M. Samuels, Richard J. Briston and Shahrokh M. Saudagaran
Volume 6:	Accounting and Accountability in Emerging and Transition Economies – Edited by Trevor Hopper and Zahirul Hoque (Guest Editors)
Volume 7:	Accounting, Banking and Corporate Financial Management in Emerging Economies – Edited by Victor Murinde (Guest Editor)
Volume 8:	Corporate Governance in Less Developed and Emerging Economies – Edited by Mathew Tsamenyi and Shahzad Uddin
Volume 9:	Accounting in Emerging Economies – Edited by Mathew Tsamenyi and Shahzad Uddin
Volume 10:	Research in Accounting in Emerging Economies – Edited by Mathew Tsamenyi and Shahzad Uddin

RESEARCH IN ACCOUNTING IN EMERGING ECONOMIES
VOLUME 11

ACCOUNTING IN ASIA

EDITED BY

S. SUSELA DEVI
Faculty of Business and Accountancy,
University of Malaya, Malaysia

KEITH HOOPER
Faculty of Business and Law, Auckland
University of Technology, New Zealand

Emerald

United Kingdom – North America – Japan
India – Malaysia – China

Emerald Group Publishing Limited
Howard House, Wagon Lane, Bingley BD16 1WA, UK

First edition 2011

British Library Cataloguing in Publication Data
A catalogue record for this book is available from the British Library

ISBN: 978-1-78052-444-3
ISSN: 1479-3563 (Series)

Emerald Group Publishing
Limited, Howard House,
Environmental Management
System has been certified by
ISOQAR to ISO 14001:2004
standards

Awarded in recognition of
Emerald's production
department's adherence to
quality systems and processes
when preparing scholarly
journals for print

INVESTOR IN PEOPLE

CONTENTS

LIST OF CONTRIBUTORS

Modar Abdullatif	Middle East University, Amman, Jordan
Orhan Akisik	Isenberg School of Management, University of Massachusetts, Amherst, MA, USA
Yu-Shan Chang	Tamkang University, Taipei, Taiwan
Wuchun Chi	National Chengchi University, Taipei, Taiwan
S. Susela Devi	University of Malaya, Malaysia
Simon S. Gao	Napier University Business School, Edinburgh, UK
Keith Hooper	Auckland University of Technology, New Zealand
Long-Jainn Hwang	National Chengchi University, Taipei, Taiwan
Guangyou Liu	Sun Yat-sen Business School, Sun Yat-sen University, Guangdong, China
Sherliza Puat Nelson	International Islamic University Malaysia, Malaysia
Afzalur Rashid	University of Southern Queensland, Australia
Hong Ren	Sun Yat-sen Business School, Sun Yat-sen University, Guangdong, China
Min-Jeng Shiue	National Taipei University, Taipei, Taiwan

Siti Norwahida Shukeri	Universiti Malaysia Perlis, Malaysia
Walid Siam	Hashemite University, Zarqa, Jordan
Jinyu Zhu	Yunnan University of Finance & Economics, Kunming, P.R. China

LIST OF REVIEWERS

Ratnam Alagiah
University of South Australia,
Australia

Jahangir Ali
Latrobe University, Australia

S. Susela Devi
University of Malaya, Malaysia

Charles Elad
University of Westminster

Keith Hooper
Auckland University of
Technology, New Zealand

Zahirul Hoque
Latrobe University,
Australia

Che Ruhana Isa
University of Malaya, Malaysia

Orthodoxia Kyriacou
Middlesex
University, UK

Keith Maunders
Universities of Hull and Fiji

Saadiah Munir
University of Malaya, Malaysia

Venancio Tauringana
University of Bournemouth, UK

Mathew Tsamenyi
Birmingham Business School,
University of Birmingham, UK

Shahzad Uddin
Essex Business School,
University of Essex, UK

Prem Yapa
RMIT, Melbourne, Australia

ABOUT THE VOLUME

Research on accounting in Asia has continued to focus on corporate governance issues since the Asian financial crisis in 1997 and the major corporate scandals since 2000. Furthermore, as most Asian countries have announced their intentions to converge by 2011 and 2012 to a single set of global financial reporting standards, corporate governance reforms are also converging. However, the debate is growing as to whether true convergence is achievable. Generally, there is consensus that sharing rules is not a sufficient condition to create a common business language. Clearly, management incentives and national institutional factors play an important role in framing financial reporting quality. This in particular has made corporate governance reforms, implemented in a coordinated effort by all key stakeholders in the financial reporting process, an essential element of enhancing the financial reporting regime.

The papers in the volume are entwined and interlinked by the central concern for corporate governance and financial reporting quality. Overall, the volume advances the debate on implementation issues and theoretical considerations. Emerging countries in Asia are contemplating full convergence with the International Financial Reporting Standards because they believe that convergence to a single set of global financial reporting standards will enhance financial reporting quality and lead to lower cost of capital. Mirroring these practical concerns, it is hoped that readers will find the papers insightful in terms of theoretical development, practices and policy implications.

INTRODUCTION TO ACCOUNTING IN ASIA

ABSTRACT

Purpose – *This paper introduces the special issue on accounting in Asia. It summarises and reflects on themes and findings emerging from the papers in this volume.*

Design/Methodology/Approach – *The findings reported in the paper are based on desk research and review of the papers contained in the volume.*

Findings – *The papers evidence that corporate governance and financial reporting quality are interlinked. Accounting in Asia is preoccupied with the corporate governance–financial reporting quality nexus in the face of convergence with International Financial Reporting Standards (IFRS).*

Research limitations/Implications – *Policy makers in Asian countries need to develop appropriate regulatory mechanisms to address cultural issues, namely, attitudes towards secrecy and fraud, to ensure effective implementation of IFRS. This entails sound grounding in ethics and integrity within the financial reporting stakeholder community. Additionally, unintended consequences of fair value application need to be examined in the Asian context.*

Originality/Value of paper – *This paper is a summary of seven studies in Asia. The studies highlight critical issues emerging from Asia's experience with corporate governance reforms and the move to IFRS convergence, and set the agenda for future research in accounting in Asia, specifically, and emerging economies, generally.*

Increasingly, countries are converging to a single set of global financial reporting standards. Similarly, corporate governance reforms are also converging. Thus far, mixed results are evident as to whether true convergence is achievable (Peng & Bewley, 2010). Jeanjean and Stolowy (2008) confirm that sharing rules is not a sufficient condition to create a common business language. It is clear that management incentives and national institutional factors play an important role in framing financial reporting quality. It is envisaged that an enhanced corporate governance regime will go hand in hand with an enhanced financial reporting regime, under a coordinated effort by all key stakeholders in the financial reporting process (Melis & Carta, 2010).

Fair Accounting Value (FVA), culture and ethics emerge as research areas, where improved governance structures may impact on financial reporting to yield higher quality reports and therefore facilitate investor confidence. How governance and reporting can be improved is therefore the focus of the papers presented in this special issue.

This special issue hopes to provide a platform for scholars to share insights on accounting in Asia. Corporate governance has received much attention over the last two decades, partly due to the 1997–1998 Asian financial crisis, the collapse of Enron and other corporate failures. Researchers continue to focus on corporate governance and financial reporting quality issues in Asia. Hence, the seven papers in this volume are entwined and interlinked by the central concern for corporate governance and financial reporting quality. We believe the special issue is timely given the increasing momentum with which emerging economies in Asia are adopting the IFRS in the belief that convergence to a single set of global financial reporting standards will enhance financial reporting quality and lead to lower cost of capital.

The seven papers in this volume focus on the corporate governance–financial reporting quality nexus. Six papers are based on a single country context, one each from Bangladesh (Rashid), Jordan (Siam and Abdullatif), Malaysia (Puat Nelson and Shukeri), Taiwan (Chang, Chi, Hwang and Shiue) and two from China (Liu and Ren; Zhu and Gao), whilst the seventh paper (Akisik) discusses 29 emerging economies of which 9 are from Asia (China, Hong Kong, India, Indonesia, Korean Republic, Malaysia, Philippines, Taiwan and Thailand) and the remaining 20 encompass Argentina, Brazil, Bulgaria, Chile, Colombia, Czech Republic, Estonia, Greece, Hungary, Lithuania, Mexico, Poland, Romania, Russia, Slovakia, Slovenia, South Africa, Turkey, Ukraine and Venezuela.

The methods adopted are varied. Four papers use qualitative methods whilst the remaining three are quantitative. The methods adopted reflect the need for scholars to consider qualitative methods to illuminate local nuances and peculiarities in the Asian context.

Rashid explicates the key institutional forces reinforcing corporate governance practices in Bangladesh. The Bangladesh experience highlights the importance of institutional regulatory and enforcement regimes as well as isomorphic pressures to enhance corporate governance practices in Asia.

Liu and Ren discuss the Chinese attempt to adapt the International Federation of Accountants (IFAC) Code of Ethics. They use a content analysis approach to compare the IFAC and the Chinese Code. They conclude that a full convergence to the IFAC Code is not practicable given the Chinese culture. The paper reveals potential tensions that may arise as emerging countries, specifically in Asia, attempt to align their ethical framework to a principles based one from a traditionally rigid and legalistic culture. This echoes the concern, raised by many researchers, on the move by many countries around the world to converge to IFRS (Hail, Leuz, & Wysocki, 2009). The paper raises a significant issue on ethics; the need to align and converge ethical standards is paramount as countries in Asia move to IFRS convergence.

Zhu and Gao investigate the nature and type of fraudulent financial reporting methods adopted by Chinese listed companies. Their paper provides deeper understanding of corporate behaviour and management fraud. The study adopts a descriptive approach, analysing 182 punishment bulletins and a sample of 83 cases during the period 2002–2006. It is observed that some frauds continue for long periods. This raises concern and questions the efficacy of Chinese corporate governance mechanisms as well as the regulatory environment. As mentioned earlier, convergence to full adoption of IFRS requires a strengthened regulatory regime, with enforcement powers granted to the Chinese Securities Regulation Commission. This goes hand in hand with the enforcement of a Code of Ethics that is suitably aligned to an IFRS principles-based framework as discussed in Liu and Ren. However, it is noted that Chinese corporate governance mechanisms were strengthened in 2007 and examination of post-2007 corporate behaviour will be useful to evidence the efficacy of the enhanced corporate governance regime.

Puat Nelson and Shukeri provide evidence on the enhanced Malaysian corporate governance regime after 2007. Whilst closely linked to the subject of financial reporting quality, they examine the audit report timeliness of Malaysian listed companies in 2009 and examine the association between this and selected corporate governance characteristics.

On a similar vein, Chang, Chi, Huang and Shue examine the association between related-party transactions, CEO duality and audit quality. Audit quality in this case is proxied by auditors giving a going concern opinion for a sample of financially distressed companies. Interestingly, their evidence is drawn from data of both public-listed and privately held companies. They provide useful insights on how corporate governance mechanisms function differently between public and private companies.

Siam and Abdullatif examine Jordanian bankers' perceptions regarding the implementation of FVA. Their paper raises concerns for the profession and policy makers in emerging countries to ensure the implementation of FVA is addressed in a holistic manner to avoid unintended economic consequences. This call echoes the trepidations in the United States in converging to IFRS (Hail et al., 2009).

Lastly, Akisik examines the association between efficient management of shareholder value and countrywide components of stakeholder governance in 29 emerging economies, of which 9 are in Asia. The major aspects of stakeholder governance examined in this paper are corporate social responsibility, employment and customer satisfaction. The paper provides support for the view that companies that focus on meeting expectations of their stakeholders will ultimately enhance their shareholder value.

Whilst these papers do not provide a coherent accounting of accounting in Asia, they are related in many ways. The underlying concern is with improving financial reporting quality through enhanced corporate governance mechanisms, convergence to IFRS and ethical codes of conduct. A number of significant implications emerge. Firstly, the papers serve as a wake up call to policy makers in Asian countries, specifically, and emerging economies, generally, to develop appropriate regulatory mechanisms to address cultural issues, namely, attitudes towards secrecy and fraud, to ensure effective implementation of IFRS.

Secondly, FVA, which is imbued in IFRS, entails a fair amount of subjectivity and necessitates the exercise of professional judgement. This calls for sound grounding in ethics and integrity within the financial reporting stakeholder community.

Thirdly, unintended consequences of fair value application need to be examined in the Asian context. Given the different business and institutional context within which Asia operates, the application of FVA needs to be managed cautiously and gradually. A holistic approach encompassing all stakeholders in the financial reporting value chain needs to be adopted. The Asian context differs significantly from more advanced western economies by its predominantly relationship-based capitalism and cultural idiosyncrasies.

We conclude this review by identifying five research gaps that could possibly provide directions for future research. Firstly, extant literature has not shown whether banks, institutional investors or equity analysts take any active role in enhancing corporate governance in Asian countries. We believe the overall development of a country's financial system may affect the degree to which corporations are subject to market discipline and experience corporate governance pressures.

Secondly, extensive government involvement in corporate Asia provides opportunities to examine the application of extant finance theories, such as free cash flow and contracting theories in financing and investment decisions, and to investigate the moderating effects of corporate governance mechanisms thereon and the implications for adoption of a set of global financial reporting standards.

Thirdly, little is known thus far about how corporate governance effectiveness in Asia varies with the stage of adoption of IFRS. Has adoption of IFRS led to enhancement of corporate governance practices or vice versa?

Fourthly, there is also limited evidence on the interaction between corporate governance and public governance. This is particularly relevant given the political economy of the region. Listed companies' corporate governance practices are likely to be influenced by the rules, in particular how and to what degree the rules are enforced. There is limited evidence on how corporate governance practices of a country are shaped by the quality and the integrity of its government and its regulatory policies.

Lastly, whilst empirical corporate governance research has advanced significantly in Asia, the relationships between institutional frameworks, financial market development, firm behaviour and firm financing structures are unclear. Furthermore, it will be useful to have more evidence of the link between growth (economic development) and corporate governance (Globerman, Peng, & Shapiro, 2011). Whilst it is observed that economic growth is slow in countries with weak institutions, which provide weak protection of property rights for investors or fail to constrain corruption and self-interested politicians and their elites, the evidence on the link between corporate governance and growth is not clear. Evidence of this relationship will go a long way to convince policy makers in emerging economies to seriously implement corporate governance reforms and ensure appropriate mechanisms to assess the efficacy of IFRS convergence.

ACKNOWLEDGEMENTS

We are grateful to the authors who contributed papers to the volume. We sincerely thank all the referees for contributing their time and expertise by conducting their meticulous reviews in a timely manner. We are also grateful to Emma Wakefield and Gareth Bell of Emerald Group Publishing for their assistance in bringing this volume to fruition. We also thank Mritunjai Sahai of MPS Limited, Chennai, India, for his support and encouragement in editing the volume. Finally, we thank Shahzad Uddin, Mathew Tsamenyi and Shahrokh M. Saudagaran for giving us the opportunity to edit the volume.

REFERENCES

Globerman, S., Peng, M. W., & Shapiro, D. M. (2011). Corporate governance and Asian companies. *Asia Pacific Journal of Management, 28,* 1–14.

Hail, L., Leuz, C., & Wysocki, P. (2009). Global accounting convergence and the potential adoption of IFRS by the United States: An analysis of economic and policy factors. A Research Report to FASB. Electronic copy available from http://ssrn.com/abstract=1357331.

Jeanjean, T., & Stolowy, H. (2008). Do accounting standards matter? An exploratory analysis of earnings management before and after IFRS adoption. *Journal of Accounting and Public Policy, 27*(6), 480–494.

Melis, A., & Carta, S. (2010). Does accounting regulation enhance corporate governance? Evidence from the disclosure of share-based remuneration. *Journal of Management and Governance, 14,* 435–446.

Peng, S., & Bewley, K. (2010). Adaptability to fair value accounting in an emerging economy: A case study of China's IFRS convergence. *Accounting, Auditing & Accountability Journal, 28*(8), 982–1011.

S. Susela Devi
Keith Hooper

CORPORATE GOVERNANCE IN BANGLADESH: A QUEST FOR THE ACCOUNTABILITY OR LEGITIMACY CRISIS? ☆

Afzalur Rashid

ABSTRACT

Purpose – *This study aims at presenting an overview, development, and process of current corporate governance practices in Bangladesh.*

Design/Methodology/Approach – *Based on New Institutional Sociology (NIS) as a theoretical framework and by using archival data, this study highlights the roles of key institutional forces in reinforcing the existing corporate governance practices in Bangladesh.*

Findings – *This study notes that corporate governance practices in Bangladesh are still at infancy. While Bangladesh is trying to adopt many international corporate governance best practices for institutional legitimacy, the weak institutional enforcement regime, along with the absence of an effective check and balance, poses serious challenges to the firm-level good corporate governance practices in Bangladesh.*

☆ This study is based on my Ph.D. thesis completed at the University of Wollongong, Australia.

Accounting in Asia
Research in Accounting in Emerging Economies, Volume 11, 1–34
Copyright © 2011 by Emerald Group Publishing Limited
All rights of reproduction in any form reserved
ISSN: 1479-3563/doi:10.1108/S1479-3563(2011)0000011006

1

The absence of isomorphic pressures to regulate the firms leads to many incidences of noncompliance.

Practical implications – *This study takes part in the following global debate: whether corporate governance in an emerging economy is a reality or an illusion.*

Originality/Value – *This study seeks to contribute to the increasing literature by recognizing the interest of readers, academics, practitioners, and regulators to gain more insight and understanding of corporate governance practices in an emerging economy, such as Bangladesh.*

Keywords: Bangladesh; compliance; corporate governance; culture; law; new institutional sociology

INTRODUCTION

Both the *pull* effect, such as international development of corporate governance practices following the mega corporate collapses and scandals that broke out around the world in the early 2000s (in particular, the collapse of Enron, WorldCom, and HIH Insurance), "Asian Financial Crisis" in 1997, and the *push* effect, such as an increased interest in corporate governance practices in Bangladesh by international donor agencies, such as Asian Development Bank (ADB), International Monetary Fund (IMF), World Bank, and other international donor agencies along with the speculative event in the Bangladesh stock market in 1996, give rise to the corporate governance debate in Bangladesh. The "Global Corporate Governance Forum," an IFC multidonor trust fund facility, argues that corporate governance is a powerful tool to battle against poverty (World Bank, 2007). In the context of Bangladesh, it is so warrant that the World Bank has imposed conditions requiring the improvement of corporate governance practices in order to get financial assistance (Solaiman, 2006). The choice of Bangladesh for this study is important to the accounting and business community as Bangladesh is ranked 57th among the largest economies in the world (World Bank, 2009). Its economic freedom scored 53, making its economy the 130th freest economy in 2011 (Index of Economic Freedom, 2011). Despite these facts, Bangladesh is one of the world's poorest and most densely populated nations; weak institutions, poverty, and corruption undermine economic development and fuel social and political unrest (Index of Economic Freedom, 2011).

Given the increased interest in corporate governance practices in Bangladesh, this study aims at contributing to the growing literature by providing an insight and understanding of current corporate governance practices in Bangladesh. An earlier study (Uddin & Choudhury, 2008) provided an account of corporate governance practices in Bangladesh and noted that a traditionalist/family culture mediates the rationalist/legalistic regulatory process of corporate governance in Bangladesh. In a recent study, Siddiqui (2010) investigated the development of corporate governance codes/ regulations in Bangladesh and concluded that Bangladesh adopted the donor-prescribed codes of corporate governance due to legitimacy threats rather than efficiency reasons (p. 254). This study differs from earlier studies in terms of theoretical, methodological, and contextual approach. By using archival data, such as academic literature, newspaper reports, publications of relevant authority including the web pages of the key institutions, revisions of relevant laws and legislations, and the disclosure documents of listed companies, this study presents the roles of key institutional forces (isomorphic pressures) in reinforcing the existing corporate governance practices in Bangladesh. The prime motivation of this study is to seek the improvements in the regulatory process to bring accountability in the Bangladesh corporate sector. This paper adopts new institutional sociology (NIS) as theoretical foundation and as a means of understanding the weaknesses of the conformance and legitimization process. This study asks some key questions: Are the corporations in Bangladesh following the authoritative guidelines (good corporate governance practices) to be good corporate citizens? Are the institutions (regulatory bodies) in a position to exert pressures on the corporations to follow the authoritative guidelines; or, are the companies facing pressures from the institutions (regulatory bodies), which they rely on, to legitimize their existence? Are the corporations in Bangladesh imitating each other in their field (the good corporate governance practices of one firm being followed by others) to be more legitimate or successful? And, does culture have any relevance with respect to how corporate governance is exercised in Bangladesh? This study noted that many of the institutional reforms and corporate governance changes occurred due to isomorphic pressures from donor agencies. However, subsequent institutional failures in reinforcing isomorphic pressures on the corporations to follow the authoritative guidelines and the absence of the culture of care by the principal players led to many incidences of noncompliance.

The remainder of this study is organized as follows: the second section provides the theoretical foundation; the third section presents an overview of corporate governance in Bangladesh; the fourth section presents the key institutions insisting the corporate governance practices in Bangladesh; the fifth section presents the legal systems, which exert great influence in framing corporate governance practices of a country; the sixth section presents corporate control mechanisms in Bangladesh; and the seventh section presents the firm-level corporate governance practices in Bangladesh. The final section has the discussion and draws a conclusion.

THEORETICAL FOUNDATION: NEW INSTITUTIONAL SOCIOLOGY

This study is drawn on new institutional sociology (hereinafter referred to as NIS) as the theoretical foundation which is concerned with the processes by which schemes, rules, norms, and routines become established as authoritative guidelines for social behavior (DiMaggio & Powell, 1983, 1991; Meyer & Rowan, 1977; Scott, 2005). This theory suggests that organizational survival is subject to some form of conformity to prevailing values or standards for appropriate behavior (Fogarty, 1996). Organizations adopt such behavior and norms in response to market and institutional pressures and to legitimize their existence; firms under the influence of legitimization effects will adopt similar structures through a process called *institutional isomorphism* (DiMaggio & Powell, 1983, 1991; Meyer & Rowan, 1977).

The process of *institutional isomorphic* change may occur in three ways: *coercive isomorphism*, *mimetic isomorphism*, and *normative isomorphism* (DiMaggio & Powell, 1983, p. 150). "*Coercive isomorphism* occurs from both the formal and informal pressures exerted on companies by other organizations upon which they are dependent and by cultural expectations in the society within which organizations function … in some circumstances, organizational change is a direct response to government mandate: manu-facturers adopt new pollution control technologies to conform to environ-mental regulations; nonprofits maintain accounts, and hire accountants, in order to meet tax law requirements; and organizations employ affirmative-action officers to fend off allegations of discrimination" (DiMaggio & Powell, 1983, p. 150). The state, in its own right or through the delegation of its powers, becomes a central force in the coercion of organizations through its control over resources (Fogarty, 1996). *Mimetic isomorphism* occurs due to uncertainty and "organizations tend to model themselves after similar organizations in their field that they perceive to be more legitimate or successful" (DiMaggio & Powell, 1983, p. 152). Finally, *normative isomorphism* stems from pressures or intervention by professional groups. "In addition, in many cases, professional power is as much assigned by the state as it is created by the activities of the professions" (DiMaggio & Powell, 1983, p. 152). Professionals do so to legitimate themselves by providing their expertise and widely held values (Abbott, 1988). Professionals are also believed to inject a particular moral order as part of their adherence to a code of professional ethics (Fogarty & Rogers, 2005).

NIS perspectives have been extensively used in explaining the accounting and corporate governance phenomena in the literature. Tsamenyi, Cullen, María, and González (2006, p. 410) argue that "NIS is particularly relevant for analyzing organizations that are confronted with uncertainties and, as a result, compete for political and institutional legitimacy and market position." The fulfillment of institutional isomorphism lends legitimacy to organizations, which enables them to continue their operations (see Mir & Rahaman, 2005). As noted in this paper, Bangladesh went through many corporate governance reforms with the help of donor agencies to increase the institutional capabilities and legitimacy; the choice of NIS would appropriately be fitted in exploring the intuitional capability in reinforcing corporate governance practices within the listed firms in Bangladesh (interplay between the firms and on which the firms are dependent) as well as a means of understanding toward the weaknesses of conformance and legitimization process.

CORPORATE GOVERNANCE IN BANGLADESH: AN OVERVIEW

The development of corporate governance in Bangladesh is relatively new. The establishment of Dhaka Stock Exchange (DSE) in 1954 was an important landmark on corporate activity in Bangladesh. The then Companies Act 1913, passed in British Parliament, was the existing law for company governance. The trading at DSE remained suspended during the nine-month liberation war in 1971. Soon after the independence, the activities of DSE, the symbol of capitalism, were suspended again as Bangladesh adopted socialism as the economic and political framework to ensure the so-called *economic justice* or *distributive justice*.[1] Socialism was constitutionally accepted as one of the four fundamental principles of the state. Government of Bangladesh in an order (the Bangladesh Government Nationalization Order 1972) nationalized all large- and medium-sized industries including the banking and insurance sectors. Application of the Companies Act 1913 was suspended. However, socialism and the nationalization policy in Bangladesh failed. It is alleged that the biggest public failure in Bangladesh was in the state-owned enterprises (SOEs) due to corruption, mismanagement, and lack of effective monitoring, and thereby huge accumulated losses (World Bank, 1995, p. 89); the losses of those enterprises consumed 30% of annual project aid (Uddin & Hopper, 2003). Bangladesh reentered into the market economy following the change of regime in 1975. The new regime adopted the privatization policy with the hope of greater economic efficiency, superior firm performance, and promotion of capital market development. The DSE resumed its operation in 1976 only with nine (9) listed companies.

Due to increased interest in corporate governance practices in Bangladesh by international donor agencies, such as ADB, IMF, and World Bank, in mid-1990s, various corporate governance reforms were initiated with the support of them (Uddin & Choudhury, 2008; Uddin & Hopper, 2003). Securities and Exchange Commission Bangladesh (SECB) was established as a corporate watchdog (authoritative body) in 1993 under the "Securities and Exchange Commission Act 1993" to administer and enforce the securities laws and legislations. The Companies Act 1913 was repealed and the Companies Act 1994 was enacted. The Chittagong Stock Exchange (CSE), the country's second stock market, was established in 1995 to saturate the increased trading of securities in the market. While these reform initiatives were in process and the stock market was growing gradually, Bangladesh stock market went through a major turmoil in 1996. The existing coercive pressures for corporate governance reform from the international donor agencies along with this incident and the governance failures elsewhere boosted up the corporate governance debate in Bangladesh. Following this incident, further reform was initiated with the financial assistance of international donor agencies. The World Bank initiated the "Private Sector Infrastructure Development Project" of U.S. $235 million in 1997 (World Bank, 2005). The ADB provided various assistance[2] to take initiatives for an orderly growth of the capital market and helped to establish the institutional infrastructure necessary to sustain the capital market's long-term development including the institutional reform within the SECB (Asian Development Bank, 1997), such as automation of the stock exchanges and revising the capital market laws and regulations (Uddin & Choudhury, 2008), including the various initiatives to enhance the various supervisory capabilities of SECB and Stock Exchanges, the market intermediaries, and Investment Corporation of Bangladesh (ICB), such as market monitoring and surveillance systems, improve information gathering and train staff in investigating and prosecuting securities violations (Asian Development Bank, 1997, 2000a, 2008). In 1999, World Bank provided a grant of US $ 200,000 for the development of accounting and auditing standards in Bangladesh and the adoption of international accounting standards (IASs) in Bangladesh; SECB also received technical and financial assistance from ADB to ensure a smooth transition to the use of IASs (Mir & Rahaman, 2005). Many of these projects goals are already implemented. For example, DSE started screen-based trading in mid-1998. All price share index, which was started on September 16, 1986, was modified later conforming to the IFC regulation. "Central Depository Bangladesh Limited" (CDBL) was incorporated as a public limited company on August 20, 2000, following the concern of trading of fake shares (SECB, 2004). Credit rating was made mandatory for all initial public offerings (IPO), right and bonus issues, and issue of debt instruments by publicly listed companies through "Credit Rating Companies Rules 1996," with the first credit rating company starting its operations in April 2002. Further, to increase the investors' awareness in the capital market, the listed companies have been categorized by SECB as A, B, G, N, and Z, based on profit–loss, status of annual general meeting (AGM), and commercial operational status of the companies. The announcement of Corporate Governance Notification (CGN) is a broader step of corporate governance reform in Bangladesh. Finally, in order to train the capital market participants and intermediaries, "Bangladesh Institute of Capital Market" was established in 2008 (SECB, 2009). The chronological development of corporate governance in Bangladesh is shown in Table 1.

Table 1. Evolution of Corporate Governance in Bangladesh.

1954	Establishment of Dhaka Stock Exchange
1972	Nationalization of major industries
1977	Reentry into the market economy
1993	Establishment of Securities and Exchange Commission Bangladesh
1994	Revision of Companies Act
1995	Establishment of Chittagong Stock Exchange
1998	Automation of stock exchanges
1999	Adoption of IASs
2000	Central Depository Bangladesh Limited
2002	Credit rating for initial public offerings
2006	Corporate Governance Notification (CGN)
2008	Establishment of Bangladesh Institute of Capital Market

Reed (2002) maintains that reforms in developing countries occur due to past attempts at promoting "development" and recent processes of economic globalization, resulting in the movement of developing countries in the direction of an Anglo-American model of corporate governance. It is to be noted that due to past failures within the state-owned enterprises, international donor agencies have extended support (in the form of loan and financial assistance) and exerted isomorphic pressure for corporate governance reforms and for the adoption of international corporate governance best practices in Bangladesh, as they have powers (in the form of withholding resources or by not providing loans). DiMaggio and Powell (1983, p. 154) argue that "in cases where alternative sources are either not readily available or require effort to locate, the stronger party to the transaction can coerce the weaker party to adopt its practices in order to accommodate the stronger party's needs." Mir and Rahaman (2005) described it as the ability of providing resource or controlling organizations to influence resource-dependent organizations; due to such resource dependency, donor agencies are able to influence the field of policy making in the developing countries. Bangladesh is not an exception to this.

KEY INSTITUTIONAL FORCES

This study is drawn to evaluate the institutional capacity in reinforcing current corporate governance practices by firms. Therefore, in the next few subsections, this study presents the key institutional forces that can exert subsequent isomorphic pressure on firms.

Registrar of the Joint Stock Companies

The Registrar of the Joint Stock Companies (RJSC) is the sole authority to provide registration for a company in Bangladesh. The RJSC is also responsible for winding up procedures and dissolution of companies. Before applying for a registration, a new company is required to get the consent of SECB for registration (Solaiman, 2006). It is alleged that getting registration for a new company within a reasonable time in Bangladesh is impossible. It is not very uncommon that a bribe is to be paid by all applicants for obtaining registration within a reasonable time; otherwise, it may take months and years to get the same (Karim, 1995, p. 91). Such bribery is in fact widespread and there is severe corruption among government officials and police (Index of Economic Freedom, 2011).

RJSC is one of the sources of *coercive isomorphism*. It has the legal authority to enforce the provisions of Companies Act 1994. The RJSC, however, has no technical capacity to identify accounting and auditing violations (World Bank, 2003). Companies Act 1994 requires the companies to file a copy of the annual report including the audited accounts with the RJSC. Any member of the public limited company may apply to inspect any company's file for a small fee. RJSC is the statutory authority to penalize companies for failure to file their annual reports. RJSC, however, fails to enforce the timely filing of annual audited financial statements and there are many incidences of failure by companies to submit the required statements and returns on time (Karim, 1995; World Bank, 2003). It also has very little role in the regulation of the securities market (Solaiman, 2006). The RJSC is attached and accountable to the Ministry of Commerce.

Securities and Exchange Commission Bangladesh

The SECB is an autonomous statutory body and attached to the Ministry of Finance. SECB, the prime source of *coercive isomorphism* (sole authority to force the firms), may direct the firms to follow the schemes, rules, norms, and routines as part of good corporate governance practices. It is entitled to regulate overall activities of the capital market in Bangladesh. The SECB registers (issues licenses) and regulates the business of capital market participants and intermediaries, such as stock exchanges, stock brokers and dealers, sub-brokers, share transfers agents, merchant banks and portfolio managers, managers of issues, trustees of trust deeds, underwriters, investment advisors, and other intermediaries of the securities market. It takes steps to ensure proper issuance of securities (in compliance with the securities laws); protects the interests of the investors; promotes, develops, and maintains a fair, transparent, and efficient capital market; monitors and prohibits the fraudulent and unfair trade practices relating to securities trading in any securities market; undertakes investigations and inspections relating to any unfair practices and conducts inquiries and audits of any issuer or dealer of securities, the stock exchanges and intermediaries, and any self-regulatory organization in the securities market; and, overall, regulates the business of the stock exchange or any other securities market (SECB, 2006).

Stock Exchanges and Capital Markets

Although the Bangladesh capital market is one of the smallest in Asia, it is one of the oldest in this region. The capital market in Bangladesh was founded during the Mughal regime (commonly known as Mughal Bengal[3]) in the early 17th century. At present, there are two stock exchanges in Bangladesh: one is Dhaka Stock Exchange and the other is Chittagong Stock Exchange. Stock exchanges are other sources of *coercive isomorphism* that may direct the firms to follow the schemes, rules, norms, and routines as part of good corporate governance practices; otherwise, firms may be delisted from the stock exchanges.

The stock market development in Bangladesh is relatively new. Despite a lot of initiatives, the stock market growth at DSE during the period of 1977 through 1985 was nonsignificant. The number of listed companies in 1985 was only 69. There was a steady growth of the stock market from 1986 to 1995. However, there was an unusual growth during the period 1996 due to a speculative bubble, and Bangladesh capital market went through a major turmoil. It started following the withdrawal of "lock-in"[4] system on July 8, 1996, and the purposeful arrival of foreign institutional investors (Solaiman, 2006). It is alleged that the local brokers, agents, and company directors were involved in insider trading, market manipulations, and fraudulent activities with these foreign institutional investors, which may have contributed to the abnormal fluctuations of share price, leading to the market crash (Asian Development Bank, 2005). Although there is a provision of huge punishment (including civil liability, fines, and imprisonment) for manipulations, insider trading, and fraudulent activities under the "Securities and Exchange Ordinance 1969" and "Prohibition of Insider Trading Regulation 1995," it is alleged that the SECB was not fully equipped to cope with such a situation. The inquiry committee formed by SECB claimed that two DSE members and one SECB member were also involved in the activities with those foreign institutional investors that led to stock market collapse in 1996 (Solaiman, 2006). The Securities and Exchange Commission of Bangladesh obtained warrants of arrest against 32 people in 7 brokerage firms and 8 listed companies. But no proceeding could be carried on later because the proceedings were abandoned due to poor enforcement of the law (*The Economist*, 1997).

Professional Accounting Bodies

There are two professional accounting bodies in Bangladesh: the Institute of Chartered Accountants of Bangladesh (ICAB) and the Institute of Cost and Management Accountants of Bangladesh (ICMAB). ICAB became the member of the International Accounting Standards Board (IASB) in 1983.

ICAB prescribes separate Bangladesh Accounting Standards (BASs) and Bangladesh Standards of Auditing (BSAs). Both the accounting bodies are autonomous institutions and attached to the Ministry of Commerce.

So far, ICAB adopted twenty nine (29) BASs on the basis of forty one (41) IASs and all eight (8) International Financial Reporting Standards (IFRSs) as Bangladesh Financial Reporting Standards (BFRSs). However, BASs are heavily aligned with the European "concept and/or principles-based" as opposed to U.S. "rules-based" accounting standards (see Hoque, 2007, p. 25). ICAB also adopted thirty one (31) BSAs on the basis of thirty five (35) ISAs and four (4) Bangladesh Auditing Practice Statements (BAPSs) on the basis of thirteen (13) International Auditing Practice Statements (IAPSs).

ICAB is the sole authority for regulating the accounting profession in Bangladesh. However, it does not have direct influence (exert *coercive pressure*) on firm governance (as shown by the dotted line in Fig. 1). ICAB however, exerts *normative pressure* on firms through professional accountants who work as internal as well as external (independent) auditors to ensure that the internal control function works adequately and effectively. The listed firms are required to comply with the financial reporting practices

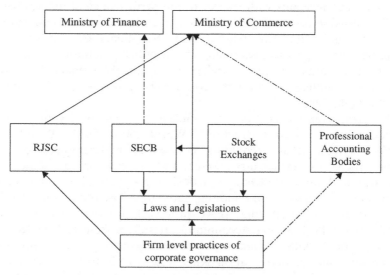

Fig. 1. Key Legal Institutions (Who are Accountable to Whom) and Their Roles on Firm-Level Corporate Governance Practices. *Source*: Partly adapted from Uddin and Choudhury (2008).

of professional accounting bodies under the provisions of various laws and legislations. Section 212 of Companies Act, 1994, allows only the members of the ICAB (chartered accountants) to act as external auditors to audit the company's financial affairs to ensure that their accounts conform to all BASs as adopted by ICAB. Therefore, there is very little role of the members of ICMAB (cost and management accountants) in company auditing.

It is argued that the work of professionals is not fully a neutral or technical exercise; institutionalized expectations surround its practice (Fogarty & Rogers, 2005); they are also subject to the same coercive and mimetic pressures as are organizations (DiMaggio & Powell, 1983, p. 152). DiMaggio and Powell (1983, p. 152) further maintain that "two aspects of professionalization are important sources of isomorphism. One is the resting of formal education and of legitimization in a cognitive base produced by university specialists; the second is the growth and elaboration of professional networks that span organizations and across which new models diffuse rapidly. Universities and professional training institutions are important centers for the development of organizational norms among professional managers and their staff." It is, however, complained that the ICAB has limited capacity to adequately function as an effective professional accountancy body; it has not yet implemented adequate quality assurance arrangements with respect to the performance of its members; it does not provide sufficient guidance to its members on how to improve the quality of audits; its "Investigation and Disciplinary Committee" is not proactive with respect to disciplining errant public practitioners; and it has no effective measures to ensure that its members maintain current professional standards through continuous professional development (World Bank, 2003).

The professional education in Bangladesh lacks quality in terms of curriculum and skilled instructions (World Bank, 2003). World Bank (2003) maintains that accounting courses at undergraduate program mainly focus on elementary topics and application of some basic standards and do not include practical application of national and/or international accounting and auditing standards. The training provided by ICAB does not meet the IFAC-proposed International Education Standards for Professional Accountants. It suffers from lack of technical and functional skills, organizational and business management skills, interpersonal and communication skills, and skills in forming professional judgments. Continuing professional education and development arrangement by ICAB is weak and lacks effective monitoring or enforcement mechanism.

LEGAL ENVIRONMENT

The corporate legal statutes in Bangladesh consists of certain acts and ordinances, numerous legislative instruments such as orders, notifications, rules, regulations, and circulars, which are issued by the government, SECB, stock exchanges, and other relevant governmental agencies. The Companies Act 1994, a law of the Ministry of Commerce, is the main statute for corporate governance in Bangladesh. Further, many notifications, orders, directives, and guidelines issued by SECB and stock exchanges are also considered to be the statutes for corporate governance in Bangladesh (Fig. 1).

Although many laws and legislations in Bangladesh originate from the sociocultural and religious guidelines, Bangladesh was a former British colony and it inherited the common legal systems based on English common law (as opposed to civil law). Although "the existence of a common legal environment affects many aspects of an organization's behavior and structure" (DiMaggio & Powell, 1991, p. 150), it provides stronger investor protection than that of civil law countries (La Porta, Lopez-de-Silanes, Shleifer, & Vishny, 1998).

However, like many emerging economies, the enforcement of law is very poor in Bangladesh as the courts are underfinanced and underresourced (see, Ararat & Ugur, 2003). In November 2007, Bangladesh separated the judiciary from the executive function of the government; however, the lower courts are considered to be part of the executive function and suffer from serious corruption (Index of Economic Freedom, 2011).

Unlike in a culture with high "uncertainty avoidance," company officials are found to prefer implicit or flexible rules or guidelines. The poor legal enforcement leads to many instances of noncompliance by firms. Common noncompliances are not holding AGM on time, nonpayment of declared dividend, nondelivery of shares, and noncompliance of securities laws. Insider trading is a common problem, which is evident in 1996 share market scandal. Due to long process of settlement, it encourages the companies to repeat the noncompliance and violations.

CORPORATE CONTROL MECHANISMS IN BANGLADESH

Unlike the firms in Anglo-American countries, firms' economic activities in Asia (particularly East, Southeast Asia and Japan) and in many continental European countries (such as Germany, Finland, and the Netherlands) are based on personal or mutual relations, outside the formal legal and institutional arrangement of "rule-based" governance, which is also known as "relationship-based capitalism" (Li, 2003; Li, Park, & Li, 2004; Wade, 2000). Bangladesh is not an exception to this. Corporate control mechanisms in Bangladesh are mostly insider (internal) oriented, such as ownership structure, as the core investors own the significant stakes of shares, which is also known as *ownership control* approach and, in general, is the board of directors (see Rashid & Lodh, 2008). These core investors have huge role in disciplining the firms and the firms keep a close relationship with them. Although the board of directors have very limited roles, they are responsible for duty of care and diligence that includes ensuring that financial controls are effective. However, similar to firms in Anglo-American countries, such financial controls are reinforced through disclosure and transparency (financial audit). The CGN can so far be considered as the "Code of Corporate Governance Best Practices" in the context of Bangladesh. CGN imitates many international (Anglo-American) corporate governance practices. Among many other requirements, it requires the listed firms to have Anglo-American type outside independent directors in their boards and an Anglo-American type audit committee, a board committee to oversee the audit functions. The noncompliance requires an explanation.

Due to highly concentrated ownership, lack of takeover regulations, a nonefficient market, and huge transaction costs associated with the takeover process, some of the important external control mechanisms, such as a market for corporate control or takeovers, are largely absent in the Bangladesh corporate sector. In the absence of a liquid capital market, other dominant control mechanisms, such as executives' compensation in the form of stock options is also absent in Bangladesh. Similar to firms in East and Southeast Asia, Japan, and many continental European countries, capital market has a little role in providing finance and there is a significant reliance on debt financing, leading to a higher corporate debt ratio. However, unlike the firms in Anglo-American countries, the primary source of corporate borrowing in Bangladesh is from banks (private debts). Public debt in the form of corporate bond is almost absent in Bangladesh corporate sector. Similar to firms in Anglo-American countries, firms' borrowing from banks is primarily short-term and banks simply keep an arm's-length relationship with their corporate clients and are not involved in monitoring activity. Thus, unlike the firms in many continental European countries, the role of banks as lender is less central and thus the ability to use debt covenants as a corporate control mechanism is absent in Bangladesh corporate sector.

Unlike the firms in Anglo-American countries, external board members (outside directors), financial analysts, and financial press and media have little role in monitoring and disciplining the firm management (see, Rashid, De Zoysa, Lodh, & Rudkin, 2010). Therefore, boards and management are not fearful of being criticized. Finally, the role of other intermediaries, such as investment banks, financial analysts, and credit rating agencies are less central in Bangladesh corporate sector.

FIRM-LEVEL PRACTICES OF CORPORATE GOVERNANCE IN BANGLADESH

The firm-level corporate governance practices are the practices of corporate governance within the listed firms. A firm's corporate governance tradition has a great influence in protecting the shareholders' rights (Baker & Kolb, 2009). It is argued that the corporate collapses in the early 2000s, such as collapse of Enron, WorldCom, and HIH Insurance, were due to the absence of firm-level corporate governance practices within the respective firms (Mardjono, 2005). As noted, Bangladesh is struggling toward the institutional sweeping change in strengthening the corporate governance practices in line with the international corporate governance best practices. Many reforms were initiated with the help of donor agencies to increase the institutional capabilities. The following paragraphs extend the firm-level practices of corporate governance in Bangladesh. The exploration of these practices aims at presenting the interplay between the firms and on which the firms are dependent. The Hofstede (1980) culture, such as "power distance," "individualism versus collectivism," "masculinity versus femininity," and "low versus high uncertainty avoidance" have some relevance to how corporate governance practices are exercised in Bangladesh. The exploration also aims at presenting any relevance that the culture has to corporate governance practices in Bangladesh. Answers to many of the key questions asked earlier in this paper are apparent from such exploration.

Corporate Ownership Structure and Control

Unlike the firms in Anglo-American countries, corporate share ownership in less-developed countries is predominately concentrated in the hands of a small number of controlling shareholders who are in fact family members and have an active interest in running a corporation (Ararat & Ugur, 2003;

Li, 2003). Bangladesh is not an exception to this. Apart from a few controlling ownership by foreign investors, government, and financial institutions, the joint stock companies in Bangladesh are mainly controlled by founding sponsors/directors who are in fact the family members, leading to a high degree of ownership control. From a sample of 107 listed nonfinancial companies, it appears that on an average, the single largest shareholder holds 29.77% shares and the top three largest shareholders hold 46.87% of the shares of the listed firms (Table 2).

As the presence of pyramidal or cross-shareholding structure is not very common in Bangladesh, individual shareholdings are also quite large. It leads to high inequality or power distance between the insiders and outsiders. Therefore, it is very hard for average noncontrolling shareholders to achieve necessary votes to pose a threat to the poorly performed company management as there is no guideline regarding the "ultimate controlling share ownership" in the Bangladesh Companies Act 1994. While insider ownership has great influence on firm economic performance, the study by Rashid (2011) in the context of Bangladesh confirmed that there is a nonlinear (or curvilinear) relationship between insider shareholding and firm's economic performance.

Although the concept of institutional shareholding came to light in Bangladesh a long time ago (following the establishment of Investment Corporation of Bangladesh (ICB) on October 1, 1976), it appears that unlike the firms in Anglo-American countries, institutional investors do not own the majority of stakes in the listed firms. The average institutional investment is only 18.33% in Bangladesh, while the Anglo-American standard is found to be 60% (Farrar, 2005, p. 339). Due to huge dominance of family shareholding, the institutional investors are not in a position to force the

Table 2. Ownership Structure Within the Listed Firms.

Shareholding Category	Mean	Minimum	Maximum
Sponsors/Directors	41.40	0	95.97
Institutions	18.33	0	57.61
Government	1.12	0	52.94
Foreigners	5.07	0	85.43
General public	34.26	0.79	81.78
Single largest shareholder	29.77	2.73	95.00
Ownership by top three shareholders	46.87	5.64	98.52

Source: Respective company annual report for the year ending 2007–2008. The largest shareholder is a single person or a single institution.

companies on behalf of their clients to improve performance, disclose voluntary information or improve their corporate governance practices, and/ or to add value to the firm. This is because they are not able to effectively narrow the gap between the ownership and control in the context of Bangladesh. All of these lead institutional investors to simply become secondary market traders, not equity partners (Uddin & Choudhury, 2008). There is also a dearth of foreign institutional investors in Bangladesh capital market (Solaiman, 2006). The flow of private institutional funds to the capital market is also very limited. There are no "pension funds" or "provident funds" in the market. The study by Rashid (2011) also confirmed that institutional shareholding has no role in influencing firm performance in Bangladesh.

Board of Directors

Bangladesh Companies Act 1994 provides the guidelines for the appoint-ment, qualifications, and disqualifications of board members (directors). However, there is no guideline in the Companies Act 1994 on the roles and responsibilities of directors and penalties for noncompliance of fiduciary duty (duty of care); there is no guideline on board composition and board leadership structure. As Bangladesh is perceived to be a society of high power distance, the less powerful accept power relations that are autocratic or paternalistic. Subordinates acknowledge the power of others based on their formal, hierarchical positions in Bangladesh. Therefore, most of the corporate decision-making power is concentrated in the hands of few persons (corporate managers who are representative of the family). Sometimes, they abuse their entrusted powers for private gains. Unlike a low individualism society, corporate directors and executives in Bangladesh place great importance on themselves, who are in turn family members, as opposed to the importance on the greater good for the organization.

The shareholders have very little role in the process of election and reelection of directors for the listed companies in Bangladesh in an AGM. It is very common that the sponsor directors manipulate the AGM so that their chosen individual can be elected (Bangladesh Enterprise Institute; 2004; Uddin & Choudhury, 2008). Sobhan and Werner (2003) noted that in about 73% of the nonbank listed companies, the boards are heavily dominated by the sponsor shareholders who generally belong to one family – the father as the chair and the son as the CEO. Due to huge family dominance in the board, the board meetings become the family meeting and the outcomes are not disclosed, making confidentiality as an excuse (Uddin & Choudhury, 2008).

Although there is no provision for shadow directors in the board, some shareholders from the family-controlled firms exercise huge powers, which reduce the effectiveness of the board. While the board of directors is expected to monitor management and give strategic guidelines, the board members of some listed companies were involved in malpractices that led to the stock market scandal in 1996 (discussed earlier).

The CGN, which is imitated from Anglo-American countries, requires the board to have at least one-tenth (or minimum one) independent directors. It may lead to high inequality (off-balance) or power distance between the inside and outside directors. The United Kingdom "Cadbury Report 1992" suggests that there should be a minimum of three nonexecutive (outside) directors in the board and the United Kingdom "Higgs Report 2003" suggests that at least half of the board members should be the nonexecutive directors.

There is no legislative definition of "independent director"; there are no legislative guidelines for their qualifications and experience and there is no stringent condition for appointing them into the board. Further, as this guideline allows the appointments of such directors by inside elected directors, there is a provision for appointing the outside independent directors into the board due to having personal close relationship with the family, existing board members, company management, and large share-holders or having some other connections that can be used for the company in the future, rather than their expertise.

The United Kingdom "Tyson Report 2003" recommends the appointment of nonexecutive directors with diversity in background, skills, and experience to enhance board effectiveness and improve stakeholders' relationship. The United Kingdom Higgs Report 2003 suggests that the independent directors should not have any "relationships or circumstances which could affect, or appear to affect, the directors' judgment." Further, the United Kingdom "Cadbury Report 1992" suggests that the independent directors should not be a former executive of a company. The "pilot study" of many companies' annual reports reveals that a number of independent directors who were appointed following the CGN were the former executive directors of the company. They managed a position in the board after changing their hat. The WorldCom's board was made up of more than 50% nonexecutive directors; however, it was ineffective as most of them were somehow the beneficiary of WorldCom (Kaplan & Kiron, 2004). Sobhan and Werner (2003) argue that the directors who would fit the definition of "independent" in Bangladesh are often current or former government officials or bureau-crats. They are appointed to help the company get licenses or as payback for previous favors. When boards need an independent opinion, they rely on employing outside consultants or advisors. Therefore, independent directors may not be able to serve as an advocate for minority shareholders or as a source of new and different ideas.

The empirical study on board composition (in the form of representation of outside independent directors) by Rashid et al. (2010) reveals that the board composition has no influence on firm economic performance in Bangladesh. Therefore, while CGN was based on explanation or compliance basis, it can be argued that many firms may not have appointed outside independent directors (imitated each other) due to uncertainty or to become more legitimate or successful.

Management and CEO

The term CEO is not a familiar concept in Bangladesh corporate sector. The Bangladesh Companies Act 1994 gives some guidelines regarding the position of the managing director who is in fact the CEO. In most of the companies, the CEOs are the representatives of the controlling shareholders or family members of the controlling shareholders. Their qualifications and expertise does not always prevail in their appointment in the firm. Therefore, there is an absence of any accountability structure of management to the board. The existing laws do not require the companies to disclose the CEO pay in the disclosure documents, despite there being an increased concern in the corporate governance literature whether the well-paid CEOs are performing well (Jensen & Murphy, 1990).

Unlike the corporate boards in many continental European countries, such as Germany, Finland, and the Netherlands (except France,[5] Spain, and the United Kingdom) and due to common law tradition (see Rose, 2005), the corporate boards in Bangladesh are one-tier boards or management boards. There is no supervisory board and both the executive and the nonexecutive directors perform duties together in one organizational layer, which is most common in Anglo-American countries. Therefore, there are some incidences of CEO duality in some listed companies in Bangladesh. The CGN requires that the office of the Chairperson of the Board and the CEO preferably be filled by two different individuals. It also leads to some incidences of CEO duality in some listed companies. While the dual-leadership structure may work well in some Anglo-American countries,[6] it may not work well in an emerging economy such as Bangladesh as the CEOs have not invested undiversified human capital (managerial talent) in a single firm (many of them have large ownership stakes within the firm). It may give enormous powers (inequality or consolidation of powers) to the CEOs, reducing the check and balances or the board's ability to exercise the governance (monitoring) function and creating a conflict between the management and the board (Solomon, 2007; Zahra, 1990). Such conflict of interest may reduce the board independence and may lead to severe problems as seen in Enron (Gillan & Martin, 2007; Solomon, 2007). The empirical study by Rashid (2010) in the context of Bangladesh reveals that dual-leadership structure (CEO duality) does not influence the firms' economic performance in Bangladesh.

Shareholders Rights

Corporate law offers several basic rights to shareholders, such as right to dividend, right to company's undivided assets, and preemptive right to subscribe additional stocks. The shareholders exercise such rights through voting for directors and on other major corporate issues in shareholders meeting, such as AGM (La Porta et al., 1998). The Bangladesh Companies Act 1994 offers several provisions for such rights. For example, Section 81 (1) requires a company to hold its first AGM within a period of not more than 18 months from the date of its incorporation. AGM of a company must also be held once per calendar year and no more than 15 months after the previous. According to Section 81 (2), a court, on application of any member of the company, may call or direct the calling of a general meeting of a company in default of holding AGM. However, unlike the corporate laws in many developed countries, there is no legislative guideline for calling a "meeting of shareholders" by shareholders. Under Section 84, a director who holds not less than 10% of the shares of a company can call for an extraordinary general meeting. Shareholders should be sent the audited accounts of the company together with directors' and auditors' reports thereon, proposed to be laid before such AGM together with the notice convening such meeting. Section 85 allows shareholders to vote and Section 106 allows them to remove the directors by passing an extraordinary resolution. Section 155 (1) (a) gives shareholders the preemptive rights to buy new shares to protect them from dilution. Section 233 gives the jurisdiction of the court in protecting the minority shareholders' right. However, many shareholders are not aware of their basic rights and lack appropriate motivation to exercise their rights (Sobhan & Werner, 2003).

Although AGM is seen as a disciplining mechanism or a forum to make the corporate management accountable (La Porta et al., 1998), such a traditional forum for disciplining corporate management is often ineffective for the publicly listed Asian corporations as only a few large shareholders dominate voting at the AGMs (Asian Development Bank, 2000b, p. 77). Bangladesh is not an exception to this. In Bangladesh, the location of AGM is decided by the directors, but should normally be at the registered office of the company, so that all the books and records are at hand. Due to space constraints, the meetings are often held in places other than the registered office (Sobhan & Werner, 2003). The shareholders often misunderstand their function as shareholders; it is noted that they are happy to attend the AGM in a nice location rather than exercising their shareholding rights in the company's management (Bangladesh Enterprise Institute, 2004).

The most important right of a shareholder is the right to vote in an AGM. In Bangladesh, shareholders are required to show up in person or send an authorized representative to the AGM to be able to vote. There is no provision to mail or e-mail their proxy vote to the firm, which makes it difficult for shareholders to exercise their voting rights. Annual meeting does not require a quorum (Bangladesh Enterprise Institute, 2004). It allows the firm management to manipulate the AGM. It is not very uncommon to change the AGM venue due to so-called "unavoidable circumstances" to discourage the shareholders to attend the AGM. Uddin and Choudhury (2008) noted that many companies' AGM venues are sometimes shifted far away from the capital city, so that the shareholders will have less incentive to attend the AGM.

Although all shareholders have the right to question in an AGM, a few shareholders are allowed to question the board of directors regarding the board's actions and activities (Bangladesh Enterprise Institute, 2004). It is noted that a few organized individuals control and disrupt the AGMs, affecting the relationship between shareholders, boards, and management (Bangladesh Enterprise Institute, 2004; Uddin & Choudhury, 2008). In order to combat with this problem, SECB requires the listed companies to submit a copy of the Annual Report and proceedings (including the unedited "Audio Visual Proceeding") of AGM to the SECB, in addition to submitting these to RJSC. However, many firms fail to comply with this.

There are provisions of penalties in the Companies Act 1994 for not holding AGM on time or nonpayment of declared dividend. However, many firms are found to hold up to five AGMs and publish financial statements of up to five consecutive years on the same day (Karim, Ahmed, & Islam, 2006). A common way to punish a company (other than the financial penalty) for aforementioned irregularities is to degrade it to "Z" category. In extreme cases, if a company fails to hold an AGM in three consecutive years and fails to pay dividend for five consecutive years, it may be delisted from the stock exchanges as per the listing rules of both the stock exchanges. However, many companies are not delisted in an excuse that the investors will suffer (Solaiman, 2006).

The most common shareholders' right is the "right to dividend." There are several incentives for payments of dividends by the companies and punitive measures for nonpayments of the same (Uddin & Choudhury, 2008). However, as noted earlier, many companies fail to hold an AGM for a number of years, let alone pay the dividends, and there is a recurrence of such violations by many companies. They pay fines for several violations (including the fines for nonpayment of past dividends). Surprisingly, these companies' shares have bullish trend in the market and investors are attracted to make capital gains only. It is to be noted that although the attraction of a firm's stock lies within the dividends and capital gains, such unusual price jump is not related to the intrinsic value of stocks. The tendency of stock price manipulation started in 1996 when the stock price of some companies reached to its peak and investors rushed to the market with a hope for further increase (bullish trend) but finally their stocks ended up with pieces of papers.

Due to such bullish trend, the market in Bangladesh became so lucrative that it attracted a large number of investors to make some gains. Financial institutions (even violating the banking regulations[7]), company officials (even by borrowing from banks[8]), and general public, who have invested their last resort of saving within the stock market, are among them. Such tendency creates huge demands of securities that cannot be saturated by the existing supply of securities.

It is, however, complained that companies (the promoters[9]) go to the market not necessarily for the equity capital and many investors subscribe not necessarily to become the equity partners. Both the promoters' and subscribers' attitude is to grab the primary shares to make capital gain. Therefore, amazingly many recent IPOs are oversubscribed (even some underperforming companies' IPOs, issued at premium) and many recent IPOs are found to be issued by lottery! Many companies take this opportunity and go to public (issue IPO) through various fraudulent activities or with an intention to fraud (even though they are not in commercial operation or have the intention to commence the commercial operation soon). These companies usually do not hold the AGMs and do not declare and pay dividends. Although many investors are attracted to these companies' shares to make capital gain, the marginal investors neither receive dividends nor are able to make a capital gain.

While direct listing does not provide any benefit to the company and only the government enterprises can be listed under this rule, in early 2010, two companies were listed on the stock exchanges under "direct listing rule" (Inquiry Committee Report, 2011). Recently, many companies issued IPOs with unusual premium through "book building" method.[10] It is complained that many of these companies' accounts were fabricated and a few of these have never earned a profit in their history (*Daily Naya Diganta*, 2011). In the past, a Taka 100 IPO was issued at Taka 100. Recently, many companies split their Taka 100 shares to Taka 10, arguing that it will increase shares availability. It, in fact, gave an opportunity to the companies to increase the number of IPOs and issue the same at possible highest premium (Inquiry Committee Report, 2011). While these companies are collecting as much premium as possible from the investors, it was unknown what they will pay to the investors in return. Amazingly, the IPOs of these companies were oversubscribed.

While there is a widespread concern and criticism of price manipulations by these companies, the single-day turnover set a new benchmark in the history of Bangladesh on October 15, 2009, at DSE, exceeding the turnover of Taka 12 billion (*Daily Star*, 2009). On that day, many of the small companies' shares jumped without any justifiable reasons.[11] The regulatory body, SECB, was not in a position to interfere; rather, it argued that the market trends were under its close surveillance but also advised the investors to follow the fundamental-based investment and to avoid any rumor-based investment (*Daily Star*, 2009).

The share price index on December 5, 2010, at DSE reached its peak (at 8,900 points) in the history of Bangladesh and the turnover reached to Taka 32 billion for a single day in the history of Bangladesh, breaking the previous record (evident from Fig. 2). The reverse turn, which is very natural, started on December 8, 2010. It was apparent that many investors, including financial institutions, were leaving the market. Following the collapse in 1996, the *Economist* magazine wrote, "The Slaughter of the Innocent" (*The Economist*, 1996) and after 14 years, the *Economist* again wrote, "Fresh Innocent to the Slaughters" (*The Economist*, 2011). The market finally collapsed again on January 20, 2011. Almost after 14 years, the average investors "took a bath" again. Many dominant individual and institutional investors disappeared from the scene. It is noted that the price of many companies' stock, whose IPOs were set through book-building method, had unprecedented fall. The finance minister admitted that he and SECB made some mistakes

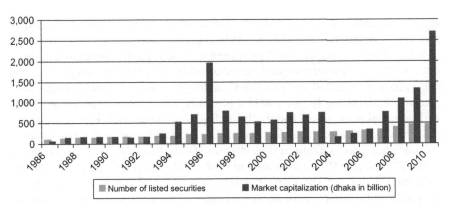

Fig. 2. Trend of Stock Market Growth During the Period of 1986–2010.
Source: Data from Dhaka Stock Exchange web page and Securities and Exchange
Commission Bangladesh Annual Reports and Quarterly Reviews (Various Years and
Quarters). The period is year ending June.

(*Prothom Alo*, 2011); he added that the companies whose share price had an
unusual fall will be investigated; institutional investors will be asked to
reinvest their profit from stock market; two proposed IPOs will be postponed;
whether any company has issued IPO by making irregularities, within book-
building method, will be investigated and it will be forced to redeem its shares
(*Daily Naya Diganta*, 2011). Subsequently, SECB suspended the trading of
six brokerage houses, alleging that they have heavily contributed to collapse
by selling their shares at unusual faster rate. However, whatever was to
happen had already happened. One young investor committed suicide after
losing all of his borrowed capital in the stock market (*Daily Sun*, 2011). The
regulators in many instances blamed the investors but failed to explain why
the stock price increased almost every day without any justifiable reasons that
attracted these investors. In 1996, there were fewer than 50,000 investors;
most of them were based in Dhaka and in 2011 there were almost 3.2 million
investors who were from other towns and cities in Bangladesh (*The
Economist*, 2011).

Financial Reporting and Disclosure

The accounting practices and company financial reporting in Bangladesh
are mainly guided under the several provisions of Companies Act 1994.

There are further guidelines for accounting practices and company financial reporting in the Banking Companies Act 1991 (for banking companies) and in the Insurance Act 1938 (for insurance companies). Securities and Exchange Rule 1987 requires all the listed companies to prepare half-yearly accounts (in the same format as the annual accounts but not required to be audited) and send the same to the SECB, the stock exchanges, and the shareholders.

Despite the above institutional arrangements, the accounting and auditing practices in Bangladesh suffer from institutional weaknesses in terms of their regulation, compliance, and enforcement of standards and professional rules (World Bank, 2003). The preparation of financial statements and conduct of audits, in many cases, are not consistent with internationally acceptable standards. There are many reasons behind this. ICAB adopted the IASs in its original form (Mir & Rahaman, 2005; Sobhan & Werner, 2003), the subsequent amendments by the International Accounting Standards Committee (IASC) have not been adopted by ICAB and, therefore, IASs and BASs differ in a number of material aspects (Sobhan & Werner, 2003; World Bank, 2003). Sobhan and Werner (2003) noted that as many of the IASs were not adopted immediately, it may have allowed the companies to fabricate the financial statement. For example, "IAS 27" requires the holding companies to prepare the "Consolidated Financial Statement." Bangladesh adopted it in 2007 and it may have allowed the companies to drain the profit from one subsidiary to another in the way of transfer pricing. Sobhan and Werner (2003) further noted that after adoption of IAS 27, companies may not have any incentive to prepare the consolidated financial statement as there is no tax benefit for a loss in one subsidiary that could be used to reduce taxes for the group as a whole. There is no disclosure on *effect of change in foreign exchange rate, related party transactions, revenue recognition, and employee benefit* by the listed companies (World Bank, 2003). Although it is Securities and Exchange Commission that regulates the financial reporting practices of listed companies, the Banking Companies Act 1991 allows Bangladesh Bank (the central bank) to regulate the financial reporting by banks and the Insurance Act 1938 allows the "The Chief Controller of Insurance" to regulate the financial reporting practices of insurance companies. It is complained that no attempt by Bangladesh Bank is made to assess the degree of compliance with financial reporting requirements and "The Chief Controller of Insurance" rarely exercised powers to ensure such compliance and the financial reporting requirements for banks and insurance companies are not consistent with IASs (World Bank, 2003).

Gary (1988, p. 8), from a review of accounting literature, designed the following framework, which linked culture with accounting values:

a. Professionalism versus statutory control.
b. Uniformity versus flexibility.
c. Conservatism versus optimism.
d. Secrecy versus transparency.

From the discussions above, it is apparent that the corporate financial reporting practices in Bangladesh lack both the professionalism and statutory control. The flexibility of financial reporting noted above leads to lack of uniformity as noted in Gary (1988). The lack of professional accountants in Bangladesh is one of the reasons contributing to poor financial reporting practices. World Bank (2003) noted that, as the best students do not come to this profession, there is a very low passing rate in the professional qualification examinations conducted by the ICAB, leading to a large supply of unqualified accountants. These accountants are also known as "CA Course Complete" (CC accountants). Because of the limited supply of well-skilled, qualified accountants (chartered accountant), companies often hire the lesser-qualified CC accountants. A lack of adequate number of accounting academics and the lack of theoretical and practical aspects of IASs and ISAs within many academics may have contributed to this. Further, due to a lack of research in the educational institutions in Bangladesh, academics usually are not concerned in directing accounting practice (as argued in positive accounting theory by Watts & Zimmerman, 1986). Rather, academics sometimes consider the poor industry practice by the accountants who have lack of adequate knowledge and do not follow the uniform practice. Howieson (1996, p. 31) argues that unwillingness to tackle this policy issue is arguably an abrogation of academics' duty to serve the community, which supports them.

The auditing practices in Bangladesh also suffer from significant institutional weakness. None of the international Big 5 audit firms have any offices in Bangladesh. As many shareholders do not understand the role of external auditors in company governance, companies and shareholders are not willing to pay high fees for an audit, which in turn does not provide an incentive for auditors to provide quality personnel and audits (Karim & Moizer, 1996; Sobhan & Werner, 2003; Uddin & Choudhury, 2008). It is one of the reasons for low remuneration structure of the accountants. Audit firms mostly employ their students (who attach to the audit firms as part of their CA Course Complete to become CC accountants) to conduct the audit tasks and the auditor simply approves it.

In order to enhance the auditor's independence, while external auditors' appointments in many developed countries are overseen by "audit committee," in Bangladesh, despite the requirement of an "audit committee" in CGN (although no requirement of expertise is mentioned for the audit committee members), many firms do not have an audit committee. The external auditors' appointments are proposed by company management in an AGM and like any other agenda, it is passed even before it is read out (see, Uddin & Choudhury, 2008). Due to low fee structure for auditing services, company management enjoys strong bargaining power while appointing an external auditor (Karim & Moizer, 1996). In order to avoid the conflict of interest, some regulations in the developed economy (such as Sarbanes–Oxley Act 2002 in the United States) and "ASX Principles of Good Corporate Governance and Best Practices Recommendations" require that the nonaudit services (such as bookkeeping and internal auditing) provided by the auditor are subject to audit committee preapproval and disclosure. CGN prohibits the company to allow external/statutory auditors to perform the services, such as bookkeeping or other services related to the accounting records or financial statements, broker–dealer services, and internal audit services. However, this is not a rigid guideline as noncompliance requires an explanation. All of these may lead to compromise of the auditor's professional judgment because of either bias or undue influence or conflict of interest,[12] leading to a poor quality of audit. It is alleged that the ICAB does not provide adequate guidelines to its members to improve the quality of audit performed by its members (World Bank, 2003). Although there are some general professional practice guidelines/"Code of Ethics" for its members, ICAB, however, has no effective measures to ensure that members maintain the highest professional standards. To date, the self-regulation functions has been largely ineffective and actions for auditing violations by its members are very rare (Siddiqui, 2010; Sobhan & Werner, 2003), even though from time to time many notices and letter of warnings are sent to many chartered accountants' firms by SECB.[13] The SECB requires auditor rotation once every three years, except where the company declares dividends at a rate prescribed by the SECB, in which case, the same auditor can continue in office; however, such practice of linking auditor rotation with the company's dividend declaration is highly unusual (World Bank, 2003). The SECB in an order required the issuer company not to appoint any firm of chartered accountants as its statutory auditor for a consecutive period exceeding three years without SECB's prior approval. Many companies failed to comply with this and it is challenged in the court by some other companies and is now pending (Uddin & Choudhury, 2008).

Due to the weaknesses in above institutional arrangements and lack of effective enforcement of the timely and accurate filing, the compliance of full and accurate disclosure is few in number (World Bank, 2003). Many companies take up to seven years to present audited financial statements before the AGM of shareholders and many companies take more than seven years just to release the audited financial statements to outsiders (Karim et al., 2006). Due to poor statutory control and high power distances, the company officials restrain the information (maintain secrecy) to preserve power inequalities as noted in Gary (1988).

DISCUSSION AND CONCLUSION

This study presents an overview, development, and process of current corporate governance practices in Bangladesh. This study is drawn on NIS in evaluating the institutional capability in reinforcing corporate governance practices as well as a means of understanding the weaknesses of conformance and legitimization process. The exploration of the interplay between firms and on which the firms are dependent reveals answers to many of the key questions asked in this study. It is noted that Bangladesh is struggling toward the institutional sweeping change to strengthen the corporate governance best practices within the listed firms, in line with international corporate governance best practices. As part of this movement, since early 1990s, various reform initiatives were undertaken, such as establishment of SECB, enactment of new Companies Act 1994, automation of the stock exchanges and revising the capital market laws and regulations, including the various initiatives to enhance the various supervisory capabilities of SECB and Stock Exchanges, adoption of IASs, and announcement of code of best practices by listed companies (CGN).

Despite such institutional reforms, the existing regulatory regime in many cases fails to exert isomorphic pressures on firms to follow the schemes, rules, norms, and routines as authoritative guidelines leading to many incidences of noncompliance. Due to absence of such pressures, the corporations in Bangladesh in many instances are failing to follow the authoritative guidelines (good corporate governance practices) to be good corporate citizens. Companies are not found to be fearful to imitate each other in their field to be more legitimate or successful due to lack of institutional and market forces (market competition). Consistent with Hofstede (1980) culture of high "uncertainty avoidance," company officials are found to prefer implicit or flexible rules. Unlike a low individualism society, it is noted that corporate directors and executives in Bangladesh place great importance on themselves, who are in turn family members, as opposed to the importance on the greater good for the organization. Due to poor statutory control and high power distances, the company officials in many instances restrain the information to preserve power inequalities. It is argued that the potential benefits of adopting international corporate governance best practices may not necessarily be same across the countries (see Zattoni & Cuomo, 2008). It is also argued that, building an effective regulatory structure in a developing country is not simply about the technical design of the most appropriate regulatory instruments, it is also concerned with the quality of supporting regulatory institutions and capacity (Jalilian, Kirkpatrick, & Parker, 2007). The regulatory body SECB suffers from significant institutional weaknesses in terms of shortage of talented people and lack of ethics by its members; SECB is unable to unveil many fraudulent activities by the firms and in many instances SECB members were found to be involved in malpractices. Institutional forces failed to mobilize professionals to standardize the norms and practices. It is questioned if such reforms and adoption of internationally accepted practices was prompted by legitimization or efficiency reasons to improve the corporate governance practices within the listed firms (see Siddiqui, 2010). It can be questioned whether there will be a sustainable enforcement of corporate governance practices without framing a strong institutional regime and the code of ethics by the members of the regulatory body. DiMaggio and Powell (1983, p. 152) argue that "one important mechanism for encouraging normative isomorphism is the filtering of personnel. Within many organizational fields, filtering occurs through the hiring of individuals from firms within the same industry; through the recruitment of fast-track staff from a narrow range of training institutions; through common promotion practices, such as always hiring top executives from financial or legal departments; and from skill-level requirements for particular jobs."

Although by law the management of joint stock companies was entrusted to managers, such institutional weaknesses and poor or ineffective legal enforcement along with the absence of effective check and balance pose serious challenges to the firm-level effectiveness of good corporate governance practices in Bangladesh. It allows the company officials to become opportunists and abuse the entrusted power for private gain. They are effectively working to beat the system due to some situational factors. Therefore, it can be argued that although Bangladesh adopted the corporate governance best practices in line with the international corporate governance best practices for institutional legitimacy, in fact, there is a legitimacy crisis.

Regulation in the rigorous format is needed to deal with the opportunists, as market plays a very little role. It is also very important to update the stock exchange listing requirement and to make sure that the firms that have good fundamentals and comply with the regulations are coming to the market. Change in culture of ethics and value system is imperative for the public interest. Changes in rules and legislations and their effective enforcement should be made in a way so as to lead to a change in values (Ararat & Ugur, 2003). Educating the investors is another way to make the firm accountable. They may be encouraged to become the equity participants instead of simply becoming the market traders to make the firm accountable. Achieving these targets for firm-level compliance is not a long way off. The characteristics of corporate governance practices in a country are the result of forces aimed at increasing their efficiency as well as legitimization effects because of path dependence (Zattoni & Cuomo, 2008). Therefore, there should not be any haste and the reform is to be initiated in a clever way to keep up with the change and complexity to bring the accountability.

NOTES

1. It is concerned with equitable distribution of resources which is prevalent in a socialist economy as opposed to capitalist economy.

2. These include a loan of U.S. $80 million for Capital Market Development Program (CMDP) in 1997; technical assistance grant of U.S. $2.04 million in 1997, U.S. $1.07 million in 2000, and U.S. $4.0 million in 2003 (see Asian Development Bank, 1997, 2000a, 2008).

3. The Mughals are a line of Muslim emperors who reigned the divided Afghanistan, Pakistan, Kashmir, and Northern India from 1526 to 1858.

4. It was introduced on February 11, 1995 so that the shares under IPO issued in favor of local or foreign investors would not be permitted to trade (or transfer) such shares before one year.

5. France has a mixture of unitary and two-tier board system (see Charreaux & Wirtz, 2007).

6. The Anglo-American based "Cadbury Report 1992" and "Higgs Report 2003" suggested separating the executive function of the board from the monitoring function by splitting the role of chairperson and CEO.

7. A commercial bank is not allowed to invest more than 10% of its capital in the stock market.

8. Recently a director of a listed company borrowed huge money from a commercial bank under industrial loan facility and have invested the whole money in the stock market (*Prothom Alo*, 2010).

9. They are the sponsor and/or founding directors.

10. "Book building," a method of setting IPO price, was introduced in Bangladesh in 2009.

11. For example, Marico's share of Taka 10 jumped to Taka 368 on the first day of subscription on September 1, 2009.

12. IFIC Code of Ethics for Professional Accountants requires the members of the profession not to compromise their professional or business judgment because of bias, conflict of interest, or the undue influence of others.

13. In September 2002, the ICAB, for the first time in its 38 years of existence suspended the membership of an audit firm auditor for 3 years (see Siddiqui, 2010).

ACKNOWLEDGMENT

I acknowledge the helpful comments from the anonymous reviewers on the earlier drafts of this paper. I also recognize the support from Professor Shazad N. Uddin of the University of Essex.

REFERENCES

Abbott, A. (1988). *The system of professions*. Chicago, IL: University of Chicago Press.

Ararat, M., & Ugur, M. (2003). Corporate governance in Turkey: An overview and some policy recommendations. *Corporate Governance*, 3(1), 58–75.

Asian Development Bank. (1997). *News release: ADB loan to Bangladesh to reform capital market*. Retrieved from http://www.adb.org/Documents/News/1997/nr1997121.asp. Manila: The Asian Development Bank. Accessed on June 7, 2005 and April 30, 2008.

Asian Development Bank. (2000a). Technical assistance to the People's Republic of Bangladesh for capacity building of the SEC and selected capital market institutions. Project #: BAN 33226, November 2000. Retrieved from www.adb.org/Documents/TARs/BAN/R281-00.pdf. Accessed on August 28, 2009.

Asian Development Bank. (2000b). Corporate governance and finance in East Asia, a study of Indonesia, Republic of Korea, Malaysia, Philippines and Thailand, a consolidated report (Vol. 1). Manila: The Asian Development Bank.

Asian Development Bank. (2005). *Capital market development program in Bangladesh*. Manila: Asian Development Bank.

Asian Development Bank. (2008). Technical assistance loan improvement to capital market and insurance. Project #: BAN 36197, March 2008. Retrieved from http://www.adb.org/Documents/PAMs/BAN/36197-BAN-PAM.pdf. Accessed on August 28, 2009.

Baker, H. K., & Kolb, R. W. (2009). *Dividends and dividend policy*. NJ: Wiley.

Bangladesh Enterprise Institute. (2004). *The code of corporate governance for Bangladesh*. The Taskforce on Corporate Governance and Bangladesh Enterprise Institute. Dhaka: Bangladesh Enterprise Institute.

Charreaux, G., & Wirtz, P. (2007). Corporate governance in France. In: A. Kostyuk, U. C. Braendle & R. Apreda (Eds.), *Corporate governance*. Ukraine: Virtusinter Press.

Daily Naya Diganta. (2011). General news item. *The Daily Naya Diganta*, January 24. Retrieved from http://www.dailynayadiganta.com. Accessed on January 24, 2011.

Daily Star. (2009). Single-day turnover sets new benchmark on DSE. *The Daily Star*, October 15. Retrieved from http://www.thedailystar.net. Accessed on October 15, 2009.

Daily Sun. (2011). Bangladesh fund prevents further share price fall. *The Daily Sun*, May 10. Retrieved from http://www.hawker.com.bd. Accessed on May 12, 2011.

DiMaggio, P. J., & Powell, W. W. (1983). The iron cage revisited: Institutional isomorphism and collective rationality in organizational fields. *American Sociological Review, 48*(2), 147–160.

DiMaggio, P. J., & Powell, W. W. (1991). Introduction. In: W. W. Powell & P. J. DiMaggio (Eds.), *The new institutionalism in organizational analysis*. Chicago, IL: University of Chicago Press.

Farrar, J. (2005). *Corporate governance: Theories, principles and practice* (2nd ed.). South Melbourne, VIC: Oxford University Press.

Fogarty, T. J. (1996). The imagery and realty of peer review in the U.S.: Insights from institutional theory. *Accounting, Organizations and Society, 21*(2/3), 243–267.

Fogarty, T. J., & Rogers, R. K. (2005). Financial analysts' reports: An extended institutional theory evaluation. *Accounting, Organizations and Society, 30*, 331–356.

Gary, S. J. (1988). Towards a theory of cultural influence on the development of accounting system internationally. *Abacus, 24*(1), 1–15.

Gillan, S. L., & Martin, J. D. (2007). Corporate governance post-Enron: Effective reforms, or closing the stable door? *Accounting and Finance, 13*, 929–958.

Hofstede, G. (1980). *Culture's consequences – International differences in work-related values*. Beverly Hills, CA: Sage Publications.

Hoque, Z. (2007). An interview with Zahirul Hoque: Interview by Sarah Powell. *Strategic Direction, 23*(6), 25–28.

Howieson, B. (1996). Whither financial accounting research: A modern day Bo-Peep? *Australian Accounting Review, 13*(3), 251–262.

Index of Economic Freedom. (2011). *Bangladesh: Economic freedom score* (Retrieved from http://www.heritage.org/. Accessed on September 12, 2011). Washington, DC: The Heritage Foundation.

Inquiry Committee Report. (2011). *Enquiry commission on stock market collapse 2011*. Dhaka: Government of Bangladesh.

Jalilian, H., Kirkpatrick, C., & Parker, D. (2007). The impact of regulation on economic growth in developing countries: A cross-country analysis. *World Development, 35*(1), 87–103.

Jensen, M. C., & Murphy, K. J. (1990). CEO incentives – It's not how much you pay, but how. *Harvard Business Review, 68*(3), 138–153.

Kaplan, R. S., & Kiron, D. (2004). Accounting fraud at WorldCom. In: L. Cummings & B. Millanta (Eds.), *Financial accounting theory and practice* (2nd ed.). Sydney: McGraw Hill Australia Pty Ltd.

Karim, A. K. M., & Moizer, P. (1996). Determinants of audit fees in Bangladesh. *International Journal of Accounting, 31*(4), 497–509.

Karim, A. K. M. W. (1995). *Provision of corporate financial information in Bangladesh*. Unpublished Ph.D. thesis, University of Leeds, England.

Karim, A. K. M. W., Ahmed, K., & Islam, A. (2006). The effect of regulation on timeliness of corporate financial reporting: Evidence from Bangladesh. *Journal of Administration and Governance, 1*(1), 15–35.

La Porta, R., Lopez-de-Silanes, F., Shleifer, A., & Vishny, R. W. (1998). Law and finance. *Journal of Political Economy, 106*(6), 1113–1155.

Li, J. S. (2003). Relationship-based versus rule-based governance: An explanation of the East Asian miracle and Asian crisis. *Review of International Economics, 11*(4), 651–673.

Li, S., Park, S. H., & Li, S. (2004). The great leap forward: The transition from relation-based governance to rule-based governance. *Organizational Dynamics, 33*(1), 63–78.

Mardjono, A. (2005). A tale of corporate governance: Lessons why firms fail? *Managerial Auditing Journal, 20*(3), 272–283.

Meyer, J. W., & Rowan, B. (1977). Institutionalized organizations: Formal structure as myth and ceremony. *American Journal of Sociology, 83*(2), 340–363.

Mir, M. Z., & Rahaman, A. S. (2005). The adoption of international accounting standards in Bangladesh: An exploration of rationale and process. *Accounting, Auditing and Accountability Journal, 18*(6), 816–841.

Prothom Alo. (2010). General news item. *Prothom Alo*, November 5. Retrieved from http://www.prothom-alo.org/. Accessed on November 5, 2010.

Prothom Alo. (2011). General news item. *Prothom Alo*, January 21. Retrieved from http://www.prothom-alo.org/. Accessed on January 21, 2011.

Rashid, A. (2010). CEO duality and firm performance: Evidence from a developing country. *Corporate Ownership and Control, 8*(1), 163–175.

Rashid, A. (2011). Corporate governance, ownership structure and firm performance: Evidence from an emerging economy. *Corporate Ownership and Control, 9* (Forthcoming).

Rashid, A., & Lodh, S. C. (2008). The influence of ownership structure and board practices on corporate social disclosures in Bangladesh. In: S. Uddin & M. Tsamenyi (Eds.), *Research in Accounting in Emerging Economies*, (Vol. 8, pp. 211–237).

Rashid, A., De Zoysa, A., Lodh, S., & Rudkin, K. (2010). Board composition and firm performance: Evidence from Bangladesh. *Australasian Accounting Business and Finance Journal, 4*(1), 76–95.

Reed, D. (2002). Corporate governance reforms in developing countries. *Journal of Business Ethics, 37*, 223–247.

Rose, C. (2005). The composition of semi-two tier corporate boards and firm performance. *Corporate Governance: An International Review, 13*(5), 691–701.

Scott, W. R. (2005). Institutional theory: Contributing to a theoretical research program. In: K. G. Smith & M. A. Hitt (Eds.), *Great minds in management: The process of theory development*. New York, NY: Oxford University Press.

SECB. (2004). *Annual Report 2003–04*. Securities and Exchange Commission Bangladesh, Dhaka. Retrieved from http://www.secbd.org/annual.html. Accessed on November 18, 2005.

SECB. (2006). *Investors information*. Securities and Exchange Commission Bangladesh. Retrieved from http://www.secbd.org/investor.html. Accessed on July 8, 2006.

SECB. (2009). *Annual Report 2008–09*. Securities and Exchange Commission Bangladesh, Dhaka. Retrieved from http://www.secbd.org/annual.html. Accessed on March 10, 2010.

Siddiqui, J. (2010). Development of corporate governance regulations: The case of an emerging economy. *Journal of Business Ethics, 91*(2), 253–274.

Sobhan, F., & Werner, W. (2003). *A comparative analysis of corporate governance in South Asia: Charting a roadmap for Bangladesh* (Retrieved from http://www.bei-bd.org/documents/cg%201.pdf. Accessed on July 5, 2005). Dhaka: Bangladesh Enterprise Institute.

Solaiman, S. M. (2006). Recent reforms and development of the capital markets in Bangladesh: A critique. *Journal of Asian and African Studies, 41*(3), 195–228.

Solomon, J. (2007). *Corporate governance and accountability* (2nd ed.). Chichester: Wiley.

The Economist. (1996). Slaughter of innocents. *The Economist,* December 7. Retrieved from http://www.economist.com. Accessed on October 28, 2006.

The Economist. (1997). Revenge of the innocents. *The Economist,* April 12. Retrieved from http://www.economist.com. Accessed on October 28, 2006.

The Economist. (2011). Fresh innocents to the Slaughter. *The Economist,* January 18, 2011. Retrieved from http://www.economist.com. Accessed on January 23, 2011.

Tsamenyi, M., Cullen, J., María, J., & González, G. (2006). Changes in accounting and financial information system in a Spanish electricity company: A new institutional theory analysis. *Management Accounting Research, 17,* 409–432.

Uddin, S., & Choudhury, J. (2008). Rationality, traditionalism and state of corporate governance: Illustrious from a less-developed country. *Accounting Auditing and Accountability Journal, 21*(7), 1026–1051.

Uddin, S., & Hopper, T. (2003). Accounting for privatization in Bangladesh: Testing World Bank claims. *Critical Perspectives on Accounting, 14*(7), 739–774.

Wade, R. (2000). Wheels within wheels: Rethinking the Asian crisis and the Asian models. *Annual Review of Political Science, 3,* 85–115.

Watts, R. L., & Zimmerman, J. L. (1986). *Positive accounting theory.* Englewood Cliffs, NJ: Prentice-Hall Inc.

World Bank. (1995). *Bangladesh: From stabilization to growth. A World Bank country study.* Washington, DC: The World Bank.

World Bank. (2003). *Report on the Observance of Standards and Codes (ROSC) Bangladesh.* The World Bank, May 16.

World Bank. (2005). *The World Bank in Bangladesh: Country brief* (Retrieved from http://siteresources.worldbank.org/INTBANGLADESH/Resources/BD06.pdf. Accessed on April 20, 2008). Washington, DC: The World Bank.

World Bank. (2007). *Corporate governance: A powerful tool in the battle against poverty.* Washington, DC: World Bank.

World Bank. (2009). *World development indicators database.* Retrieved from http://siteresources.worldbank.org/DATASTATISTICS/Resources/GDP.pdf. Accessed on September 12, 2011.

Zahra, S. A. (1990). Increasing the board's involvement in strategy. *Long Range Planning, 23*(6), 109–117.

Zattoni, A., & Cuomo, F. (2008). Why adopt codes of good governance? A comparison of institutional and efficiency perspectives. *Corporate Governance: An International Review, 16*(1), 1–15.

A CONTENT ANALYSIS ON THE NEWLY REVISED CODE OF ETHICS FOR PROFESSIONAL ACCOUNTANTS IN CHINA

Guangyou Liu[1] and Hong Ren[2]

ABSTRACT

Purpose – *The paper presents a content analysis of the 2009 Exposure Draft of Code of Ethics for Professional Accountants in China. It aims to investigate how equivalently the Chinese Institute of Certified Public Accountants (CICPA) adopts the International Federation of Accountants (IFAC) Code with certain adjustments due to specific national circumstances. The investigation is intended to highlight the principles-based conceptual framework approach to settlement of ethical standards and regulation for professional conduct.*

Design/Methodology/Approach – *Regarding the codes of ethics for professional accountants as a genre of discourse text, this paper applies a content analysis method to the investigation of how the newly revised Code of Ethics for Professional Accountants in China adopts the IFAC Code of the same type. Both semantic content and presentation format are considered in the content analysis.*

Accounting in Asia
Research in Accounting in Emerging Economies, Volume 11, 35–60
ISSN: 1479-3563/doi:10.1108/S1479-3563(2011)0000011007

Findings – *This study puts forward the argument that even though CICPA claims to have equivalently adopted the principles-based conceptual framework of the IFAC ethical codification, the rigid legalistic presentation format might, however, deviate from the newly revised codification of CICPA from ethical principles to regulatory rules. Our findings prove a practical and nation-specific form of combining direct import and legal enhancement at a time when the Chinese accounting profession is on its way to converging with the IFAC Code of Ethics.*

Research limitations/Implications – *One limitation of the current study is the lack of information about the motivation of CICPA in adopting the principles-based conceptual framework approach to ethical codification, besides the pragmatic needs of global economic and business environments. Also, the current study focuses its comparison on IFAC and CICPA, without limited consideration of differences in cultural traits.*

Practical implications – *Content analysis results and conclusions of the study might render pragmatic the implications for future adoptions of the IFAC Code by various national or regional professional bodies.*

Originality/Value – *This paper proposes a content analysis, in terms of semantic units and legislative formats in ethical codification documents, to identify the principles-based conceptual framework approach in the IFAC and CICPA codes of ethics.*

Keywords: Content analysis; codes of ethics; principles-based; rules-based; conceptual framework approach

INTRODUCTION

Responding to the increasing demands for more reliable public accounting services from domestic and international business communities, the Chinese Institute of Certified Public Accountants (CICPA) has attempted to tighten the screening of its members' conduct by setting up a more authoritative special committee, the disciplinary committee. Accordingly, the practices of public accounting will be monitored more closely and the violators of professional ethics and conduct will be brought to disciplinary action more quickly and properly by CICPA (Lin, 1998). The first Chinese rules-based codification of conduct for professional accountants was drawn up in 1995 when CICPA was established. The second effort of this sort was CICPA's

SAVE THIS BOX AND PACKING MATERIAL IF DAMAGED BOOKS ARE RECEIVED

1. This package was shipped insured by FedEx Ground Service. Please save the books, carton, and packing materials for fifteen business days in case FedEx wants to inspect the damage.
2. Call 1-800-325-8833 to report shipment damage to your Library Service Representative.
3. Report the books damaged and the Invoice number.
4. Midwest Library Service will process a credit to you for the damaged books.
5. FedEx will settle the claim with Midwest.

If you have any other questions about shipment damages please call your Library Service Representative at 1-800-325-8833. Thank you.

MIDWEST LIBRARY SERVICE

guidance for the Codes of Accounting Professional Ethics, which was enacted effectively in 2002. The International Federation of Accountants (IFAC) Code of Ethics cast observable influences on these two Chinese ethical codes for accountants. In 2009, the IFAC Code of Ethics was officially adopted into the CICPA Exposure Draft of Codes of Ethics for Professional Accountants. With a tradition of legislation-based accounting practices, the 2009 CICPA Exposure Draft of Codes of Ethics produces not only a set of professional standards but also a set of rules in legalistic format. We are interested by this approach to convergence with the international accounting standards and try to exhibit its references to the international convergence in other emerging Asian countries.

The primary aim of this study is to examine the rationale of a principles-based ethical conceptual framework which CICPA claims to have transplanted from the IFAC Code of Ethics into its 2009 Exposure Draft of Codes of Ethics. A content analysis is conducted on the IFAC Code of Ethics for Professional Accountants (revised in July 2009 and expected to be effective in January 2012) and CICPA's Exposure Draft of Codes of Ethics revised in 2009. After considering available methodologies for this research, we have determined that a content analysis fits well in exploring how general ethical principles and enforcement rules construct the conceptual framework approach to solving professional ethical problems.

With the passing of time and the approaching globalization of accounting, the IFAC Code of Ethics will be more and more influential around the world, and it will provide increased guidance for professional accountants in different nations and regions.

We find out that the 2009 CICPA Exposure Draft of Codes of Ethics exhibits China's intention of improving the professional ethics in accounting practices and its efforts of convergence with the international ethical standards. In particular, the legalistic format shaping the newest CICPA Code of Ethics needs to be reflected with care in other emerging Asian countries when they consider convergence with the IFAC Code of Ethics.

Besides this introduction, this study is structured as follows: The following section will provide a background review of the accounting profession and ethical regulations for professional accountants in China; then a literature review will be provided for a debate of the principles-based versus rules-based codes of ethics, and investigation of the principles-based ethical conceptual framework, which leads to research hypotheses of this study; this will be followed by a methodological description of content analysis; the next section will provide the results and discussion in relation to content analysis, followed by an explanatory section on inter-coder reliability in this content analysis. The last section presents conclusions, limitations and suggestions for future research.

THE ACCOUNTING PROFESSION AND ETHICAL REGULATIONS IN CHINA

Accounting has gained an important role in China's economic and social development since the 'open-door' policy reform. However, the modern accounting profession in China is newly established and inexperienced compared to most Western countries. The CICPA was founded in November 1988 as the first professional accounting body in the People's Republic of China. The later-established Chinese Association of Certified Public Auditors (CACPA) was merged in 1995 to form a new professional body by the current name of CICPA, under the direct control of the Ministry of Finance (MOF), resulting in the unification of name, institution and regulations (Lin & Chan, 2000). In 1997, CICPA joined the International Federation of Accountants (IFAC) after a 9-year delay following clearance of the political and sovereignty issues relating to application and approval. In recent years, CICPA has developed its own globalization strategy, in order to perform well in its leading role in the process of internationalizing the Chinese accounting profession and developing a world-class accounting profession for China. Currently, besides having IFAC membership, CICPA is one of the founding members and sits on its Executive Committee of the Confederation of Asian and Pacific Accountants (CAPA) which is the leading accounting professional body and plays a key role in providing high-quality accounting services throughout the Asia-Pacific region. CICPA nowadays is the sole professional accounting organization in China authorized to issue Chinese CPA qualifications and supervise the self-regulation of the Chinese accounting profession. CICPA exercises the management and service functions by virtue of the powers vested by the *Law of the People's Republic of China on Certified Public Accountants*, the *Charter of the Chinese Institute of Certified Public Accountants* and relevant laws and regulations.

The first annual nationwide CPA examination was initiated by CICPA in 1990. To qualify for CICPA membership, all applicants are required to have a bachelor's degree, pass the CPA examination and have at least 3 years' work experience in the accounting or auditing professions. Continuing professional education is mandatory for all CICPA members to hold membership. Around 2002, universities offered business ethics courses and CPA firms started to conduct professional ethical training programmes (Wu, 2003).

Continuous efforts have been made by CICPA, ever since its inception, in promulgating its guidance and principles for all its members nationwide.

The latest document for those aforementioned purposes was the CICPA guidance for the Codes of Accounting Professional Ethics enacted effectively in 2002. This revolutionary revision had assumed its programmatic applications in establishing professional image and credibility, and adequately regulating professional behaviour in Chinese accountancy.

However, with drastic changes occurring in the new millennium in terms of accounting environments where accounting practices are subject to increased international impact and extensions, accounting professional ethics is going global as well. CICPA, with its sharp awareness of this significant globalization process, assumes its leading role in converging Chinese codes and principles of ethical conducts for professional conducts with those of the international accounting communities, to accommodate the demands of the new era.

The issuance of the Exposure Draft of the CICPA Guidance for the Codes of Ethics for Professional Accountants (namely, the CICPA Code of Ethics which is equivalent to that of IFAC) was to mark the year of 2009 as a period of evolution in the Chinese accounting profession. The Code of Ethics for Professional Accountants issued by CICPA is largely based on the IFAC Code of the same name. New trends are observed in CICPA's efforts to construct an integrative ethical conceptual framework to guide the application of ethical principles and rules, highlighting the priorities of public interest and converging with the current codes of ethics established by major international accounting communities. CICPA has sought to adapt the IFAC Code to Chinese circumstances, both by changing the IFAC wording where appropriate and by the insertion of legislative power in rigid legalistic forms. This legalistic format is unique in the codification of professional conduct in global accounting.

LITERATURE REVIEW AND RESEARCH HYPOTHESES

Principles-Based versus Rules-Based Codes of Ethics

A code of ethics has been the traditional means by which a profession assures the public and its clients of its responsibilities and thereby the maintenance of its integrity and reputation (Velayutham, 2003). A code of ethics for professional accountants can be expressed as either principles-based and high level or rules-based and detailed (ICAEW, 2009), which is similar to the two differentiated approaches in establishing the generally accepted accounting principles for financial reporting.

Recent high-profile events in the United States indicate that the accountants and auditors involved have followed rules-based ethical perspectives and have failed to protect investors and stakeholders, resulting in a wave of scandals and charges of unethical conduct (Satava, Caldwell, & Richards, 2006). However, Herron and Gilbertson (2004) find that accounting professionals are more likely to consider their independence impaired, and are more likely to reject a questionable audit engagement, when they are provided with principles-based codes.

In practice, codes of ethics for professional accountants are a mixture of principles and rules. The rules should support the underlying principles of the code (ICAEW, 2009). Whether a code is described as principles- or rules-based will be dependent on whether the principles are built into the foundations of the code and the extent of the rules. An outstanding example is the AICPA Code of Professional Conduct (Code) which provides guidance in both forms: principles and rules (Herron & Gilbertson, 2004).

The IFAC Code of Ethics for Professional Accountants establishes the international standard of codified ethics on which IFAC members or their national/regional standards should be modelled. Farrell and Cobbin (2000) conclude that the Ethics Committee of IFAC has chosen to provide a model code of ethics in the quest for harmonization of measurable behavioural standards for professional accountants throughout the world. The IFAC Code of Ethics echoes the popularity of the view that rules-based standards are undesirable and focuses weight upon the establishment of principles-based framework for ethical reasoning and judgment. The view of IFAC that the principles-based approach is best suited to a rapidly changing business and accounting professional environment is widely recognized by most influential professional bodies (e.g. ACCA, 2003; CIMA, 2007; FEE, 2003; ICAEW, 2009). FEE (2003) states that by focusing on the underlying aim rather than detailed prohibitions, the principles-based approach combines flexibility with rigour in a way that is unattainable with a rules-based approach.

The Chinese accounting system was initially based on the former Soviet system of uniform accounting. Since then, economic reform and emerging market growth in the last three decades have driven the Chinese accounting profession reasonably close to the requirements of international accounting communities. An abundance of literature has been dedicated to searching for the cultural and contextual factors to explain the differences in

China's accounting and auditing, and the progress of convergence with international accounting standards (Lin & Fraser, 2008; Xiao, Weetman, & Sun, 2004). Through its great efforts in converging with the international financial accounting and auditing standards, CICPA has incorporated the concept of a principles-based approach into the CICPA Code of Ethics for Professional Accountants. This leads to our first research hypothesis as follows:

H1. The CICPA Code focuses its content on ethical principles not on enacting rules, in the same manner as the IFAC Code.

Conceptual Framework in the Code of Ethics

Ever since a conceptual framework was defined by the FASB (1976, p. 2), there has been a persistent urge to search for a conceptual framework which has proved irresistible to standard setters in the English-speaking world (Page, 2005).

IFAC's proposition of an ethical conceptual framework in establishing the codes of ethics for professional accountants constructs another platform for the principles-versus-rules debate. By nature, the concept of a conceptual framework is more intangible in terms of linguistic expression and apparently overrides the presentation formats expressed by the concepts of fundamental principles and rules. The IFAC conceptual framework approach has earned strongly voiced support from many influential professional bodies. ACCA states its full support for the principles-based approach and welcomes the move to place the whole of the Code on a threats and safeguards footing, declaring that this will provide a framework for analysing the threats and safeguards which accountants can use to determine appropriate courses of action (ACCA, 2003). Fédération des Experts Comptables Européens (FEE), the representative organization for the accountancy profession in Europe, interprets the IFAC conceptual framework of threats and safeguards to assure the professional accountant's compliance with the fundamental principles as such that while the conceptual framework approach to establishing the code of ethics includes examples of threats that might arise and appropriate safeguards to deal with them, these examples are clearly stated to be illustrative and not comprehensive (FEE, 2003). ICAEW (2009) appreciates the IFAC conceptual framework approach from the perspective of active consideration and demonstration of conclusions for ethical professional conducts: A framework of principles places the onus on the accountant to actively consider independence for every given situation, rather than just agreeing a checklist of forbidden items; it also requires him to demonstrate that a responsible conclusion has been reached on ethical issues.

However, considerable concerns with rules are also articulated in their comments on the IFAC Code of Ethics relating to the conceptual framework. FEE (2003) states that the conceptual approach can be virtually indistinguishable from rule making, for example, in a case where there are no adequate safeguards against severe actual or apparent threat to independence; it would amount to a rule on prohibiting the activity. The Chartered Institute of Management Accountants (CIMA, 2007), while supporting the Code of Ethics for Professional Accountants being developed by the International Federation of Accountants, warns that the newly revised IFAC Code of Ethics could potentially transform the code from a conceptual framework into a rules-based approach by an increase in detail to the Code of Ethics, eventually resulting in making the code too rule-based. ICAEW (2009) comments that the IFAC Code tends to be in the form of a principles-based framework, a framework of principles rather than a set of rules, containing some rules, but in the main being flexible guidance.

Opening up the Chinese accounting profession to the globalization and harmonization of ethical standards lends powerful support to the healthy and vigorous growth of the national accounting profession. As a young and inexperienced professional institute, CICPA contributes its current efforts in revising the CICPA Code of Ethics and adopting the ethical conceptual framework in accordance with the IFAC Code, responding to the requirements of the Chinese accounting evolution towards internationalization. An observable effort is the fact that the conceptual framework approach in the IFAC Code has been adopted and rooted in the text of the CICPA Code of Ethics, but again, the effectiveness and efficiency in presenting the conceptual framework approach in another accounting context are worthy of further investigation. Extant literature on accounting conceptual framework discloses different viewpoints. Davidson and Gelardi (1996) identify the similarities of China's conceptual framework with those found in Western accounting standards and recognize the differences resulting from China's unique cultural, political and economic features. Rayman (2007) proposes an alternative conceptual framework for fair value accounting, and Whittington (2008) even criticizes the role of IASB conceptual framework in his review of international accounting convergences.

We intend to investigate the application of conceptual framework in ethical codes by testing the following two research hypotheses:

H2a. The CICPA Code adopts the same ethical conceptual framework of threats and safeguards as the IFAC Code.

H2b. The CICPA Code adopts the same presentation format as the ethical conceptual framework of the IFAC Code.

RESEARCH METHODOLOGY

Content Analysis

Content analysis is a systematic, replicable research technique for compressing large blocks of text into fewer content categories based on explicit rules of coding (Stemler, 2001). In the studies of ethical standards, content analysis is extremely useful for spotting trends and patterns in documents of ethical codification. The most important outcome of content analysis is a simple aggregation of qualitative data so that the researcher may compare the categorical variables in a quantitative method. The power of content analysis applied in the current study on the ethical conceptual framework in textual code documents is ensured by adopting the syntactical paragraphs as the coding units, which result in numerical description and comparison of the two ethical codes under investigation. The content analysis includes determining the coding units, defining the research categories, collecting the data (documents), coding the textual materials and analysing the data.

The current study involves a comprehensive review of the two newly revised contemporary Exposure Drafts of Codes of Ethics for Professional Accountants by CICPA and IFAC respectively. A number of key categories and sub-categories measuring the principles-based conceptual framework approach will be developed from the textual document of the two codes of ethics under investigation for the purposes of content analysis. Content analysis in the studies of ethical codes enables the researchers to clearly investigate the rationale underpinning the formation and implementation of ethical codes in different national contexts. Also, the typical features drawn from this analysis can be concisely and accurately descriptive of the principles-based conceptual framework approach to setting up the ethical codes.

Coding Process and Coding Units of Current Study

Following the instructions by content analysis textbooks (e.g. Weber, 1990; Stemler, 2001), two coders with similar but inter-supplementary academic background and research fields have independently accomplished all the coding procedures on the main bodies of the two codes of ethics under investigation. Accuracy in defining the coding units and coding results has been assured by a trial coding on some sample texts of ethical codes other than the studied ones. The trial coding has made the coding schemes clear to both coders. In the process of coding the two codes of ethics for professional accountants which are written in two different languages, special care has been exercised to ensure that the coding schemes shared by two coders. Once the formal coding starts, both coders work independently till they finalize their coding results. Statistical tests on the codification reliability of the current study will be presented in section 'Tests on the Codification Results: Kappa Statistics for Inter-coder Reliability'.

There are several different ways of determining coding units in the content analysis. The current study adopts syntactical definition of paragraphs as the coding units. A total of 420 paragraphs are identified as coding units from the IFAC Code of Ethics and 401 paragraphs from the CICPA Code of Ethics. Overarching the coding units, sections are structured to indicate the preamble and practical application of principles-based conceptual framework into specific areas of professional accounting.

Definition and Coding of Categories

As noted by Stemler (2001), content analysis extends far beyond the technique of counting words, and more meaningful research implications lie in coding and categorizing of the data under investigation. Categorizing means the mutually exclusive and exhaustive grouping of words with similar meaning or connotations (Weber, 1990, p. 37). There are four content categories under investigation in the content analysis of textual content. They are *Principles*, *Rules*, *Threats/Safeguards* and *Assumptions*. Based on these content categories, seven categories of different legislative forms are also coded.

Principles include five fundamental principles in the preamble section of the codes plus *independence*. Six principles fall into this category.

They are denoted by 'Integrity', 'Objectivity', 'Professional competence and due care', 'Confidentiality', 'Professional behaviour' and 'Independence'.

Applications are defined in this study as another category in terms of *threats* and *safeguards*, following the descriptive definition of IFAC's 'conceptual framework approach' which states, 'this Code establishes a conceptual framework that requires a professional accountant to identify, evaluate, and address threats to compliance with the fundamental principles (IFAC Code: 100.6)'; for the definition of threats, they 'may be created by a broad range of relationships and circumstances, and when a relationship or circumstance creates a threat, such a threat could compromise, or could be perceived to compromise, a professional accountant's compliance with the fundamental principles (IFAC Code: 100.12)'. For the safeguards, they 'are actions or other measures that may eliminate threats or reduce them to an acceptable level (IFAC Code: 100.13)'. As threats and safeguards are normally interactive and responsive to each other in the text of ethical codes, the coding scheme combines these two categories and they are denoted by the variable *Applications*.

Rules are studied as a variable composed of rule statements on both general and specific issues. Although fundamental principles can incorporate prohibitions, a principles-based framework still contains certain prohibitions where these are necessary. As noted by Bagshaw (2006), the principles, rules and the expressions of 'shall' and 'must' drive the principles-versus-rules debate into a quagmire; thus classifying these two categories largely relies on the coders' subjective judgment, based on the criteria that rules in a code of ethics are statements which clarify what should and should not be done in certain circumstances or with specific relationships.

Assumptions, as thresholds for applying the principles or rules, include public interests and materiality, and they act as an important variable in this investigation. As the primary ethical feature, the accounting profession wishes to achieve public recognition. Ethical codes are promoted by accounting bodies as serving a public interest role in that they 'protect the economic interests of professional members' clients and of third parties who place reliance on the pronouncements and advice delivered by both the professional body and its members' (Canning & O'Dwyer, 2002). Consideration of materiality is vital to the application of fundamental principles in the codes of ethics as it is closely associated with the significance of the financial interests and relationships in professional judgment and decisions.

Equipped with the foregoing determination of coding units and research categories, and conceptualization of studied categories, two coders of similar research fields rate separately the two textual documents, that is, the Exposure Draft of IFAC Code of Ethics and the Exposure Draft of CICPA Code of Ethics, both of which were revised in 2009. The studied categories are collected by two individual coders through separate coding of both documents and then aggregated into the values of these categories in expressions of frequencies and percentages. The coding scheme shared by both coders is stated in Table 1.

Presentation Formats of Coded Categories

Presentation format analysis of this study intends to investigate how the IFAC Code of Ethics and its CICPA equivalent version structure their ethical conceptual framework in the respective documents. The presentation formats underlying the texts are coded on the basis of the categories. There is no prior accounting research literature mentioning the structural implications of an ethical code; however, the coding results in terms of presentation formats shall fit in the inspection of ways in which the conceptual framework is presented in the two ethical codes under investigation. This logic adds up to a coding scheme categorizing eight presentation formats, and each of these coded patterns is explained in Table 2.

Table 1. Coding Schemes for Content Categories.

Content Categories	Sub-categories	Coding
Principles	Integrity	PRNCPL1
	Objectivity	PRNCPL2
	Due care	PRNCPL3
	Confidentiality	PRNCPL4
	Competence	PRNCPL5
	Independence	PRNCPL6
Applications	Scope of application	APLKN1
	Examples of threats	APLKN 2
	Examples of safeguards	APLKN 3
Rules	General rule statements	RUULS1
	Rules on specific issues	RUULS2
Assumptions	Public interest	ASUMPN1
	Materiality	ASUMPN2
Others	Paragraph(s) fall into none of the above	Others

Table 2. Coding Schemes for Presentation Format Categories.

Format Categories	Explanation of Coded Patterns
Pure P	Paragraph(s) solely on principles (including conceptual framework)
Pure R	Paragraph(s) solely on rules (both general and specific rules)
Pure T/S	Paragraph(s) solely explaining threats and safeguards
P + T/S and T/S + P	Paragraphs shaping a pattern with principle(s) and illustrative threats and safeguards
R + T/S and T/S + R	Paragraphs shaping a pattern with rule(s) and illustrative threats and safeguards
P + R	Paragraphs shaping a pattern with principle(s) and rule(s)
P + T/S + R	Paragraphs shaping a pattern with principle(s), illustrative threat(s) and safeguard(s), and rule(s)
Others	Paragraph(s) fall into none of the above-listed categories

Note: P refers to statements of Fundamental Principles; R refers to paragraphs of Rules; T/S refers to paragraphs of threats–safeguards illustration; Variable Assumptions is excluded from this statistical description due to a significantly small number of frequencies in the coding result.

RESULTS OF CONTENT ANALYSIS AND DISCUSSION

Coding Results and Discussion on Hypothesis 1

Semantic analysis based on the coding units refers to the differentiation between paragraphs predominated by principles and those by rules. Results from this analysis depict the predominance of judgmental principles or regulatory rules in the two ethical codes under investigation. The total frequencies and percentages of counts on statements of pure principles (112.5, 13.70%) and pure rules (179, 21.80%) in the IFAC and CICPA codes illustrate the differences between the two ways of expressing ethical requirements and regulation. A larger gap between the principles and rules can be observed within the CICPA Code. The simple statistical summary of frequency counts supports Hypothesis 1, namely, the CICPA Code focuses its content on ethical principles not on enacting rules, in the same manner as the IFAC Code.

Assumptions relating to public interest and materiality are rarely stated with specific dedications in both codes, and they are usually requirements underlying the other components of the code statements, for example, the concept of 'materiality' appears 19 times in the threats–safeguards sections of the IFAC Code, and 23 times in the CICPA Code; however, only 5.5 times are 'materiality' and 'public interest' identified in the statement which specifically clarifies the threshold for professional judgment and decision. Basic assumptions, or threshold for ethical judgment and decision, can be traced in both codes of ethics. This might imply that through readily declaring the public interest and considering materiality, the codes of ethics have required professional accountants to act in the public interest while remaining powerful in protecting professional reputations (Parker, 1994).

The proportion of relationships resulting from this study directly addresses the concerns of some international professional bodies on the tendency of the IFAC Code of Ethics to become more rules-based instead of focusing more on the fundamental principles and giving more room to professional judgment and decision. Professional bodies advocate that care should be taken that principles do not become rules and that professional accountants need to be able to exercise their own judgment. This concern is even sterner in the expression of the CICPA Code, in which the principles-based rather than rules-based approach is adopted from the IFAC Code. However, our findings here show a wider gap between principles and rules in the CICPA Code than in the IFAC Code. The version adopted by CICPA embraces more rules in its legalistic form.

A breakdown of the three thematic parts helps illustrate further the extent of adopting the principles-based conceptual framework approach by the two codes of ethics. As an adopted version of the IFAC Code, the CICPA Code follows the same overall structure of three major thematic parts: general introduction to fundamental principles and conceptual framework approach, application of the fundamental principles and conceptual framework approach in public practices, and application among business accountants.

Coding Results and Discussion of Hypotheses 2a and 2b

Coding Results and Discussion of Hypothesis 2a

The threats–safeguards conceptual framework approach tends to take its straightforward shape in each code. Statements on applications of fundamental principles by means of threats and safeguards stand out as the highest count frequencies (421.5) and percentages (51.34%) in both codes of ethics. It can be found in Table 3 that the CICPA Code puts considerably more effort into embedding the IFAC-defined conceptual framework of threats and safeguards into its code of ethics.

Table 3. Frequencies and Percentage of Total Counts for Content Categories.

Content Categories	Total of Both Codes				IFAC Code		CICPA Code	
	Coder 1	Coder 2	Average		Average		Average	
	No.	No.	No.	%	No.	%	No.	%
Principles	118	107	112.5	13.70	71.5	17.02	41	10.22
Applications	416	427	421.5	51.34	199.5	47.50	222	55.36
Rules	190	168	179	21.80	99.5	23.69	79.5	19.83
Assumptions	13	12	12.5	15.23	5.5	1.31	7	1.75
Others	84	107	95.5	11.63	44	10.48	51.5	12.84
Total	821	821	821	100	420	100	401	100

One commonplace feature which can be summarized here is the fact that the enforcement of the conceptual framework of threats and safeguards has been clearly presented in both codes of ethics. As is widely recognized and accepted by most professional bodies in the international accounting communities, the codes' threat-and-safeguard approach better serves the public interest and professional reputation in nearly all circumstances. Propensity and preference for the threats–safeguards approach has been echoed by the International Organization of Securities Commissions (IOSCO) by recognizing the benefits of a threats and safeguards approach on the basis of a framework of principles and referring them to the IFAC Code of Ethics (IOSCO, 2007). It should be noted that the CICPA Code highlights the threats–safeguards approach more than the IFAC Code, that is, 55.36% versus 47.5% expressed as a percentage of coverage in the code text.

Fig. 1 depicts the de-structured relationships between the studied categories and the principles-based conceptual framework approach, and findings are summed up as follows.

It is clear in the IFAC Code that principles (35, 40.7%), together with rules (33, 38.37%), dominate the preamble of Part A, while applications of fundamental principles and conceptual framework in terms of threats and safeguards outperform the rest of the categories in both Parts B and C, in which principles and conceptual framework are referred to as the different fields of accounting practice. This finding just fits in the declaration of IFAC's adoption of the principles-based conceptual framework approach, at least in its expression of semantic structure.

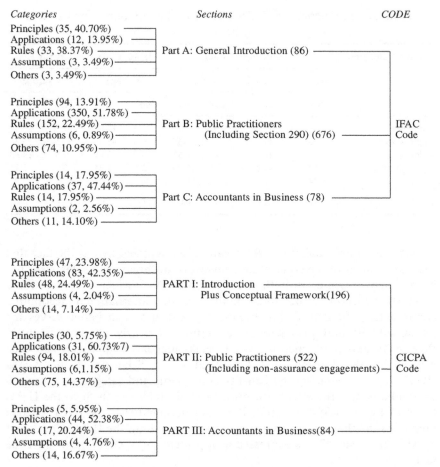

Fig. 1. Semantic relationships with conceptual framework. *Note:* For each of the two ethical codes under investigation, the coding results of the two coders are aggregated for the purpose of this illustrative diagram.

It is also clear in the CICPA Code that the framework of threats and safeguards dominates all the three parts (42.35%, 60.73% and 52.38%, respectively). Even more impressively, Part I of the CICPA Code is dedicated to a description of threats and safeguards more than of fundamental principles. This finding is consistent with the overall analysis of CICPA's tendency to rely strongly on the threats–safeguards approach. However, this may lead to a lack of adequate coverage of fundamental principles and conceptual framework approach, especially in Part I of the general introduction. Further analysis results in another finding that the legalistic form of CICPA lends its remarkable influences to the semantic expression of principles and rules.

To sum up, Hypothesis 2a has been largely supported by the coding results. As is stated in the hypothesis, the CICPA Code adopts the same ethical conceptual framework of threats and safeguards as the IFAC Code. The principles-based conceptual framework approach to establishing the code of ethics has been presented in an adequately clear and powerful way of focusing on the fundamental principles and a framework of threats and safeguards. Still some differences exist between the IFAC and CICPA codes with regard to the extent of being consistent with the principles-based conceptual framework approach. The IFAC Code tends to balance between the principles-versus-rules debate and the threats–safeguards framework approach in its expression, while the CICPA Code, an adopted version of the IFAC Code, has even gone a bit further beyond the principles-based conceptual framework approach with its imposed legalistic form.

Coding Results and Discussion on Hypothesis 2b
A concise description of the presentation formats underlying the two codes of ethics is presented in Table 4. This table depicts the forms of presenting the principles-based conceptual framework in the two codes under investigation. It is quite striking that in both codes of ethics, the most-weighted presentation format is R + T/S, that is, 35.37% on average for the total counts of the two codes. This implies that rules are closely associated with the framework approach of threats and safeguards. More impressively, for the CICPA Code, the percentage of R + T/S pattern has been found to be more than double the second largest percentage in the same text.

The fact is apparent that threats and safeguards (T/S) play a critical role in constructing the principles-based conceptual framework as they are uttered either alone (47.5, 21.54%) or combined with other presentation formats, for instance, P + T/S (16, 7.26%), R + T/S (78, 35.37) and P + T/S + R (24.5, 11.11%).

The traditional pattern of P + R takes up only 7.03% of the total, and the newly established P + T/S + R pattern based on the framework of threats and safeguards amounts to 11.11%.

Although both IFAC and CICPA declare a principles-based approach in their ethical codification, the two codes differ in presentation formats.

Table 4. Frequencies and Percentage of Total Counts for Presentation Format Categories.

Legislative Formats Categories	Total of Both Codes				IFAC Code		CICPA Code	
	Coder 1	Coder 2	Average		Average		Average	
	No.	No.	No.	%	No.	%	No.	%
Pure P	27	15	21	9.52	14	12.02	7	6.73
Pure R	19	17	18	8.16	8.5	7.30	9.5	9.13
Pure T/S	52	43	47.5	21.54	26	22.32	21.5	20.67
P + T/S[a]	15	17	16	7.26	11	9.44	5	4.81
R + T/S[b]	75	81	78	35.37	32.5	27.90	45.5	43.75
P + R	15	16	15.5	7.03	11	9.44	4.5	4.33
P + T/S + R	23	26	24.5	11.11	13.5	11.59	11	10.58
Total	226	215	220.5	100.00	116.5	100.00	104	100.00

Notes: 1. (a) This category also includes T/S + P; (b) This category also includes T/S + R.
2. P refers to statements of fundamental principles; R refers to paragraphs of rules; T/S refers to paragraphs of threats–safeguards illustration; category *Assumptions* is excluded from this statistical description due to an exceptionally small number of frequencies in the coding results.

P-related patterns (including Pure P, P + T/S, P + R and P + T/S + R) in the IFAC Code take up 42.49%, while R-related patterns (including Pure R, R + T/S, P + R and P + T/S + R), 56.23%. However, P-related patterns in the CICPA Code only take up 26.45%, while R-related patterns take up 67.79%. The differences in legislative formats prove to be parallel with those in terms of semantic units in the foregoing analysis of the principles-based approach in the codes of ethics.

A breakdown analysis of presentation format into the above-mentioned three thematic parts also helps illustrate further the extent of adopting and the way of presenting the principles-based conceptual framework approach by the two codes of ethics. Fig. 2 depicts the associations between the studied presentation formats and the presentation of principles-based conceptual framework approach, and findings are summed up as follows.

A part-by-part comparison in Fig. 2 sorts out some common structuring features shared by both codes. Firstly, P + R pattern is important in the preamble of ethical codes (26.83% in the IFAC Code and 22.5% in the CICPA Code), and usage of this pattern declines in the remaining parts of the application. Secondly, Pure T/S pattern takes significant roles in all parts of both codes of ethics, which again echoes the advocate for the framework

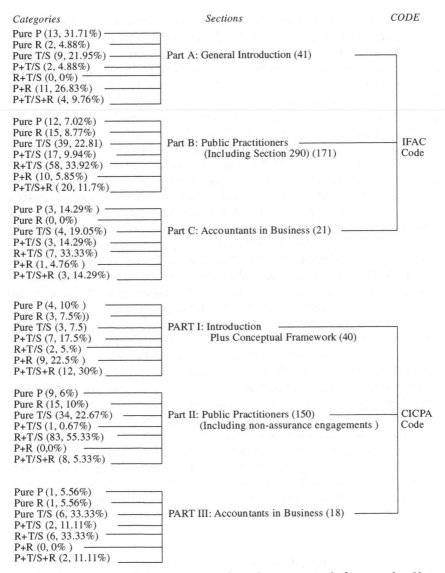

Categories

Pure P (13, 31.71%) ————
Pure R (2, 4.88%)   ————
Pure T/S (9, 21.95%) ———— Part A: General Introduction (41)
P+T/S (2, 4.88%)   ————
R+T/S (0, 0%)   ————
P+R (11, 26.83%)   ————
P+T/S+R (4, 9.76%) ————

Pure P (12, 7.02%)   ————
Pure R (15, 8.77%)   ————
Pure T/S (39, 22.81) ———— Part B: Public Practitioners ————   IFAC
P+T/S (17, 9.94%)   ————   (Including Section 290) (171)   Code
R+T/S (58, 33.92%)   ————
P+R (10, 5.85%)   ————
P+T/S+R (20, 11.7%) ————

Pure P (3, 14.29%) ————
Pure R (0, 0%)   ————
Pure T/S (4, 19.05%) ———— Part C: Accountants in Business (21) ————
P+T/S (3, 14.29%)   ————
R+T/S (7, 33.33%)   ————
P+R (1, 4.76%)   ————
P+T/S+R (3, 14.29%) ————

Pure P (4, 10%)   ————
Pure R (3, 7.5%))   ————
Pure T/S (3, 7.5)   ———— PART I: Introduction ————
P+T/S (7, 17.5%)   ————   Plus Conceptual Framework (40)
R+T/S (2, 5.%)   ————
P+R (9, 22.5%)   ————
P+T/S+R (12, 30%)   ————

Pure P (9, 6%)   ————
Pure R (15, 10%)   ————
Pure T/S (34, 22.67%) ——— Part II: Public Practitioners (150) ———— CICPA
P+T/S (1, 0.67%)   ————   (Including non-assurance engagements) Code
R+T/S (83, 55.33%)   ————
P+R (0,0%)   ————
P+T/S+R (8, 5.33%)   ————

Pure P (1, 5.56%)   ————
Pure R (1, 5.56%)   ————
Pure T/S (6, 33.33%) ———— PART III: Accountants in Business (18) ————
P+T/S (2, 11.11%)   ————
R+T/S (6, 33.33%)   ————
P+R (0, 0%)   ————
P+T/S+R (2, 11.11%) ————

Fig. 2. Presentation formats constructing the conceptual framework. *Note:* Two coding results of two coders are aggregated for the purpose of this illustrative diagram.

approach of threats and safeguards in the current international accounting communities. Thirdly, the P + T/S + R pattern in each part of both codes ethics is moderately adopted (around 10%), which shows the potential convergence of the newly established framework of threats and safeguards with the tradition P + R pattern. Last but not least, R + T/S pattern is most frequently used in the third part of both codes, which might lead to a perception that the principles-based conceptual framework is too much public practice oriented, leaving rigid ethical rules for accountants in business.

Sharp contrasts in terms of presentation formats are also observed between the IFAC and CICPA codes in presenting the principles-based conceptual framework. As an example, Pure P pattern is a key to the preamble of the IFAC Code (31.71%) while this pattern only takes up 10% of the introductory part of the CICPA Code. Normally, fundamental principles are expected to be determined and explained in the first part of a code of ethics. As another example, R + T/S pattern ranks much higher in Part II of the CICPA Code (55.33%) than in Part B of the IFAC Code (22.81%). The second parts of both codes of ethics are given most material volume because they are dedicated to the application of fundamental principles and conceptual framework approach in the assurance and non-assurance fields of public practices, and the structural differences in this part between the two codes of ethics shed light on the different perceptions and presentations of the principles-based conceptual framework approach to establishing the codes of ethics for professional accountants.

Both overall and breakdown analyses of the presentation formats underlying the texts of the IFAC and CICPA codes of ethics reveal the fact that the threats–safeguards framework has been introduced into the principles-based approach, and both codes of ethics under investigation are geared towards using it as the best way of presenting a conceptual framework with either principles or rules. Hypothesis 2b has been majorly supported, and the CICPA Code adopts the same presentation formats with the ethical conceptual framework of the IFAC Code. To be concrete, both codes are presented largely in the formats of P-R and R + T/S.

Tests on the Codification Results: Kappa Statistics
for Inter-coder Reliability

Stability and reproducibility are two important factors that the researcher using content analysis should take into consideration for research validity (Stemler, 2001). In the process of coding the two codes of ethics for professional accountants which are written in two different languages, special care has been exercised to ensure that the coding schemes in Tables 1 and 2 shared by two coders of similar but inter-supplementary academic background and research fields lead to the same textual materials being coded in the same category.

Statistically, inter-coder reliability is a critical measure to determine the research validity of a content-analysis-based study. This validity measure, describing the generalizability of results and findings, indicates how well two or more coders reached the same judgments in coding the textual documents. Among various methods of estimating inter-coder reliability, the current study produces on the basis of two individual coders the Kappa statistic K, which is a very robust measure for nominal-level variables, and this statistic can be computed by standard statistical packages such as the SPSS crosstab (Landis & Koch, 1977).

The Kappa statistics for validity of coding the studied categories and presentation formats are computed in Table 5. Significantly valid agreement between the coding results of two separate coders has been achieved in terms of coding both semantic units and presentation formats. The Kappa is 0.887 and 0.781 respectively, significant at 0.001.

IMPLICATIONS AND CONCLUSIONS

The current study has conducted a content analysis of the latest Exposure Draft of the two codes of ethics by IFAC and by CICPA. Semantic units are

Table 5. Symmetric Measures (for Coding Categories Presentation Formats).

		Value	Asymp. Std. Error(a)	Approx. T(b)	Approx. Sig.
Categories	Measure of Agreement Kappa	0.887	0.014	41.536	0.000
	N of Valid Cases	821			
Legislative	Measure of Agreement Kappa	0.781	0.022	38.846	0.000
formats	N of Valid Cases	821			

Notes: 1. Not assuming the null hypothesis; using the asymptotic standard error assuming the null hypothesis.
2. In order to computation of Kappa for format categories, all paragraphs were coded with the coding schemes in Table 2.

coded to identify the significant components of a principles-based approach, and presentation formats are classified to illustrate how the principles-based conceptual framework is presented in each code of ethics.

The results of content analysis reveal several explanatory findings on how extensively CICPA has adopted the IFAC approach in revising its national ethical code. We find that with its new revision of the national Code of Ethics for Professional Accountants, CICPA has adopted, to a great extent, the principles-based conceptual framework for accounting ethics, in terms of both codification contents and presentation formats. However, CICPA still shows traces of tilting towards the rules-based approach. To name a couple of evidences, the entire codification is promulgated in legalistic formats, and it strongly corresponds to the *Laws for Accounting* in China. Also, extensive concrete rules or prohibitions are listed to illustrate the conceptual framework of threats–safeguards. With our content analysis and observations in place, we conclude that CICPA, with some reservations of its legalistic tradition, has partially moved to a principles-based approach to ethical codification of accounting profession.

Without doubt, these findings could be important and instructive to the accounting professional bodies in other emerging markets when they are about to get involved in converging with the IFAC ethical regulations. The practical implications of conclusions for other emerging markets are summarized as follows.

In the first place, based on the results of content analysis, one tentative conclusion is that the CICPA legalistic focus on the code of ethics for professional accountants goes a bit far in terms of the principles-based conceptual framework as per the IFAC Code of Ethics. Compared with the principles-based conceptual framework rooted in the IFAC Code of Ethics, the CICPA Code in its rigid legalistic format detracts its focus from the principles-based conceptual framework approach. Codification of ethical professional behaviour can be closely connected with the legalistic regulation of accounting standards or commercial codes, but by nature ethical principles are different from those legal doctrines and laws. Establishing a principles-based ethical conceptual framework proposed by IFAC is expected to entail more robustness and flexibility for professional accountants in their reasoning and judgment when confronted with infinite variations in circumstances that arise in both business and practice, and by no means implies setting up a series of legal doctrines which would transform the conceptual framework into rules-based norms. This legalistic form of ethical accounting regulations results from the authoritative role of CICPA in the Chinese professional accounting community. If national cultures are considered as a factor to influence the focus on principles or rules in ethical accounting codification, emerging economies such as China tend to exercise more authoritative powers on professional codes of ethics by means of stricter legalistic formats. Our finding in this regard proves a practical and nation-specific form of combining direct import and legal enhancement for the Chinese accounting profession as it moves to converge with IFAC's code of ethics.

Secondly, the observations made in the current study on the extensive adoption of the framework of threats and safeguards help affirm a conclusion that this conceptual framework has become increasingly important in implementing the principles-based codes of ethics for professional accountants. Identification of material threats to fundamental principles and provision of adequate safeguards is not only an indispensible part of the principles-based conceptual framework, but also a set of flexible building blocks which can accommodate rapidly changing environments in the business and accounting professions. However, the power of the threats–safeguards framework in applying fundamental principles could be limited if it is extensively associated with statements of legalistic rigid rules. In practice, the CICPA Code is evidenced with more rule orientations than the IFAC Code in applying the framework of threats and safeguards.

The last but not least valuable pragmatic point inferred from this study is that a principles-based conceptual framework in a code of ethics would theoretically be best expressed in the form of Principle(s) + Threat(s)/ Safeguard(s) + Rule(s). In this legislative form, principles are highlighted ahead of further investigations into threats to fundamental principles and the safeguards to reduce or eliminate those threats, then rules put forward prohibitions on conduct if no effective safeguards are available to achieve the defined goal. In practices exemplified by the IFAC and CICPA codes of ethics, threats and safeguards combined with either principle(s) or rule(s) prevail in the presentation of their ethical conceptual framework approach.

However, in practice when presenting the principles-based conceptual framework in terms of threats and safeguards, it should be borne in mind that the framework of threats–safeguards could be clad with a rules-based codification given the imposition of rigid legalistic formats.

REFLECTION ON LIMITATIONS AND SUGGESTION FOR FURTHER RESEARCH

One limitation of the current study is a lack of information about the motivation of CICPA to adopt the principles-based conceptual framework approach to ethical codification, besides the pragmatic needs of global economic and business environments. The current study focuses its comparison on IFAC and CICPA, without limited inclusion of differences in cultural traits. Cultural differences have been introduced into accounting ethics research (Cohen, Pant, & Sharp, 1996; Roxas & Stoneback, 1997).

With full awareness of those limitations which might influence the results of content analysis and adequate controls to ensure research validity, those findings in the current study of the IFAC and CICPA codes of ethics for professional accountants have significant implications for convergence of accounting professions in other emerging economies with the international accounting ethical codification. This study also implies possible directions for further research in the future. On the one hand, should in-depth surveys be accessible at a higher organizational level, implicative findings would be obtained on the internationalization of professional accounting bodies in the emerging markets. On the other hand, analyses based on these cross-cultural factors are suggested for future research into the behavioural consequences of applying fundamental principles, rules or frameworks of threats and safeguards in accounting practices.

NOTES

1. He once served as a UN auditor practising audits on ethical issues and programme management in United Nations organizations, and was also selected by the Chinese Institute of Certified Public Accountants as the first intern to conduct research studies in Scotland on the codification of professional ethics for Chinese accountants. His research interests include business and accounting ethics, and international auditing and accounting.

2. She is interested in the research fields of international organizations and strategic management.

ACKNOWLEDGEMENT

The authors thank Sun Yat-sen University for the generous support provided by the 'Fundamental Research Funds for the Central Universities'.

REFERENCES

ACCA. (2003, November). *Comments from ACCA on proposed revised code of ethics: An exposure draft issued by the international federation of accountants.* Retrieved from http://www.accaglobal.com/general/activities/policy_papers/archive/other/1106003. Accessed on October 1, 2009.

Bagshaw, K. (2006, December). Principles v rules. *Accountancymagazine.com.* Retrieved from http://www.icaew.com/index.cfm/route/149273/icaew_ga/pdf. Accessed on January 1, 2011.

Canning, M., & O'Dwyer, B. (2002). A critique of the descriptive power of the private interest mode of professional accounting ethics. *Accounting, Auditing & Accountability Journal, 16*(2), 159–185.

CIMA. (2007, May 18). Institute issues statement in response to IFAC proposal. *Accountancy Age.* Retrieved from http://www.accountancyage.com/accountancyage/news/2190182/cima-warns-code-ethics-become. Accessed on October 1, 2009.

Cohen, J. R., Pant, L. W., & Sharp, D. J. (1996). A methodological note on cross-cultural accounting ethics research. *The International Journal of Accounting, 31*(1), 55–66.

Davidson, R. A., & Gelardi, A. M. G. (1996). Analysis of the conceptual framework of China's new accounting system. *Accounting Horizon, 10*(1), 58–74.

Farrell, B. J., & Cobbin, D. M. (2000). A content analysis of codes of ethics from fifty-seven national accounting organizations. *Business Ethics: A European Review, 9*(3), 180–190.

FASB (Financial Accounting Standards Board). (1976). *Scope and implications of the conceptual framework project.* New York, NY: FASB.

FEE. (2003, November). *A conceptual approach to safeguarding integrity, objectivity and independence throughout the financial reporting Chain.* Retrieved from http://ec.europa.eu/internal_market/securities/docs/analysts/contributions/fee_en.pdf. Accessed on October 1, 2009.

Herron, T., & Gilbertson, D. L. (2004). Ethical principles vs. ethical rules: The moderating effect of moral development on audit independence judgments. *Business Ethics Quarterly, 14*(3), 499–523.

ICAEW. (2009). *Professional_ethics/Principles_versus_rules_debate.* Retrieved from http://www.icaew.com/149274/ciaew_ga/en/Technical_and_Business_Topics/. Accessed on October 1, 2009.

IOSCO. (2007). *A survey on the regulation of non-audit services provided by auditors to audited companies.* Technical committee and emerging markets committee of the IOSCO. Retrieved from http://www.betterregulationcom/doc/17/1705. Accessed on October 1, 2009.

Landis, J. R., & Koch, G. G. (1977). The measurement of observer agreement for categorical data. *Biometrics, 33*, 159–174.

Lin, Z. J. (1998). Internationalization of public accounting: Chinese experience. *Managerial Auditing Journal, 13*(2), 84–94.

Lin, K. Z., & Chan, K. H. (2000). Auditing standards in China: A comparative analysis with relevant international standards and guidelines. *The International Journal of Accounting, 35*(4), 559–577.

Lin, K., & Fraser, I. A. M. (2008). Auditors' ability to resist client pressure and culture: Perceptions in China and the United Kingdom. *Journal of International Financial Management & Accounting, 19*(2), 161–183.

Page, M. (2005). The search for a conceptual framework: Quest for a holy grail, or hunting a snark? *Accounting, Auditing & Accountability Journal, 18*(4), 565–576.

Parker, L. D. (1994). Professional accounting body ethics: In search of the private interest. *Accounting, Organization and Society, 19*(6), 507–525.

Rayman, R. A. (2007). Fair value accounting and the present value fallacy: The need for an alternative conceptual framework. *The British Accounting Review, 39*(3), 211–225.

Roxas, M. L., & Stoneback, J. Y. (1997). An investigation of the ethical decision making process across varying cultures. *The International Journal of Accounting, 32*(4), 503–535.

Satava, D. C., Caldwell, C., & Richards, L. (2006). Ethics and the auditing culture: Rethinking the foundation of accounting and auditing. *Journal of Business Ethics, 64*(3), 271–284.

Stemler, S. (2001). An overview of content analysis. *Practical Assessment, Research & Evaluation, 7*(17) Retrieved from http://PAREonline.net/getvn.asp?v=7&n=17. Accessed on October 1, 2009.

Weber, R. P. (1990). *Basic content analysis* (2nd ed.). Newbury Park, CA: Sage.

Whittington, G. (2008). Harmonisation or discord? The critical role of the IASB conceptual framework review. *Journal of Accounting and Public Policy, 27*(6), 495–502.

Wu, C. (2003). A study of the adjustment of ethical recognition and ethical decision-making of managers-to-be across the Taiwan Strait before and after receiving a business ethics education. *Journal of Business Ethics, 45*, 291–307.

Velayutham. (2003). The accounting profession's code of ethics: Is it a code of ethics or a code of quality assurance? *Critical Perspectives on Accounting, 14*, 483–503.

Xiao, J. Z., Weetman, P., & Sun, M. (2004). Political influence and coexistence of a uniform accounting system and accounting standards: Recent developments in China. *Abacus, 40*(2), 193–218.

FRAUDULENT FINANCIAL REPORTING: CORPORATE BEHAVIOR OF CHINESE LISTED COMPANIES

Jinyu Zhu and Simon S. Gao

ABSTRACT

Purpose – *This study investigates the nature, types, and methods of fraudulent financial reporting committed by Chinese listed companies with a view to understanding corporate behavior relating to management fraud in China. Such an understanding is important for preventing frauds and achieving better financial reporting compliance.*

Design/Methodology/Approach – *This study adopts a descriptive research approach using the data based on 182 punishment bulletins issued by the China Securities Regulatory Commission from 2002 to 2006. The study considers three categories of frauds (i.e., false income statements, false balance sheets, and insufficient or false disclosure) and uses these categories to describe and analyze the fraud cases.*

Research findings/Insights – *Based on the sample of 83 cases over the 5-year period from 2002 to 2006, this study finds that all the frauds in the sample involved the manipulation, alteration, and falsification of reported financial information. Fraud schemes often contained more than one*

Accounting in Asia
Research in Accounting in Emerging Economies, Volume 11, 61–82
Copyright © 2011 by Emerald Group Publishing Limited
All rights of reproduction in any form reserved
ISSN: 1479-3563/doi:10.1108/S1479-3563(2011)0000011008

technique to misstate financial statements, typically through overstating revenues and assets, and understating liabilities and expenses. Most of the sample companies committed several frauds simultaneously. This study also reveals that most of the frauds committed by Chinese listed companies lasted more than 2 years, with the longest being 9 years, and common intervals between the initial fraud year and the announcement year of punishment were more than 3 years, with the longest being 11 years.

Theoretical/Academic implications – *This study provides an empirical analysis of fraudulent financial reporting cases committed by Chinese listed companies. These cases were rarely studied in the Western literature. This study contributes to the extant literature by providing an insight into management fraud in China. Research into fraudulent financial reporting in the largest developing economy is certainly of interest as prior research into this area is mostly based on developed economies.*

Practitioner/Policy implications – *The implications drawn from this study could be useful for a better understanding of the management behavior of companies in developing and transitional economies. This study has a potential to assist regulators and accounting professional bodies to set guidelines facilitating corporate compliance of regulated financial reporting.*

Keywords: Accounting profession; audit; Chinese listed company; financial irregularities; management frauds

INTRODUCTION

Corporate fraud has recently received considerable attention from the business community, accounting profession, academicians, and regulators (Kedia & Philippon, 2009; Rezaee, 2005). Fraud may be defined as intentional deception, cheating, or stealing. It can be committed against users such as investors, creditors, customers, or government entities (Weirich & Reinstein, 2000). The US Statement on Auditing Standards (SAS) No. 82 identifies two types of corporate fraud: financial reporting fraud and misappropriation of assets. Financial reporting fraud (also called management fraud) refers to management behavior that seeks to inflate reported profits or other assets by deliberately overstating assets and revenues or understating expenses and liabilities in financial statements (Rezaee, 2005; Zahra, Priem, & Rasheed, 2005). Misappropriation of assets (also called employee fraud) is the behavior of employees stealing money or other property from their employers (e.g., embezzlement, theft, and kickbacks). This study is concerned with management fraud.

In the international arena, numerous examples of corporate failures (e.g., Bank of Credit and Commerce International (BCCI), Barings Bank, Enron, Worldcom, Societe Generale, and Parmalat) occurred over the decades, which are fundamentally the results of fraudulent activities performed either individually or collectively at the top level of organizations (Karpoff, Lee, & Martin, 2008). In the United States, annual fraud costs to American companies exceeded 6 percent of their revenues in the beginning of this century (ACFE, 2004). In the United Kingdom, fraud cost £13.9 billion in 2005 (ACPO, 2007). The collapse of Enron resulted in about US$70 billion lost in market capitalization, which was devastating for a significant number of investors, employees, and pensioners (Rezaee, 2005). As management fraud is a serious threat to market participants' confidence in audited financial statements, the society, investors, and accounting profession thus have a vested interest in the prevention and detection of such fraud (IAASB, 2004; Karpoff et al., 2008; Nor, Ahmad, & Saleh, 2010; Zahra et al., 2005). In response to the public outcry in the United States, the Sarbanes–Oxley Act of 2002 was passed by the US Congress in June 2002, laying down fines ranging between US$1 million to US$5 million and imprisonment ranging from 10 to 20 years for knowingly certifying false statements; the deliberate destruction of any audit work papers or other documents; and any mail, wire, bank, or securities fraud.

China began its economic reform three decades ago and has since achieved a great success. Chinese economy is now ranked the second largest in the world in terms of GDP, according to International Monitory Fund's (IMF) World Economic Outlook (2010). Along with the economic growth, China's capital market has also developed rapidly. As of May 26, 2010, companies listed on the Shanghai and Shenzhen Securities Exchanges reached 1,860 with the market capitalization of over US$3.13 trillion. In 2009, the Shanghai Stock Exchange was the sixth largest stock exchange in the world, ranking just below the London Stock Exchange. Over 150 companies have also been listed overseas (including Hong Kong) (CSRC, 2010). In 2006, China's Ministry of Finance issued the latest accounting and auditing standards, which were to a large extent converged with international standards. This was widely recognized as a very important step forward in promoting Chinese economic development and enhancing China's position in global capital markets (Zhong, 2006).

Transition economies provide much scope for corporate fraud (Chen, Firth, Gao, & Rui, 2006; Nor et al., 2010). Like many other transition economies in the world, China is currently facing the challenge of fighting corporate frauds and irregularities. While Chinese media has reported several cases of management frauds committed by Chinese listed companies (e.g., the case of *Yinguangxia*), there have been very few studies in the academic literature that have examined the nature, significance and characteristics of those frauds. The aim of this study is to present an empirical investigation of management frauds in China by analyzing the types and methods of management fraud committed by Chinese listed companies. Based on the sample of 83 cases over the 5-year period from 2002 to 2006 this study examines the main types, methods, and duration of Chinese listed companies' management fraud, and the period between the initial irregularity year (i.e., the first fraud year in the case) and the announcement of punishment by the China's Securities Regulatory Commission (CSRC).[1] In an attempt to reduce egregious acts of fraud, China has strengthened the powers and effectiveness of the CSRC since 2000s (Chen et al., 2006). The enforcement actions of the CSRC have provided the fraud data for this study.

This paper is organized as follows: The next section provides a general review of the literature on management fraud and the characteristics and schemes of such fraud. The third section describes the sample and data. The fourth section presents the results and analyzes various fraud methods committed by Chinese listed companies. The fifth section highlights some strategies that could be considered to prevent management fraud. The final section concludes the paper.

THE NATURE OF MANAGEMENT FRAUD AND LITERATURE REVIEW

Management fraud is a deliberate attempt of corporations to deceive or mislead users of published financial statements (especially investors and creditors) by preparing and disseminating materially misstated financial statements (Rezaee, 2005). While management fraud can be shown in a variety of ways, the fraud schemes are usually more specific. For example, the fraudulent financial reporting methods frequently used by the management of

American and European listed companies that have been detected since 2001 mainly include the following:

- fictitious or fabricated revenues,
- altering the times at which revenues are recognized,
- improper asset valuations and reporting,
- concealing liabilities and expenses, and
- improper financial statements disclosures (Badawi, 2005).

The following techniques have also been identified in the literature:

- Recording fictitious journal entries, particularly close to the end of an accounting period, to manipulate operating results or achieve other objectives (Dooley, 2002; Nguyen, 2008);
- Inappropriately adjusting assumptions and changing judgments used to estimate account balances (Powell, Jubb, de Lange, & Langfield-Smith, 2005);
- Omitting, advancing, or delaying recognition in the financial statements of events and transactions that have occurred during the reporting period (McNichols & Wilson, 1988; Nguyen, 2008);
- Concealing, or not disclosing, facts that could affect the amounts recorded in the financial statements (Bhamornsiri & Schroeder, 2004; James, 2003);
- Engaging in complex transactions that are structured to misrepresent the financial position or financial performance of the entity (Dooley, 2002; Nguyen, 2008); and
- Altering records and terms related to significant and unusual transactions (Dooley, 2002; Johnson & Rudolph, 2007).

Deloitte Forensic Center (2007) classifies the frauds into 12 categories based on how the fraud was committed including (1) aiding and abetting, (2) asset misappropriation, (3) bribery and kickbacks, (4) goodwill, (5) improper disclosures, (6) investments, (7) manipulation of account receivables, (8) manipulation of assets, (9) manipulation of expenses, (10) manipulation of liabilities, (11) manipulation of reserves, and (12) revenues recognition. Earnings management (i.e., distorting earnings to achieve earnings targets) is the most common method of management fraud. Management fraud can also vary in terms of direct falsification of transactions and events or intentional delay (early) recognition of transactions or events that eventually occur. Fictitious transaction frauds are often considered more aggressive methods of fraud schemes and occur more frequently and draw more attention from auditors and regulators than the intentional early (delayed) recognition of transactions (Rezaee, 2005).

In today's technological era, fraud has become very complicated and it is increasingly difficult to detect, especially when it is collusive in nature and committed by top management who are capable of concealing it (Alleyne & Howard, 2005; Chen & Sennetti, 2005; Holtfreter, 2004). Following the traditional audit procedures, external auditors have enormous difficulties to detect management frauds as the management that commits frauds intends to cover them through a variety of complex means (Holtfreter, 2004; Karpoff et al., 2008). This often leads to an increase of audit failures that occurs when there is a serious distortion of the financial statements that is not reflected in the audit report, and the auditor has made a serious error in the conduct of the audit (Arens, Elder, & Beasley, 2003). However, a properly done audit does not guarantee that there will be no serious deceptions in the financial statements (Tackett, Wolf, & Claypool, 2004).

Various theories and approaches have emerged over the past decades to detect fraudulent financial reporting and identify the determinants of management fraud (e.g., Apostolou, Hassell, Webber, & Sumners, 2001; Cecchini, Aytug, Koehler, & Pathak, 2010; Cullinan & Sutton, 2002; Durtschi, Hillison, & Pacini, 2004; Kaminski, Wetzel, & Guan, 2004; Karim & Siegel, 1998; Kirkos, Spathis, & Manolopoulos, 2007; Krambia-Kapardis, Christodoulou, & Agathocleous, 2010; Lou & Wang, 2009; Pai, Hsu, & Wang, 2010; Robinson & Santore, 2011; Wilks & Zimbelman, 2004). For example, Lou and Wang (2009) find fraudulent reporting positively correlated to one of the following conditions: more financial pressure of a firm or supervisor of a firm, higher percentage of complex transactions of a firm, more questionable integrity of a firm's managers, or more deterioration in relation between a firm and its auditor.

A number of auditing standards have also been established, providing guidelines concerning fraudulent financial reporting and the responsibility of auditors in detecting frauds. For example, the US Statement on Auditing Standards 1 (AU110) "Codification of Auditing Standards and Procedures" states that "The auditor has a responsibility to plan and perform the audit to obtain reasonable assurance about whether the financial statements are free of material misstatement, whether caused by error or fraud. Because of the nature of audit evidence and the characteristics of fraud, the auditor is able to obtain reasonable, but not absolute, assurance that material misstatements are detected" (AICPA, 2006). Although audit is not intended to target the existence of fraud, auditors do plan their work in such a way that errors and irregularities material to financial statements would be detected (Hemraj, 2002). Audit, by its design, is capable of providing reassurance that financial statements are not materially misleading due to fraud or error; however, an auditor is not responsible for finding fraud or other intentional misstatements (Hemraj, 2002). Management fraud is one of the roots resulting in audit failures.

Research on management fraud was predominately concerned with the cases from developed economies (e.g., Beasley, 1996; Bonner, Palmrose, & Young, 1998; Cox & Weirich, 2002; Holtfreter, 2004; Humphrey, Turley, & Moizer, 1993; Karpoff et al., 2008). Since 2000, fraudulent financial reporting has attracted the attention of Chinese accounting academicians, and a number of studies have been published in China to examine fraudulent financial reporting (e.g., Liu, 2002, 2005; Wang, 2005; Wu, 2003; Zhu, 2004). For example, Liu (2002) proposes various techniques to identify false financial statements in Chinese listed companies. While Zhu (2004) examines the duality control model of financial reporting frauds, Wu (2003) investigates fraud-detecting techniques and suggests various approaches to spot window-dressed financial statements. Integrating with auditing financial reports, Wang (2005) develops the model of "management fraud-oriented auditing." Liu (2005) empirically analyzes the characteristics of fraudulent financial reports of the listed companies from 1991 to 2004, but the study does not provide an analysis of specific types and methods of management frauds. This current study extends Liu's (2005) work by focusing on an analysis of the types and methods of fraudulent financial reporting of Chinese listed companies based on 83 cases. It intends to make a contribution to the literature by providing a detailed analysis of the nature, incidence, and characteristics of management fraud cases in China, the largest developing economy.

SAMPLE, DATA, AND DEFINED SCHEMES

This study uses the data from 182 punishment bulletins issued by the CRSC from 2002 to 2006 and adopts a descriptive approach. Identifying the sample of firms involved in management fraud is always problematic, as fraud samples are limited to only frauds exposed (Kaminski et al., 2004). Two types of management fraud cases are not available for study: frauds never being discovered and frauds that are caught by the auditor and/or firm and subsequently remedied within the firm as in this case the information is generally not revealed publicly. This study is therefore limited to the cases that have been exposed and made available publicly in China. The sample of management fraud cases was chosen from the CSRC's "Punishment Bulletins" from 2002 to 2006 published on its official website (http:// www.csrc.org.cn). We use the cases from the punishment bulletins of the CSRC, because these fraudulent financial reporting cases have been verified by the CSRC; this ensures the data and sample reliable. There were no bulletins available prior to 2002. In 2007, China adopted new accounting standards that differ significantly from the old accounting rules. In this study we used the cases took place during the period of 2002 to 2006 to ensure that all the cases follow the same accounting standards.

We obtained 182 punishment bulletins in total issued by the CRSC from 2002 to 2006. Table 1 shows the numbers of fraud cases punished by the CSRC over the period from 2002 to 2006, including committed listed companies, accounting firms, certified public accountants (CPAs), securities firms, and futures brokers. Over the period 83 listed firms were disciplined by the CSRC with financial penalty. Nineteen accounting firms and CPAs were punished because of their negligence of "management faults" in the auditing of their clients' financial statements. For example, Jiaxinda CPA Ltd. that carried out the auditing of 1998 and 1999 annual reports of Zhuhai Xinguang Group Limited did not provide any assessment of Zhuhai Xinguang's bad debts and associated party transactions and provided an unqualified report, which resulted in an overstatement of RMB6.49 million (about US$1 million) profits in Zhuhai Xinguang's accounts. The senior accountants of Jiaxinda were fined between RMB50,000 to RMB30,000.

Table 1.   The Number of Fraud Cases Penalized by the CSRC (2002–2006).

Year	No.	Listed Companies				Accounting Firms and CPAs		Others	
		No.	%	Total number of listed companies	% of listed companies	No.	%	No.	%
2002	17	6	35.3	1243	0.48	4	23.5	7	41.2
2003	35	15	42.9	1312	1.14	5	14.3	15	42.9
2004	49	27	55.1	1376	1.96	5	10.2	17	34.7
2005	43	12	27.9	1376	0.87	3	7.0	28	65.1
2006	38	23	60.5	1434	1.60	2	5.3	13	34.2
Total	182	83	45.6			19	10.4	80	44.0

Source: The punishment bulletins released by the CSRC from 2002 to 2006 (http:// www.csrc.org.cn).

Henan Huawei CPAs Partners (now Henan Huawei Accounting Consulting Limited) was fined RMB300,000 in 2002 because it did not provide an assessment of its client's (Zhenzhou Yutong Coach, Ltd.) 1999 annual report, which contained a false balance of bank accounts and impairment of assets. Huawei did not detect the reduction of assets and liabilities with a total amount of RMB13,500 million. Also, 80 securities firms, futures brokers, and others were penalized by the CSRC because of their violation against pertinent regulations relating to securities and markets.

Of total 83 listed companies disciplined, 19 (22.9 percent) were punished by the CSRC because they did not publish their financial information on time; among them 14 firms failed to publish their periodic reports on time. Examples include Chongqing Dongyuan Steel Co., Ltd., which failed to publish its 2002 interim financial report on time, and Nantong Tonmac International Co., Ltd., which delayed the publishing of its 2002 annual report due to a dispute with its auditors concerning the audit report. Our study excludes such cases, as in most of these cases they are essentially not fraudulent financial reporting. Yet, if some significant events were not disclosed on time and not properly disclosed in the periodic reports by a firm, they would be considered fraudulent financial reporting and included in our sample for analysis.

In the initial scrutiny of these cases, we observe that all the cases exhibit some level of "management fraud." Of 83 cases in the sample, 5 were punished at least twice by the CSRC, as reported in Table 2, which is about 6 percent of total sample cases.

To examine specific reasons of punishments, we exclude 14 cases that were punished as a result of the failure to publish their periodic reports on time because they were relatively easy to be identified by the regulatory authorities and information users. Three companies were punished twice (e.g., Nantong Tonmac, Chongqing Dongyuan, and Dalian Beida); for the purpose of analysis we accounted them as three listed companies, instead of six cases. Two companies punished in 2004 were excluded from the initial sample because they committed deceptions in appraising their physical assets, not reporting in financial statements. After the above adjustments, 64 firms were finally selected as the sample for a further analysis of this study. Among the 64 companies, the earliest year when the company exposed fraudulent financial reporting was 1994 and the latest year was 2004. For the purpose of this study, the "fraud year" is defined as the first year for which financial statements included fraudulent data or a company failed to publish its interim reports on time. In most cases, the actual discovery of a fraud occurs in subsequent years to the fraud year.

Table 2.   Case Companies Were Fined Twice and More.

Company	The First-Time Fine and Reason	The Second-Time Fine and Reason	The Third-Time Fine and Reason
Nantong Tonmac International Co., Ltd.	2003 – did not disclose 2001 annual report on time	2004 – in 2000 annual report there were flawed revenues and profits, deceptive disclosure of grants and funds, and non-disclosure of significant loan guarantee	
Chongqing Dongyuan Industry Development Co., Ltd.	2003 – did not disclose 2002 interim report on time	2005 – 2003 interim annual report did not disclose significant loan guarantee	
Dalian Beida Technology (Group) Co., Ltd.	2004 – 2001 annual report contains overstated revenue and profits; deliberately change the amount of payments on loan to advanced payments	2005 – the report in January 2004 does not follow the principles of true, accuracy and comprehensiveness	
China Kejian Co., Ltd.	2004 – in 2001 annual report and 2002 interim report there were omission of three major guarantees; as well during June 2000 to Dec 2001 the company did not report major guarantees on time	2005 – did not disclose 2004 annual report	2006 – did not follow the rules to report on 2004's provision of guarantee towards other parties; omission of substances of guarantees in 2004's interim report
Guangdong Kelon Electrical Holdings Ltd.	2006 – in its 2000 and 2001 interim, business and annual reports deliberately withhold items relating to significant cash transaction and loan guarantees, and major business contracts	2006 – over the period from 2002 to 2004 overstate profits through fake revenues and underreported expenses; non-disclosure of accounting policy changes and related party transactions; reporting artificial 2003 cash flow statement	2006 – did not disclose 2005 annual report on time

ANALYSIS OF MANAGEMENT FRAUD

We use three categories to distinguish fraud cases in the sample: (1) false income statements, (2) false balance sheets, and (3) insufficient or false disclosure. Under the double-entry accounting system, a fraud that leads to a false income statement always results in a false balance sheet. Therefore, we classify the fraud that leads to a false income statement into the category of false income statements and do not reclassify it into the type of false balance sheets. Further, the fraud that leads to a false cash flow statement always leads to a false income statement or/and a false balance sheet. In this study we do not classify false cash flow statements as a separate category of fraudulent financial reporting. There is no case in our sample that just falsifies the cash flow statement.

Table 3a shows the distribution of three fraud categories of the sample. Over the period of 5 years, 64 punished companies had committed 104 frauds. The most common type of fraudulent financial reporting was insufficient or false disclosure, which takes up more than a half of the total committed frauds.

Often, companies committed more than one category of fraudulent financial reporting at the same time. Table 3b reveals that 42.2 percent of the companies engaged in one category of fraudulent financial reporting, 42.2 percent of the companies had two types at the same time (mostly false income statements and false disclosure), and 15.6 percent of the companies committed all three types. For example, Guangxia (Yinchuan) Industry Co., Ltd., made false disclosure of its 1997, 1999, 2000, and 2001 annual accounts. Overall, 57.8 percent of the companies fined by the CSRC committed two or

Table 3. The Main Categories of Fraudulent Financial Reporting (Sample Case Size: 64).

Category	False Income Statements	False Balance Sheets	Insufficient or False Disclosure	Total
(a) No. of fraud cases	30	19	55	104
Percentage (%) of total frauds	28.8	18.3	52.9	100
(b) Resulting in the number of category	One type	Two types	Three types	Total
No. of companies	27	27	10	64
Percentage (%)	42.2	42.2	15.6	100.0

three types of frauds, and they were mainly related to false disclosure and false income statement.

The companies under this study adopted a variety of fraud methods to achieve their objectives. A number of companies overstated their profits through the following:

- recording fictitious revenue (including recording premature revenue)[2] (e.g., Guangxia overstated its profit RMB8.94 million over the period of January–June 2001),
- underrecording cost and expense (e.g., Sichuan Electrical Apparatus Co., Ltd., during the period of 1996–1998 did not record sales expenses of RMB8.79 million of its three subsidiaries in its consolidated accounts),
- underestimating loan and loan interests (e.g., over the period from March 1999 to April 2004, Tianshan Cement Co., Ltd., failed to disclose RMB330 millions of borrowings including bank loans of RMB305 million and other commercial loans of RMB25 million),
- lowering the allowance for asset impairment (e.g., Shandong Zhonglu Oceanic Fisheries Co., Ltd., lowered asset impairment in 2001, boosting its profit by over RMB6 million), and
- changing accounting policies without justifications (e.g., Luyin Investment Group in 2001 did not report the change of its accounting policy for various transactions including accounting for investment, bad loan, provision of doubtful debt, and prepayments, which resulted in over RMB 3 million profits).

Table 4 presents the main methods adopted by the punished companies of the "false income statement" fraud. As shown in Table 4, the main methods included recording fictitious revenue (e.g., Guangdong Kelon Electrical Holdings during the period of 2002–2004 adopted the method of reporting on false business revenues, lowering bad debt provision, and legal charges, which led to the overstatement of profits of RMB119.9 million in 2002, RMB118.5 million in 2003, and RMB148.75 million in 2004, respectively), underrecording expense, lowering the allowance for asset impairment, and recording made-up investment profits. The methods infrequently adopted by the companies included underestimating loan interests and costs, changing accounting policies, and consolidating false statements. While the main methods of recording fictitious revenue were recording untrue sales and premature recognition of revenue, delaying recognized administrational costs and operational expense were the main approaches to underrecording expense. Reducing the allowance for bad

Table 4. The Main Methods of False Income Statements.

Methods	No.	%
Recording fictitious revenue	24	35.3
Underrecording cost	6	8.8
Underrecording operation or/and administration expenses	13	19.1
Underestimating loan interests	2	2.9
Lowering the allowance for asset impairment	8	11.8
False increasing investment profit	10	14.7
Changing accounting policies without justification	2	2.9
Improper consolidating statements	3	4.4
Total cases	68	100

debts and the value of fixed assets and inventories were the main methods of lowering the allowance for asset impairment.

A number of the listed companies window-dressed their financial position through falsifying their balance sheet by overstating (or understating) assets and equities and understating liabilities with recording fictitious transactions and/or neglecting material transactions. Of 64 companies in the sample, 19 companies attempted to report fraudulent balance sheets.[3] Table 5 lists main methods adopted by the listed companies to falsify their balance sheet. Recording fictitious constructing project, accounts receivable or others receivable, intangible assets, or joint-venture investment were the main ways to falsify assets, while recording artificial paid-in-capital, underrecording of paid dividends were the main tactics to deceptively increase equities.

According to China's accounting law and accounting standards, a listed company must fairly present its financial position, operation results, and cash flow in its financial statements; fully disclose its selection of significant accounting policies including significant estimates and their changes; and provide explanatory materials for significant items of financial statements, related parties and their transactions, contingent and commitment events, events after balance-sheet-date event, and other significant events in notes to the financial statements. In practice, however, "insufficient or false disclosure" became the major type of financial irregularities committed by the Chinese listed companies as noted in Table 3. Table 6 presents the main displays of "insufficient or false disclosure" including concealing warranty, material events, and capital occupied by related parties, and untruthfully disclosing the actual use of raised capital. For example, during the period of April 21, 2003, to April 21, 2005, Sichuan Direction Photo electricity Co., Ltd., and its subsidiaries provided 81 warranties with the total value of over

Table 5.   The Main Methods of Falsifying the Balance Sheet (No. 28).

Methods	Fictitious Assets		Fictitious Liabilities		Fictitious Equities	
	Increase	Decrease	Increase	Decrease	Increase	Decrease
No. of total fraud firms (%)	10	8	0	5	4	1
	15.6	12.5	0.0	7.8	6.3	1.6

Table 6.   The Main Methods of "Insufficient or False Disclosure".

Methods	No.	%
False disclosure of the actual use of raised capital	14	12.5
Concealing mortgage of assets or/and equities	12	10.7
Concealing warranty or/and guarantee events	25	22.3
Concealing capital occupied by related parties	15	13.4
Disguising joint-venture investment	7	6.3
Concealing buy or sell goods between related parties	8	7.1
Concealing lawsuits	8	7.1
Concealing others significant events	23	20.5
Total	112	100

RMB2,401 million. Under 81 warranties, there were 208 borrowing transactions with the value of RMB1,867 million. However, Sichuan Direction disclosed only 15 transactions with the value of RMB 142.2 million. All others warranties were concealed.

Table 7 shows the number of fraud methods employed by the listed companies in the sample. It indicates that 85 percent of the companies used more than two methods simultaneously, and 33 percent of the companies employed four or more methods, all at once. Three companies even adopted 10 tactics of management fraud at the same time. In the majority of the cases, if a company committed one type of fraud, probably it also tied with other kinds of deception.

Moreover, the longer the duration of fraud committed by a listed company, the greater the impact on the capital market. The length of management fraud also reflects the effectiveness and efficiency of external supervision and control. For the purpose of this study, the "the duration of fraud" is defined as the number of years in which a company has fraudulent data in its financial statements. It is calculated from the first fraud year to the last year referred in the punishment bulletin of the CRSC. The first fraud year is the beginning year for which financial statements

Table 7.   The Number of Frauds Committed by the Listed Companies (Sample Size: 64).

No. of frauds	1	2	3	4	5	6 and above
No. of firms	9	19	15	6	6	9
Percentage (%)	14.1	29.7	23.4	9.4	9.4	14.1

Table 8.   The Lasting Years of Fraudulent Financial Reporting of Listed Companies (Sample Size: 64).

No. of lasting years	1 Year	2 Years	3 Years	4 Years	5 Years	6 Years and above
No. of firms	13	22	8	8	8	5
Percentage (%)	20.3	34.4	12.5	12.5	12.5	7.8

included fraudulent information. Table 8 reveals the duration of management fraud committed by the Chinese listed companies over the period from 2002 to 2006. It shows that 20.3 percent of the frauds committed by these listed companies lasted about 1 year; one-third lasted 2 years; 45 percent lasted 3 or more years, and 20.3 percent lasted 5 or more than 5 years, with the longest one being 9 years.

The sooner the company committing financial irregularities be punished, the better the punitive effect. However, due to the complexity of most frauds, the process from discovering frauds to imposing disciplines on the firm can take much longer time. Also, in the case of China the investigation process of alleged frauds can be very complicated because of various connections and the wide impacts, which could end in a way different from expected. The more deeply the irregularities are hidden, the longer the intervals between the initial irregularity (fraud year) and the time when the firm was actually punished will be. Table 9 presents the intervals between the initial irregularity of the listed companies in China and the year when it was actually punished. Forty-two percent of the company cases had the intervals of 3–4 years. The shortest interval was just 1 year and the longest was 11 years.

Management Fraud Prevention: Actions Needed

The above management frauds have raised serious concerns about (1) the effectiveness of corporate governance in some Chinese listed companies

Table 9.   The Intervals Between the Initial Irregularity and the Punished
of Listed Company (Sample Size: 64).

Interval	1 Year	2 Years	3 Years	4 Years	5 Years	6 Years	More than 6 years
No.	1	8	14	12	9	11	9
Percentage (%)	1.6	12.5	21.9	18.8	14.1	17.2	14.1

(Chen & Cheng, 2007); (2) the integrity and ethical conduct of top managements of these companies, as well as adequacy and efficacy of their internal control; and (3) the reliability of financial reports produced by these Chinese listed companies. Indeed, many factors have contributed to the frauds. The usual factors outlined in the studies of management fraud in other countries would be generally applicable in the case of China. Rezaee (2005) recapitulates these factors, including (1) lack of vigilant oversight functions (e.g., the board of directors, the audit committee); (2) arrogant and greedy management; (3) improper business conducts by top executives; (4) ineffective audit functions; (5) lax regulations; (6) inadequate and less transparent financial disclosures; and (7) inattentive shareholders. To prevent the fraud, it apparently requires a joint effort from various stakeholders (e.g., shareholders, regulatory supervisors, audit committee, and auditors). The establishment of effective corporate governance has been widely recommended to address the above concerns and prevent management frauds. Unlike employee fraud, management fraud is less likely to be detected by low-level controls because of management override. Typical internal control systems cannot be counted on as an effective deterrent to management fraud (Harrast & Mason-Olsen, 2007). Therefore, a high level of control and governance is required.

It is widely recognized that an independent audit committee plays a vital part in an effective corporate governance system (Myers & Ziegenfuss, 2006). This is largely due to the fact that an independent audit committee plays a central role in ensuring the credibility of financial reporting and reducing the possibility of management fraud (Harrast & Mason-Olsen, 2007). By design, audit committees are expected to maintain a line of defense against management fraud by monitoring the financial reporting function and internal controls of an organization. The US Sarbanes–Oxley Act of 2002 requires audit committees to (1) be directly responsible for the appointment, compensation, and oversight of the works of the external auditors; (2) be composed of independent members of the board of directors; (3) have authority to engage advisors; (4) preapprove any permissible nonaudit services provided by the external auditors; (5) establish procedures for employee whistleblowers to submit their concerns regarding accounting and auditing issues; (6) disclose that at least one member of its audit committee is a financial expert; (7) receive regular reports from the independent auditors on accounting treatments; and (8) receive corporate attorneys' reports of evidence of a material violation of securities laws or breaches of fiduciary duty. The Sarbanes–Oxley Act of 2002 has been widely discussed in China, and some of the rules have been incorporated into the recent corporate governance regulations by the CSRC (2007).

For the supervisory authorities, it is very important to monitor the sufficiency and authenticity of information disclosure of listed companies, especially in relation to the disclosure of warranty items, capital occupied by related parties, material buying or selling goods between related parties, lawsuits, noteworthy joint-venture investments, and others significant events. The authorities need to pay more attention to artificially recorded revenue or prematurely recognized revenue and to monitor the timeliness of disclosure of periodic reports.

To the accounting profession, it is recommended to strengthen audit procedures of sufficiency and authenticity of information disclosure, and to focus on the disclosure of warranty items, capital occupied by related parties, material buying or selling goods between related parties, lawsuits material joint-venture investments, and others significant events. External auditors should try to improve audit procedures of authenticity of profits of listed companies by focusing on the examination of falsely recorded revenue or prematurely recognized revenue, especially on the large amounts and unusual sale transaction, the recording of false investment profits, and the adequacy of estimating allowance for assets impairment. Clearly, auditors need to maintain professional skepticism during the whole auditing process. This is because the insufficiency of disclosure or misleading disclosure is usually hidden deliberately. In addition, since a company might commit various types of frauds and employ more than one deception method, the auditor should not consider a detected type or method of fraud as an isolated event. It should treat any single occurrence as a signal that there might be other types or methods of financial irregularities in the client.

CONCLUSIONS

This paper sheds light on the current status of management frauds of Chinese listed companies. Through an analysis of over 64 cases of management frauds published by the authorities over the period of 2002–2006, this paper finds that all management frauds of the Chinese listed companies involve the manipulation, alteration, and falsification of reported financial information. Fraud schemes are many and often involve more than one technique. The majority of misstatements are attained by overstating revenues and assets and understating liabilities and expenses. The main types of the frauds committed by the listed companies in China are related to insufficient or false disclosure, false income statements, falsification of a balance sheet, and not disclosing on time. False disclosure and not disclosing on time are the main likenesses of the frauds. Most of the companies in the sample simultaneously committed several frauds; *inter alia,* false profits, and insufficient or false disclosure.

Also, companies under the study have engaged in a variety of ways to deceive profits and revenues. The principal methods of falsifying profits include recording fictitious revenue, underrecording expense, lowering the allowance for asset impairments, and recording fictitious investment profits. The main method of recording fictitious revenue is recording fictitious sales and premature revenue. To lower the allowance for bad debts, fixed assets and inventories are often adopted as the major approaches to lowering the allowance for asset impairment.

Further, the main approaches to manipulating the balance sheet are related to untruly increasing assets and equities and decreasing liabilities. Recording fictitious construction projects, accounts receivable or others receivables, intangible assets, and joint-venture investments are the major means to falsify assets. Recording fictitious paid-in-capital and unrecording paid dividends are the primary ways to deceptively increase equities.

Moreover, concealing warranties, material events, and capital occupied by related parties, and falsely disclosing the actual use of raised capital are the primary means to bring about insufficient or false disclosure, along with falsely disclosing buying or selling goods between related parties, disguising mortgage of assets or equities, lawsuits, and joint venture.

Finally, this study finds that most management frauds in Chinese listed companies lasted more than 2 years, with the longest one being 9 years, and the intervals between the year of the initial irregularity exposed and the year of punishment announced were typically more than 3 years, with the longest one being 11 years.

Comparing with the results of other studies conducted in developed economies (e.g., Holtfreter, 2004; McNichols & Wilson, 1988; Rezaee, 2005) in terms of the nature and extent of frauds, Chinese fraud cases reveal more acts in concealing warranties provided to associated companies, concealing significant events, and falsifying transactions with related parties. Also, in the case of China, it took rather longer time to punish the firms and individuals that committed frauds due to the complexity of social and institution connections of those involved.

However, the above results need to be interpreted cautiously due to two limitations of the study. First, the sample size is limited to the firms punished by the CSRC during the years from 2002 to 2006. Unpunished cases were not included in the study. Second, we only investigated the data of 5 years that can be limited, as the actual discovery of management frauds normally takes more years and some frauds occurred in the study period may not be detected. The data of frauds in this study were limited to the cases exposed. Unexposed cases and cases that were under investigation were excluded from the study. We suggest that future research should use a larger sample size with a longer period of data to investigate the motivations, consequences, and market reactions of management frauds.

The findings of this study have significant implications for an understanding of corporate behaviors relating to fraudulent financial reporting. For example, there is a mixture of acts in falsifying the income statement and the balance sheet. Mostly, firms committed several frauds simultaneously; adopted more complicated approaches; and, particularly, they liked to cover up warranties, significant events, and transactions with related parties. The development of such an understanding is important for preventing frauds and improving better corporate compliance with financial reporting regulations. The paper thus contributes to the extant literature by providing an insight into management fraud from an East Asian country that is recognized as being the largest developing and transitional economy. Research into China's corporate fraudulent financial reporting is undoubtedly a core interest of the international academic community in the field. The implications drawn from this study could be useful for understanding management behavior of companies from developing and transactional countries. This study also has the potential to assist regulators and accounting professional institutions to set guidelines facilitating the supervision of corporate reporting.

NOTES

1. The CSRC is the government regulatory body with the responsibility to regulate and control securities markets in China. Its core value is to "safeguard the investors' interests". The CSRC has committed itself to fight against securities

violations and maintain the healthy development of China's securities markets through the investigation and discipline of securities violations. CSRC's official website is http://www.csrc.org.cn.

2. Recording fictitious revenue usually carries out together with recording made-up cost and expense. In this analysis, we classify them under "recording fictitious revenue." Underrecording cost is the company that intends to deceitfully bring down its operational cost.

3. In this paper, the fraud schemes of false balance sheets only affect the fair presentation of a statement of financial positions (i.e., balance sheet) and not relate to the items of an income statement. Under double-entry accounting, falsely increasing assets must lead to false increase of liabilities or/and equities, or false decrease of another assets. When we account for the number of fraud schemes, we concern about whether it involves in falsely increasing or decreasing assets, liabilities, or equities and account it only once.

REFERENCES

AICPA (American Institute of Certified Public Accountants). (2006). *SAS 1 (AU 110) – Responsibilities and functions of the independent auditor*. Durham, North Carolina: AICPA.

Apostolou, B., Hassell, J., Webber, S., & Sumners, G. (2001). The relative importance of management fraud risk factors. *Behavioral Research in Accounting, 13*, 1–24.

Association of Certified Fraud Examiners (ACFE). (2004). *Report to the Nation on Occupational Fraud and Abuse*, ACFE, Austin, TX.

Association of Chief Police Officers (ACPO). (2007). *The nature, extent and economic impact of fraud in the UK*. Retrieved from http://www.acpo.police.uk/asp/policies/Data/Fraud%20in%20the%20UK.pdf

Alleyne, P., & Howard, M. (2005). An exploratory study of auditors' responsibility for fraud detection in Barbados. *Managerial Auditing Journal, 20*(3), 284–303.

Arens, A. A., Elder, R. J., & Beasley, M. S. (2003). *Auditing and assurance services – An integrated approach*. Upper Saddle River, NJ: Prentice-Hall.

Badawi, I. M. (2005). Global corporate accounting frauds and action for reforms. *Review of Business, 26*(2), 8–14.

Beasley, M. S. (1996). An empirical analysis of the relation between the board of director composition and financial statement fraud. *Accounting Review, 71*, 443–465.

Bhamornsiri, S., & Schroeder, R. G. (2004). The disclosure of information on derivatives under SFAS No. 133: Evidence from the Dow 30. *Managerial Auditing Journal, 19*(5), 669–680.

Bonner, S. E., Palmrose, Z., & Young, S. M. (1998). Fraud type and auditor litigation: an analysis of SEC accounting and auditing enforcement releases. *Accounting Review, 73*, 503–532.

Cecchini, M., Aytug, H., Koehler, G. J., & Pathak, P. (2010). Detecting management fraud in public companies. *Journal of Management Science, 56*(7), 1146–1160.

Chen, C., & Sennetti, J. (2005). Fraudulent financial reporting characteristics of the computer industry under a strategic-systems lens. *Journal of Forensic Accounting, 6*(1), 23–54.

Chen, G., Firth, M., Gao, D. N., & Rui, O. M. (2006). Ownership structure, corporate governance, and fraud: Evidence from China. *Journal of Corporate Finance*, *12*(3), 424–448.

Chen, J. J., & Cheng, P. (2007). Corporate governance and the harmonisation of Chinese accounting practices with IFRS practices. *Corporate Governance: An International Review*, *15*(2), 284–293.

China Securities Regulatory Commission (CSRC). (2007). Retrieved from http://www.csrc.org.cn

China Securities Regulatory Commission (CSRC). (2010). Retrieved from http://www.csrc.org.cn

Cox, R. A. K., & Weirich, T. R. (2002). The stock market reaction to fraudulent financial reporting. *Managerial Auditing Journal*, *17*(7), 374–384.

Cullinan, C. P., & Sutton, S. G. (2002). Defrauding the public interest: A critical examination of reengineered audit processes and the likelihood of detecting fraud. *Critical Perspectives on Accounting*, *13*(3), 297–310.

Deloitte Forensic Center. (2007). *Ten things about financial statement fraud: A review of SEC enforcement releases, 2000–2006*. Retrieved from http://www.deloitte.com/dtt/cda/doc/content/us_forensic_tenthings_fraud200607.pdf. Accessed on November 21, 2007.

Dooley, D. V. (2002). Financial fraud: Accounting theory and practice. *Fordham Journal of Corporate and Financial Law*, *8*, S53–S84.

Durtschi, C., Hillison, W., & Pacini, C. (2004). Effective use of Benford's law in detecting fraud in accounting data. *Journal of Forensic Accounting*, *5*(1), 17–34.

Harrast, S. A., & Mason-Olsen, L. (2007). Can audit committees prevent management fraud? *The CPA Journal*, *77*(1), 24–27.

Hemraj, M. B. (2002). The utility of independence in preventing audit failure. *Journal of Money Laundering Control*, *6*(1), 88–93.

Holtfreter, K. (2004). Fraud in US organizations: An examination of control mechanisms. *Journal of Financial Crime*, *12*(1), 88–95.

Humphrey, C., Turley, S., & Moizer, P. (1993). Protecting against detection: The case of auditors and fraud? *Accounting, Auditing & Accountability Journal*, *6*(1), 39–62.

International Auditing and Assurance Standards Board (IAASB). (2004). *International Standard on Auditing (ISA) 240: The Auditor's Responsibility to Consider Fraud in an Audit of Financial Statements*.

International Monetary Fund. (2010). *World Economic and Financial Surveys – World Economic Outlook (WEO)*, International Monetary Fund.

James, K. L. (2003). The effects of internal audit structure on perceived financial statement fraud prevention. *Accounting Horizons*, *17*(4), 315–327.

Johnson, L. R., & Rudolph, H. R. (2007). The lessons of Adelphia's cash fraud. *Journal of Corporate Finance and Accounting*, *19*(1), 19–24.

Kaminski, K. A., Wetzel, T. S., & Guan, L. (2004). Can financial ratios detect fraudulent financial reporting? *Managerial Auditing Journal*, *19*(1), 15–28.

Karim, K. E., & Siegel, P. H. (1998). A signal detection theory approach to analyzing the efficiency and effectiveness of auditing to detect management fraud. *Managerial Auditing Journal*, *13*(6), 367–375.

Krambia-Kapardis, M., Christodoulou, C., & Agathocleous, M. (2010). Neural networks: The panacea in fraud detection? *Managerial Auditing Journal*, *25*(7), 659–678.

Karpoff, J. M., Lee, D. S., & Martin, J. S. (2008). The cost to firms of cooking the books. *Journal of Financial and Quantitative Analysis*, *43*, 581–611.

Kedia, S., & Philippon, T. (2009). The economics of fraudulent accounting. *Review of Financial Studies*, *22*(6), 2169–2199.

Kirkos, E., Spathis, C., & Manolopoulos, Y. (2007). Data mining techniques for the detection of fraudulent financial statements. *Expert Systems with Applications*, *32*(4), 995–1003.

Liu, M. (2005). *Research on fraudulent financial reporting of listed companies*. China: Shenzhen Securities Exchange.

Liu, S. (2002). *Identification techniques of fraudulent financial statements of listed companies*. Beijing: Chinese Finance and Economics Press.

Lou, Y. I., & Wang, M. L. (2009). Fraud risk factor of the fraud triangle assessing the likelihood of fraudulent financial reporting. *Journal of Business and Economics Research*, *7*(2), 61–78.

McNichols, M. F., & Wilson, G. P. (1988). Evidence of earnings management from the provision for bad debts. *Journal of Accounting Research*, *26*(Suppl.), 1–31.

Myers, P. M., & Ziegenfuss, D. E. (2006). Audit committee pre-Enron efforts to increase the effectiveness of corporate governance. *Corporate Governance – The International Journal of Business in Society*, *6*(1), 49–63.

Nguyen, K. (2008). *Financial statement fraud: Motives, methods, cases and detection*. Boca Raton, FL: Dissertation.com.

Nor, J. M., Ahmad, N., & Saleh, N. M. (2010). Fraudulent financial reporting and company characteristics: Tax audit evidence. *Journal of Financial Reporting and Accounting*, *8*(2), 128–142.

Pai, P. F., Hsu, M. F., & Wang, M. C. (2010). A support vector machine-based model for detecting top management fraud. *Knowledge-Based Systems*, *24*(2), 314–321.

Powell, L., Jubb, C., de Lange, P., & Langfield-Smith, K. (2005). The distinction between aggressive accounting and financial reporting fraud: Perceptions of auditors. Paper presented at the AFAANZ conference 3–5 July, 2005, Melbourne, Australia.

Rezaee, Z. (2005). Causes, consequences, and deterrence of financial statement fraud. *Critical Perspectives on Accounting*, *16*, 277–298.

Robinson, H. D., & Santore, R. (2011). Managerial incentives, fraud, and monitoring. *The Financial Review*, *46*(2), 281–311.

Tackett, J., Wolf, F., & Claypool, G. (2004). Sarbanes–Oxley and audit failure – A critical examination. *Managerial Auditing Journal*, *19*(3), 340–350.

Wu, G. (2003). *Identification and prevention of window-dressing of financial reports*. Beijing: Foreign Economics and Trade University Press.

Wang, Z. (2005). *Research on management fraud-oriented audit*. Beijing: Electrical Industry Press.

Weirich, T., & Reinstein, A. (2000). *Accounting and auditing research: A practical guide* (5th ed.). Dayton, OH: South-Western College Publishing.

Wilks, T., & Zimbelman, M. (2004). Using game theory and strategic reasoning concepts to prevent and detect fraud. *Accounting Horizons*, *18*(3), 173–184.

Zahra, S. A., Priem, R. L., & Rasheed, A. A. (2005). The antecedents and consequences of top management fraud. *Journal of Management*, *31*(6), 803–828.

Zhu, G. (2004). *Research on duality control to financial report fraud*. Beijing: China Renmin University Press.

Zhong, X. (2006). The international accounting and auditing experts highly appraised China's auditing system. *Chinese CPA* (3), 20–22.

FAIR VALUE ACCOUNTING USEFULNESS AND IMPLEMENTATION OBSTACLES: VIEWS FROM BANKERS IN JORDAN

Walid Siam and Modar Abdullatif

ABSTRACT

Purpose – *The purpose of this paper is to survey views of bankers in Jordan about the usefulness of fair value accounting and major obstacles facing its implementation in practice.*

Methodology/Approach – *A structured questionnaire was administered to individuals holding high positions in Jordanian banks. The questionnaire covered the respondents' views about the appropriateness of using fair value accounting, the usefulness of fair value figures in terms of their relevance for decision making and the obstacles facing the application of fair value accounting in practice.*

Findings – *Results of the survey showed that while there was general approval of the use of fair values in financial reporting, there were some reservations about their relevance in terms of predictive value and, more importantly, feedback value. Major obstacles facing the usefulness of fair*

Accounting in Asia
Research in Accounting in Emerging Economies, Volume 11, 83–107
ISSN: 1479-3563/doi:10.1108/S1479-3563(2011)0000011009

values in financial reporting included, according to respondents, (1) the possibility of fraud in fair value reporting, (2) the ambiguity of accounting standards on fair value application and (3) the reliability of figures measured using fair value accounting, as opposed to those measured using historical cost accounting.

Social implications – The paper discusses the positive and negative aspects of application of fair value financial reporting in accounting. It discusses how fair value financial reporting may be useful for decision making of users of financial statements and what obstacles may limit this usefulness. The paper also discusses the implications of the findings for Jordan and other emerging economies, including suggested ways to reduce the possible negative effects of fair value accounting.

Originality/Value of paper – Fair value accounting practice is relatively new to Jordan, and the Jordanian context, as a less-developed country with a low-efficiency stock market, is significantly different to the environments in which fair value accounting practices were established. The effects of applying fair value accounting in Jordanian financial reporting practices are under-researched, so this study yields views on the reliability and relevance of fair value measures and the ease of their application in practice that could be specific to the Jordanian environment and differ significantly from results from developed countries. The findings generally support this argument.

Keywords: Fair value accounting; usefulness; obstacles; relevance; reliability; Jordan

INTRODUCTION

This paper reports on a survey study of senior bank officials in Jordan about the usefulness of fair value accounting for financial reporting purposes. Fair value financial reporting has been an area of controversy as to whether, and to what extent, it should be applied in accounting (Al-Khadash & Abdullatif, 2009; Laux & Leuz, 2009a). The recent global financial crisis has increased the debate on fair value accounting, and whether or not it contributed to the crisis (see Laux & Leuz, 2009b; Yuan-yuan & Jun, 2009). The paper begins with a brief discussion of arguments for and against the application of fair values in accounting practice. It then summarises the findings of a number of empirical studies on fair value financial reporting in different countries.

The paper overviews the Jordanian environment, with particular emphasis on the special characteristics it may share with many less-developed countries, different from those of more-developed countries. Taking this into account, the paper surveys views from senior banking officials in Jordan about the usefulness of fair value accounting, its relevance and reliability and the major obstacles facing its application in Jordan as is required by the International Financial Reporting Standards (IFRS). The paper discusses the possible influence of the Jordanian context on the usefulness of fair value accounting and the obstacles facing its application, in addition to the implications of the findings for Jordan and other emerging economies. It provides suggestions for practitioners and policy makers on how to deal with the possible negative consequences of fair value financial reporting.

THE FAIR VALUE ACCOUNTING DEBATE

It has been a controversial issue whether to continue using traditional historical cost accounting measures or to replace them with measures based on fair values, and several arguments have been put forward by opponents and proponents of fair value accounting (Al-Khadash & Abdullatif, 2009; Laux & Leuz, 2009a).

International Accounting Standard (IAS) 39 (paragraph 9) defines fair value as:

> the amount for which an asset could be exchanged, or a liability settled, between knowledgeable, willing parties in an arm's length transaction.

While looking straightforward in theory, this definition requires a closer look in practice. Barth and Landsman (1995) argue that it can be applied in perfect and complete markets, which is not always the case.

The application of fair value accounting follows a three-step process. The best estimate of fair value is considered to be market prices. Second best, if market prices are not available or are not of sufficient quality, quoted market prices of comparable items are considered. Finally, fair value is applied by estimation if the first or second alternatives do not apply (Hitz, 2007). Therefore, determining fair value may be done using several different methods, including published market prices, discounted future cash flows or valuation methods (Elliott & Elliott, 2009). The recently issued proposed

IFRS 9 provides guidance on measurement of fair value for financial instruments by determining cases when cost is the appropriate estimate of fair value (such as in the cases of the existence of a wide range of possible fair value measurements and cost provides the best estimate within that range, and when more recent information to determine fair value is insufficient) (PricewaterhouseCoopers, 2011). IFRS 9 also provides indicators of cost not being the best estimate of fair value. These include significant changes in the investee's performance compared to budgets, significant changes in the market for the investee's products or significant changes in the economic environment in which the investee operates (PricewaterhouseCoopers, 2011).

Many arguments have been suggested in defence of fair value accounting. The accounting literature includes claims by scholars that historical cost accounting is irrelevant for decision making, and therefore needs to be replaced (see Deegan & Unerman, 2006; Drever, Stanton & McGowan, 2007; Riahi-Belkaoui, 2004).

The use of fair value accounting has been proposed as a replacement for historical cost accounting, especially in the area of financial instruments. In this area, fair value has been considered in many cases to be more relevant than historical cost, without impairing the reliability of the reported figure, especially if current market prices are readily available (Al-Khadash & Abdullatif, 2009). Fair value measures are seen as reflecting the market's assessment of the effects of current economic conditions on the financial instruments, and not their previous history or that of the enterprises that hold them (Carroll, Linsmeier, & Petroni, 2003). Fair values can therefore arguably be seen as reflecting economic substance (Penman, 2007). Fair value is seen as reflecting current market conditions, and therefore increasing transparency and encouraging prompt corrective actions (Laux & Leuz, 2009a). Barth (2006) concludes that the perceived usefulness of fair value accounting has shifted the argument from whether it should be used in financial statements to how it should be applied.

Fair value measurement is not without criticism. Such criticism includes the views that fair value measurements may distort net income (through recognition of unrealised holding gains and losses), are not exact, are subject to manipulation and are costly to generate (Evans, 2003). Benston (2005) criticises the implementation of market values in practice as seriously flawed. Such flaws appear in the cases of excluding held-to-maturity securities from revaluation, and measuring derivatives with fair values if managers have substantial leeway in calculating those fair values (Benston, 2005). Such practice risks being misleading since fair value expectations may end up falsified (Rayman, 2007).

Particular criticisms of fair values include the argument that a direct relation between asset prices and fair value to shareholders does not always occur. Benston (2008) criticises the use of exit values in measuring fair values of assets such as special purpose machines and work-in-process inventories, for which exit values may equal zero or even be negative. Finally, Ronen (2008) criticises the relevance of fair value accounting measures, arguing that they are not a sound base for predicting future cash flows. He also criticises the reliability of fair value accounting measures because of subjectivity of estimation, which can lead to moral hazard for managers (Ronen, 2008). Fair value accounting is also criticised because market values can be distorted due to market inefficiencies or investor irrationality (Laux & Leuz, 2009a).

A major opponent of fair value accounting is the banking industry, which has argued against fair value accounting, and lobbied against its full application (Zeff, 2010). Barth, Landsman, and Wahlen (1995) report that the banking industry in the United States accused the application of fair value accounting of causing increased volatility in earnings not related to the volatility of banks' operations, which could lead to inefficient capital allocation and increased cost of capital for banks. This extended to the European Union, where the introduction of international accounting standards (particularly IAS 39) brought strong objection from the banking industry (Larson & Street, 2004; Zeff, 2010).

INTERNATIONAL EMPIRICAL EVIDENCE ON THE APPLICATION OF FAIR VALUE ACCOUNTING

Studies covering the value-relevance of fair value accounting have found that estimates for investment securities have significant explanatory power beyond that of historical cost measures (Barth, 1994; Barth, Beaver, & Landsman, 1996; Barth & Clinch, 1998; Bernard, Merton, & Palepu, 1995). Studies have also found that fair value earnings that result from recognising unrealised holding gains and losses are more volatile than historical cost accounting earnings (Al-Yaseen & Al-Khadash, 2011; Barth et al., 1995; Bernard et al., 1995). Some studies have reported that value-relevance of fair value accounting measures also occurs under less-efficient market circumstances. For example, Carroll et al. (2003) argue that incremental value-relevance is not eliminated when an estimation of fair value for securities in thin markets is used. They found that this result applies for both fair values of securities and fair-value-based gains and losses.

However, the results of other studies have not shown positive effects of applying fair value accounting measures. For example, Eccher, Ramesh, and Thiagarajan (1996) found that in some cases historical cost measures had incremental value-relevance higher than that of fair value measures. Also, Nelson (1996) reported that fair values of investment securities have an incremental explanatory power relative to book values, but that this result applies only to investment securities, not deposits, loans, or long-term debt. Finally, Khurana and Kim (2003) found that for small bank holding companies and those with no analyst following, fair value accounting measures for loans and deposits are less informative than those of historical cost accounting measures.

The adoption of IFRS in the European Union, including IAS 32 and IAS 39, had an effect on European capital markets. For example, Armstrong, Barth, Jagolinzer, and Riedl (2006) reported that European capital markets show a positive reaction to events which increased the likelihood of adopting IFRS, and a negative reaction to events decreasing that likelihood, and that this result holds for banks, who openly opposed IAS 39. In addition, Larson and Street (2004) and Jermakowicz and Gornik-Tomaszewski (2006) found that in Europe, IAS 32 and IAS 39 were perceived as too complicated and complex in implementation, and that this was a significant barrier to IFRS convergence. Callao, Jarne, and Lainez (2007), in a study on Spain, found that the application of fair value accounting for financial instruments led to short-term weak comparability and no improved relevance for financial reporting in the local stock market. They did not find the same problem with property, plant and equipment revaluation, as this was an optional practice rejected by many companies. Ben Hamida (2007), in a study of French banks, found that the market perceived adoption of IFRS and fair value accounting as harmful to banks. She found that announcements that signalled an increased (decreased) probability of IAS 39 adoption led to negative (positive) abnormal stock price reactions.

To summarise, many studies have found that fair value accounting is value relevant and affects share prices. However, a number of studies reported concerns about the application of fair value accounting to all financial instruments and other balance sheet items, especially when there are no readily determined market values and active markets for trading.

As for emerging economies, most of them have formally adopted IFRS (such as developing countries with no existing accounting standards) or converged their existing accounting standards to IFRS (such as many previously communist countries in eastern Europe), mainly due to their willingness to adopt accounting standards acceptable to foreign parties. IFRS was seen as a relatively cheap option, compared to developing local accounting standards, that is more politically attractive than adopting the accounting standards of more-developed countries (Nobes & Parker, 2010). While formal adoption of or convergence to IFRS has arguably been without significant problems, the actual enforcement of IFRS and compliance with them in fact is questionable (Daniels, Radebaugh, & Sullivan, 2011). In particular for IFRS regarding fair value accounting, the lack of active markets for many financial statement items required or permitted to be measured by fair value is arguably a major factor affecting the practice of IFRS in many emerging economies.

The convergence to IFRS and the actual implementation of IFRS in emerging economies was the subject of some research. Peng and Bewley (2010) studied the adoption of fair value accounting and its actual implementation in China. They found that while IFRS fair value accounting standards are adopted to a high level in Chinese 2007 GAAP, they have not been widely incorporated in Chinese listed firms' financial statements, thus questioning the IFRS convergence in China. Similar results in China were reported by Olesen and Cheng (2011), who found that while Chinese companies used the fair value method in their IFRS accounts, they used the cost method in their Chinese GAAP accounts. They concluded that convergence of accounting standards did not lead to convergence of accounting practices due to political, economic and historical reasons. In a study on Bahrain, Joshi, Bremser, and Al-Ajmi (2008) reported nationalism as an important impediment to global IFRS adoption, while Irvine and Lucas (2006) argue that the United Arab Emirates has to develop appropriate regulatory systems to deal with cultural issues concerning secrecy and fraud in order to assist in adopting IFRS.

This study aims to contribute to knowledge by surveying views on arguments regarding the relevance and reliability of fair value accounting in a relatively different environment, Jordan, where the economy is less developed and market efficiency is weak. Such factors could arguably affect views on the usefulness of fair value accounting in a different manner from that in more-developed economies with high market efficiency. The Jordanian market is under-researched as to the effects of fair value accounting, with only a very few studies being conducted (see later sections for references).

THE JORDANIAN CONTEXT

Jordan is an Arab country located in the Middle East, and has a population of about 6.5 million. Arabic is the main language, but English is widely spoken, especially in business. The Jordanian culture is affected by Islam and general Arab heritage that is known for robust hospitality and an extended family system (Beard & Al-Rai, 1999). Jordan has an open economy, and is an exporter of phosphate, but has relatively limited natural resources and scarce supplies of water, and is not oil-rich.

The Jordanian economy is dominated by the service sector, which accounts for approximately 70% of GDP. It includes financial services, real estate and communications. Jordan's banking and financial services sector is generally well developed. There are over 20 banks operating in Jordan including several foreign banks, and three banks (two Jordanian and one foreign) specialising in Islamic banking. Jordanian banks have a network of branches inside Jordan, and several of them have foreign branches, subsidiaries, affiliates and/or offshore banking units. By far the largest Jordanian bank, the Arab Bank plc, also has the largest number of foreign branches and affiliates, spanning several continents. Jordanian banks generally perform both commercial and investment banking activities. They are modern institutions with contacts with numerous leading foreign banks.

Jordanian banks have since 1998 been required to use IAS/IFRS in preparing their financial statements, and to have their financial statements audited by an audit firm applying International Standards on Auditing. The vast majority of Jordanian banks are audited by international audit firms, especially Deloitte or Ernst & Young.

All Jordanian banks are required to be listed on the Amman Stock Exchange (ASE), which includes over 200 public listed companies. The ASE works in coordination with the Jordan Securities Commission, a governmental body, and is a member of the Union of Arab Stock Exchanges. During the current decade, the market capitalisation increased significantly for several reasons, including a privatisation policy under which the Jordanian government significantly reduced its ownership in many major organisations, including Jordan Telecommunications and the Royal Jordanian Airlines (Al-Akra, Ali, & Marashdeh, 2009).

Fair value accounting was required to be used by Jordanian banks early in the current decade. Due to increased trading in shares in the stock market, the effects of fair value accounting on banks' financial statements were apparent. The sharpest effects of this practice were observed in the financial statements of 2005, which showed significantly higher net profits of

Jordanian banks, given the large amount of new capital entering the market in the previous few years, some of which was contributed by non-Jordanian investors, and some of which was contributed by a large number of small Jordanian investors probably speculating on what looked like a major boom in share prices in the market. The financial statements of 2006 showed an opposite effect, leading to large volatility in share prices and net profits for Jordanian banks, with most of the changes in net profits resulting from changes in share prices rather than economic performance (see Al-Khadash & Abdullatif, 2009). Many speculators have since lost large sums on their investments in shares. In the insurance sector, Al-Yaseen and Al-Khadash (2011) reported similar evidence of increased volatility in reported net income when using fair value accounting for financial instruments. The Jordanian government reacted by proposing some solutions to the problem of the volatility in the stock market and the resulting poor investment decision making by naïve investors, given the weak efficiency of the stock market. Finally, in February 2008, a regulation was enacted that required (among other issues) the following accounting treatments for financial statements of the years ended 31 December 2007 and after (regulations on accounting principles and mandatory standards related to estimating fair value and dealing with revaluation surplus for year 2007 – amended in 2008 (The Hashemite Kingdom of Jordan, 2008)):

(1) Gains from fair value adjustments of trading securities must be disclosed as unrealised profits in the retained earnings section. These gains cannot be distributed as dividends.
(2) The cost alternative must be used for investment property under IAS 40, with fair values of these investments disclosed in the notes to the financial statements.
(3) The cost alternative must be used for property, plant and equipment under IAS 16.

These regulations effectively limited the use of fair value measurement in the financial statements of Jordanian public listed companies by only allowing recognition of what is required by IFRS (such as fair value adjustment gains/losses of trading securities in the income statement and fair value adjustment gains/losses of available-for-sale securities in the owners' equity section), while not allowing recognition in the body of the financial statements of many fair value adjustments that are optional. Such a practice is expected to limit volatility in reported results of public listed companies. While such regulations are arguably not a violation of IFRS (as the required methods do comply with IFRS), they cast a shadow on whether a full adoption of IFRS can be actually achieved in Jordan.

Local studies have concluded that ASE is not an efficient market (Al-Jarrah, Khamees, & Haddad, 2009; Alshiab & Alalawneh, 2007; Omet, 1999; Omet & Bino, 2000). Market efficiency assumes that investors see through alternative accounting choices. However, alternative accounting choices can fool investors when markets are not efficient (Drever et al., 2007). Given that fair value accounting adjustments for investment portfolios are a type of alternative accounting policy choice with no apparent major cash consequences (Jordanian tax laws defer recognition of unrealised holding gains and losses on investments until actual realisation of the gain or loss), the share price volatility after applying IAS 39 can be arguably seen as an indicator of poor market efficiency.

RESEARCH METHOD, POPULATION AND SAMPLE

A questionnaire was developed for surveying the views of bankers about the suitability of fair value accounting and the obstacles facing its application. The choice of a questionnaire rather than an interview method for collecting information was made in order to reach the largest possible number of respondents to give the results a higher generalisation potential in the Jordanian environment.

The Jordanian banking sector was used as a research population in this study due to its extensive dealing with fair value accounting through investment accounting, its clients' use of fair value accounting in their financial reporting and the potentially significant effect this issue has on banks' profits and share prices. This suggests that the bankers are one of the most knowledgeable groups of users of financial statements, and therefore can provide useful results on the issues covered in the study.

The study population consisted of all 14 Jordanian banks using traditional banking practices. The two Jordanian banks specialising in Islamic banking were excluded from the study population due to their significantly different activities, while foreign banks operating in Jordan were excluded due to the possible effects of the international background and significantly wider operations on the responses.

The questionnaire consisted of four parts. Part one included demographic data about the background of the respondents (education, highest academic qualification, job title, years of experience in banking, extent of involvement in decision making). Such data was gathered in order to be assured of the knowledge available on the part of the respondents regarding the contents of the questionnaire.

Part two was intended to find out how far the accounting officers at Jordanian commercial banks support the requirement of fair value accounting. Part three was intended to determine the extent of fair value's contribution to making the accounting information more relevant to decision makers at Jordanian banks. Finally, part four was concerned with assessing the obstacles facing the implementation of fair value accounting in Jordan. Questions included in these parts were developed after reviewing existing theory and literature and previous studies on the relevance and reliability of accounting information, and particularly fair value accounting.

A five-choices Likert scale was used, with very high agreement on the issue in question being assigned a value of 5 and very low agreement being assigned a value of 1. Face validity of the questionnaire was tested by having it reviewed by a number of accounting academics and bankers as a pilot study before formally administering it to the selected research sample. Suggested changes resulting from the pilot study were included in the final version of the questionnaire.

The researchers individually handed out the questionnaires to directors and department heads dealing with fair value reporting, and to some branch managers, and collected them later. This distribution method was opted because it is likely to generate a significantly higher response rate, compared to mail or email distribution, without seriously impairing the validity and reliability of the responses (Abdullatif, 2010), since the researchers did not interfere with the respondents while they filled in the questionnaire. Because of the high response rate (90%) and the unwillingness of some individuals included in the study sample to cooperate due to being busy, non-response bias was not tested, but it is unlikely to be significant due to the high response rate.

Ten questionnaires (written in Arabic) were distributed in 2008 to each of the 14 banks included in the study. One hundred and twenty-six usable responses (from a total of 140) were returned, giving a response rate of 90%.

FINDINGS

Characteristics of the Study Sample

Table 1 shows the characteristics of the sample of respondents to the questionnaire. The table shows that the respondents were of high rank and

Table 1.   Personal Background of Respondents.

Theme	Alternatives	Number	Percentage
Education specialisation	Accounting	84	66.7%
	Finance and banking	21	16.7%
	Business administration	13	10.3%
	Economics	8	6.3%
	Total	126	100%
Highest education achieved	Community college or lower	5	4%
	First university degree	79	62.7%
	Masters	33	26.2%
	Doctorate	9	7.1%
	Total	126	100%
Job title	General manager	12	9.5%
	Branch manager	34	27%
	Directorate manager	71	56.4%
	Department head	9	7.1%
	Total	126	100%
Experience in banking	Less than 3 years	1	0.8%
	3 to less than 6 years	2	1.6%
	6 to less than 9 years	55	43.7%
	9 to less than 12 years	32	25.3%
	12 years or above	36	28.6%
	Total	126	100%
Frequency of participation in financial decision making	Always	85	67.5%
	In most cases	27	21.4%
	Sometimes	11	8.7%
	Rarely	3	2.4%
	Total	126	100%

that 89% of them reported a high degree of involvement in the financial decision-making process. Directors and branch managers represented around 93% of respondents. This suggests the sample members' participation in the financial decision-making process and interest in the relevance and reliability of accounting information. In addition, respondents who had at least six years of banking experience amounted to about 98% of the sample. Most of the respondents had university degrees in accounting, arguably the most relevant discipline for dealing with fair value reporting.

General Acceptance of the Application of Fair Value Accounting in Financial Reporting

It can be seen from Table 2 that the Jordanian bankers have a general preference for the application of fair value accounting in financial reporting. Over 72% of the respondents to the questionnaire highly or very highly accepted the use of fair values in financial reporting.

Usefulness of Fair Value Accounting Information in the Jordanian Context

Table 3 shows that there are some concerns about the relevance of application of fair value accounting. Fair value accounting information was perceived by the vast majority of the respondents as generally relevant for decision making (statement 3.1), and particularly useful in terms of its approximately accurate value (being more up-to-date) for decision making (statement 3.2) and its perceived usefulness in terms of reducing uncertainty for decision makers (statement 3.3), perhaps due to a fact that in Jordan there is a relatively high inflation rate that can make some historical cost items reported seem out of date. However, there was some reservation (statements 3.4, 3.5 and 3.6) about the arguments that fair value reporting would lead to making accounting information, whether annual or interim, available on a suitable timely basis for decision making by external users of financial statements. This is possibly because of the lower quality of information and lower speed of its availability for external users in Jordan, compared with the same situation in more-developed countries.

Table 2. Degree of Respondents' Acceptance of the Application of Fair Value Accounting in Financial Reporting.

Degree of Acceptance	Number	Percentage
Very high acceptance	56	44.4%
High acceptance	35	27.8%
Moderate acceptance	19	15.1%
Little acceptance	9	7.1%
Very little acceptance	7	5.6%
Total number of respondents	126	100%
Mean of responses	3.984	
Standard deviation of responses	0.763	

Table 3. Degree of Agreement of Respondents that Fair Value
Accounting has Made Accounting Information more Relevant
for Decision Makers.

No.	Statement	Mean	SD
3.1	Fair value accounting information contains information relevant for decision making	4.613	0.845
3.2	Using fair value accounting leads to increased accuracy in selecting from decision alternatives	4.303	0.836
3.3	Using fair value accounting helps decision makers reduce the degree of uncertainty in decision making	4.410	0.739
3.4	Fair value accounting information is accessed by decision makers at a suitable time	3.850	1.032
3.5	Fair value accounting makes annual published financial statements available without significant additional delay	3.875	0.985
3.6	Fair value accounting makes semi-annual and quarterly interim reports available without significant additional delay	3.961	0.973
3.7	The presence of predictive value in fair value accounting information helps decision makers in making future predictions	3.891	0.967
3.8	Using fair value accounting provides the decision maker with the ability to confirm or correct previous expectations	3.369	1.287

Other reservations on the relevance and usefulness of fair value accounting
information were reported in the cases of the value of such information for
making predictions about the future (statement 3.7), and, at a higher level of
reservation, for making decisions related to the confirmation or correction of
past decisions and expectations (statement 3.8). In the Jordanian case, both
predictive ability and feedback ability of fair value information may be
limited by the fact that fair value information (although generally more
approximately accurate in terms of updated information compared to
historical cost) is still not very approximately accurate in terms of the higher
level of use of personal judgements in a small and less-efficient market. This
may make such figures less approximately accurate and more prone to
intended and unintended misjudgements, compared to the case in larger
and more developed markets where information, although still under some
level of personal judgement, is considered more trustworthy.

A suggested possible reason for the lower level of acceptance on the
usefulness of fair value accounting information for feedback value,

Table 4. Official Annual Inflation Rates in Jordan.

Year	Inflation Rate (%)
2001	1.77
2002	1.83
2003	2.34
2004	2.64
2005	3.49
2006	6.25
2007	4.74
2008	13.94
2009	−0.67
2010	5.00

Source: Department of Statistics.

compared to predictive value, is that due to the relatively high level of inflation in Jordan, fair value reported figures may be significantly different from the figures used by the decision makers for making their initial decisions. Table 4 shows the official general inflation rates (for all commodities) for Jordan in the last decade, as issued by the Department of Statistics. Other unofficial rates suggested by other parties are significantly higher. The table shows a relatively high figure for the inflation rate for 2008 compared to prior years, arguably due mainly to the global financial crisis and the increased prices of petrol and other energy resources during that year, the issue that led to rises in prices of most other goods and services (the negative rate in 2009 is because figures in the table are calculated in comparison with the previous year). The fact that Jordan is a country with a generally low GDP per capita and with a significant percentage of the population under the poverty line may make any small increase in the inflation rate or the Consumer Price Index severely felt by many people, including some financial decision makers. It is possible that the high inflation rate might make fair value figures more useful in terms of decreasing uncertainty, while also less useful in terms of feedback value, given the significantly different figures reported in different years.

Obstacles Facing the Application of Fair Value Reporting in Jordan

The application of fair value accounting in Jordan has not been without obstacles in terms of relevance and use in financial decision making.

Table 5. Degree of Agreement of Respondents on the Existence of
Certain Obstacles Facing the Application of Fair Value Accounting.

No.	Statement – Obstacle	Mean	SD
5.1	Ambiguity in practice due to the existence of many IFRS requirements related to measurement and disclosure of fair value accounting	4.217	0.707
5.2	Ambiguity of required disclosures related to fair value in IFRS	4.017	0.861
5.3	Low reliability of fair value estimates compared to historical cost information	3.994	1.104
5.4	Fair value accounting information is not objective, cannot be proved and is prone to financial statement fraud	4.320	0.837
5.5	Reliance on subjective assumptions in determining fair value when revaluing fixed assets such as property and equipment	3.217	1.017
5.6	Lack of a market price for some financial instruments makes it difficult to apply fair value accounting	3.413	1.003
5.7	Depending on market prices or expert opinions in estimating the fair value of some assets such as land and buildings	3.409	1.113
5.8	Lack of sufficient market conditions necessary for use of fair value accounting	3.556	0.991

Table 5 shows a list of eight suggested obstacles included in the study
questionnaire and the views of respondents on these issues.

It can be seen from Table 5 that the respondents find three important
obstacles facing the application of fair value accounting in Jordan. These are
(1) the possibility of fraud in fair value reporting; (2) the ambiguity of
accounting standards in their coverage of recognition, measurement and
disclosure regarding fair value reporting; and (3) the questioned reliability of
figures measured using fair value accounting, compared to those measured
using historical cost accounting.

The Jordanian business environment is one where there are some
possibilities for fraud and misstatements in financial reports. Some
suggested reasons for that include the possibility that regulations in Jordan
do not provide for strong punishment for financial statement fraud, and that
the occurrence of such punishment might not have severe negative
consequences for perpetrators. This could be exacerbated by the fact that
fair value figures are generally based on estimates and professional
judgements that are, in the case of Jordan, taken from a low-efficiency

market where much information is not readily available. This may lead to fair value reporting figures being wrong due to either unintentionally erroneous professional judgements or intentional exploitation of such an environment to deliberately report false fair value figures that cannot be easily verified. The weak position of the external auditor in the Jordanian business society (see Abdullatif & Al-Khadash, 2010, for an analysis) increases the possibilities that false fair value reporting may not be detected and/or reported by external auditors. It is interesting to see from Table 5 that statement 5.4 was the most supported statement by the questionnaire respondents, to a significantly higher level than other statements dealing with the subjective nature of fair value reporting, such as statements 5.5, 5.6 and 5.7. This suggests that it is a lack of trust and a fear of fraud that concern the respondents, to a significantly higher degree than the effects of the subjective nature of fair value accounting.

Jordanian regulations for financial reporting are very limited on detail, but require the use of IFRS for financial reporting, especially by public listed companies. However, as shown from statements 5.1 and 5.2, it seems that there is a perception of ambiguity of the requirements of IFRS regarding fair value accounting recognition, measurement and disclosure. Suggested reasons for this include the existence of several accounting standards on fair value accounting (see Abu-Harb, 2009; Lundy, 2002) and/or a lack of sufficient accounting training by the respondents. In particular, the respondents may lack recent accounting education and training, given their relatively long accounting and business experience, which suggests that most of them were employed in business before the regulations for fair value accounting were required to be used in Jordanian financial reporting.

Statement 5.3 shows a general perception that the use of fair value accounting is less reliable than the use of historical cost accounting. While that is generally agreed upon by most accountants around the world, in the case of Jordan, fair value reporting may have even lower reliability. This is because of the lack of efficient resources to draw fair value figures from. For example, market values of listed shares, while readily available, are very prone to the effects of rumours due to the weak efficiency of the stock market. Fair values of other assets that may be re-valued under IFRS (such as property, plant and equipment or investment property) are not readily available due to the lack of organised active markets of such assets. Therefore, one can get a wide range of fair value estimates on any particular asset.

Finally, responses to statements 5.5–5.8 suggest that the degree of importance of the issues covered in these statements is lower than that for the issues covered in other statements included in Table 5. It is interesting to note that statements 5.5–5.8 cover issues that relate to limitations of fair value accounting, such as the subjectivity of reported figures and disclosed information and the need to use personal judgement by accountants and other experts, especially in the cases of the lack of available market prices for assets valued using fair value accounting figures. This problem is particularly important in the Jordanian market due to the general shortage of agreed-upon market prices for most of the assets that may be valued using fair value figures, as well as for issues such as tests of impairment for goodwill, for example (see Qabajeh, 2009). Even in the case of ready availability of market prices, such as for shares of public listed companies, such figures are not reliable because they are prone to the effects of factors not related to actual economic activities due to the low efficiency of the stock market (Al-Khadash & Abdullatif, 2009).

The relatively low agreement on the importance of limitations of fair value accounting, such as the subjectivity involved in determining the reported figures, the lack of widely available market values and the lack of market efficiency suggest the possibility that the respondents to the questionnaire do not have sufficient awareness about the importance of such issues in limiting the usefulness of fair value reporting. This is especially in an environment such as Jordan, where the general lack of market efficiency and readily available market prices for assets seriously increases the possibility that reported fair value figures are wrong or misleading or fraudulently misstated (Qabajeh, 2009). If such views are expressed by bankers, among the most financially educated individuals, then the whole population of workers in accounting, auditing and financial analysis need to be adequately educated about the recent accounting practices required by IFRS, and to have up-to-date education and training on such accounting-related issues (see Al-Sa'eed, 2008). Another possible reason for the relatively low agreement on the importance of limitations of fair value accounting may be that some respondents actually believe that these limitations are not very material, and therefore should arguably not limit the use of fair value accounting.

Reliability of the Results

The questionnaire results' reliability was tested by using Cronbach's alpha, which was found to be nearly 81%, a figure significantly higher than the minimum acceptable value of 60% (Zikmund, Babin, Carr, & Griffin, 2010).

This means that the questionnaire results were acceptable in terms of their reliability.

IMPLICATIONS OF FINDINGS FOR JORDAN AND OTHER EMERGING ECONOMIES

The findings of this study show that while the application of fair value accounting was seen as a positive thing by many respondents, there were some important obstacles likely to face the implementation of fair value accounting in Jordan and probably in many other emerging economies. However, given the trend towards worldwide adoption of IFRS by developing countries, including Jordan, and the fact that IFRS are increasingly leaning towards fair value accounting practices, these countries have to deal with the possible negative consequences of the application of fair value in financial reporting. Different suggestions can be made here that may improve the application of fair value accounting in Jordan and other emerging economies.

The International Federation of Accountants (IFAC) (2004) reports several suggested solutions to challenges facing emerging economies in their convergence to IFRS in practice. The suggested solutions are based on these countries committing to successful adoption of IFRS and to integrity in applying IFRS in practice by stakeholders involved in this process. In addition, IFAC (2004) proposes that there should be urgent attention to development of implementation guidance for IFRS, and to the availability of adequate training on the implementation of IFRS. These issues are discussed below regarding Jordan in particular and other emerging economies in general, with particular emphasis on fair value accounting. Since many emerging economies have formally committed to convergence to IFRS, dealing with these issues would arguably significantly improve the efforts of these countries in achieving this convergence in practice.

First, preparers, auditors and users of financial statements generally need to be better educated about IFRS requirements regarding fair value financial reporting, and to have continuous training to be up-to-date with any new or amended requirements (Albasheer, 2006). Such training is likely to reduce any ambiguities in understanding and applying fair value-related IFRS. Kumarasiri and Fisher (2011) suggest the use of technological methods, such as knowledge-based expert systems, to enhance this education process. Another suggestion is for the accounting profession and regulatory authorities in the developing countries to establish a committee to be responsible for issuing a clear translation of IFRS and clarifying any ambiguous contents when necessary (Albasheer, 2006).

A second and major problem of fair value financial reporting is its relatively high level of subjectivity and use of professional judgement (Khouree, 2006), and that this fact may lead to fraud in the reported figures (Matar & Alsuwaitee, 2006). There are two avenues for dealing with this problem. The first is for the regulatory authorities to apply more strict penalties on clear violations of fair value reporting requirements, as a measure of discouraging fraud and earnings management (Matar & Alsuwaitee, 2006). As markets weak in efficiency lack clear and agreed-upon measures of fair value for most assets, a second avenue for dealing with the problem of subjective measurement of fair values is for regulatory authorities and professional bodies to develop or adopt a measurement and valuation base for fair value of assets. A suggested set of standards to use in asset valuation is the International Valuation Standards issued by the International Valuation Standards Council (Abu-Haltam, 2010). The use of an agreed-upon set of valuation standards is likely to significantly reduce the effects of volatility in applying personal judgement for fair valuation of financial statement items in emerging economies.

CONCLUSIONS

Fair value accounting practices for financial reporting have risen in prominence worldwide during the last two decades under pressure from the business community for accounting information that is more relevant and reflective of the market conditions, and therefore more useful for financial decision making. However, the use of fair value was, and still is, controversial.

While proponents of fair value accounting have argued in favour of its relevance and usefulness, opponents have argued that it may be misused in practice and can lead to distortions of net income through early recognition of unrealised holding gains and losses. This early recognition may lead to unwanted economic consequences, especially in institutions such as banks, where the use of fair value accounting can be relatively sensitive.

Proponents and opponents of fair value accounting have been academics and practitioners from more-developed countries, assuming conditions of higher market efficiency and more transparency in disclosures. Whether, or to what extent, this applies to less-developed countries is debatable.

Low-efficiency markets and less transparency combined with mainly closely held businesses (including public listed companies) may lead to different results from applying fair value accounting. These include possible fraud or poor personal judgements regarding the fair value measures or undesired economic consequences (in terms of poor investment decisions). In the particular case of the banking sector in Jordan, Al-Khadash and Abdullatif (2009) reported very high volatility in income of banks, in many cases several times more when unrealised holding gains and losses were included in net income than if unrealised holding gains and losses were excluded from the calculation of net income. This suggested that market prices lead banks' reported net incomes, rather than the other way around. Several negative social and economic consequences were reported as a result of this (Al-Khadash & Abdullatif, 2009).

This study surveyed views of the Jordanian bankers on the usefulness of fair value accounting and obstacles that may potentially impair this usefulness. In summary, while fair value accounting was seen as generally useful for financial decision making, there were some reservations concerning its usefulness, especially regarding its feedback value and its predictive value, due to the increased possibility of errors in personal judgements, and the relatively high inflation rates that may lead to large differences between fair values and historical costs. The main obstacles to the application of fair value accounting perceived by respondents to the questionnaire included possibilities of fraud through the misuse of personal judgement, lack of reliability of fair value reported figures compared to historical cost reported figures and ambiguity of accounting standards concerning fair value. While these issues may be important in a more-developed country setting, they are more likely to occur in less-developed countries. Therefore, these issues need more attention by international and local regulatory authorities interested in improving financial reporting.

These results leave us with the question of whether fair value accounting should be required worldwide (as is the general case of IFRS) or whether some alternative can be proposed and permitted for financial reporting in less-developed countries, where the full application of fair value accounting may lead to more negative economic consequences since, while in more-developed countries using market prices is generally seen as more relevant and not seriously impairing reliability in many cases, in less-developed countries reliability may be seriously impaired. The findings from this study do not provide conclusive evidence on this, but they highlight issues that international standard setters may find important when considering the application of fair value accounting standards. In addition, the findings show the need for Jordan and other emerging economies to implement adequate training for preparers, auditors and users of financial statements on the application of IFRS on fair value accounting, and to develop adequate guidance for practical application of IFRS on fair value accounting.

Several suggestions for future research on fair value accounting can be developed from the results of this study. These include in-depth studies of the actual practice of fair value accounting by reporting entities in developing countries and studies of the methods of application of personal judgement in the valuation of assets. It is also important to study the effects of fair value reporting in developing countries on security prices and how such an effect may be different from what exists in more-developed contexts. A related issue also worth exploring in developing countries is the use of fair value reported items by users of financial statements and how the presence of fair values may affect the users' decision making. The potential effect of fair value reporting on the auditing function in developing countries and how auditors in these countries adjust their audit practices as a result of that is also worth further exploration.

REFERENCES

Abdullatif, M. (2010). Audit programme adjustments and fraud risk factors: Evidence from Jordan. Paper presented at the Second Kuwait Association of Accountants and Auditors Conference: The Role of Accounting in the Stability and Support of Financial Markets, 1–2 December, Kuwait.

Abdullatif, M., & Al-Khadash, H. (2010). Putting audit approaches in context: The case of business risk audits in Jordan. *International Journal of Auditing, 14*(1), 1–24.

Abu-Haltam, I. M. (2010). What after applying International Financial Reporting Standards? It is International Valuation Standards. *Almudaqqeq*, No. 85–86, 23.

Abu-Harb, M. (2009). *The extent of the reliability and relevance for the outcomes of accounting information systems under the application of the fair value concept in the Jordanian commercial bank*. Unpublished Ph.D. dissertation, The Arab Academy for Banking and Financial Sciences, Amman, Jordan.

Al-Akra, M., Ali, M. J., & Marashdeh, O. (2009). Development of accounting regulation in Jordan. *International Journal of Accounting, 44*, 163–186.

Albasheer, M. (2006). Fair value and Jordanian regulations related to the accounting and auditing profession. Paper presented at the Jordanian Association of Certified Public Accountants Seventh Conference: Fair Value and Financial Reporting, 13–14 September, Amman, Jordan.

Al-Jarrah, I. M., Khamees, B. M., & Haddad, F. S. (2009). The effect of anomaly in monthly trading in Amman Stock Exchange over the period 2002–2006. *Jordan Journal of Business Administration, 5*(4), 523–532.

Al-Khadash, H., & Abdullatif, M. (2009). Consequences of fair value accounting for financial instruments in developing countries: The case of the banking sector in Jordan. *Jordan Journal of Business Administration, 5*(4), 533–551.

Al-Sa'eed, M. A. (2008). *The impact of disclosure – Applying the concept of fair value according to changes in the International Financial Reporting Standards on financial reporting of insurance companies in Jordan.* Unpublished doctoral thesis, Amman Arab University, Amman, Jordan.

Alshiab, M., & Alalawneh, A. (2007). Common shares performance evaluation for companies listed at Amman Stock Exchange. *Dirasat: Administrative Sciences, 34*(1), 210–220.

Al-Yaseen, B. S., & Al-Khadash, H. (2011). Risk relevance of fair value income measures under IAS 39 and IAS 40. *Journal of Accounting in Emerging Economies, 1*(1), 9–32.

Armstrong, C., Barth, M. E., Jagolinzer, A., & Riedl, E. J. (2006). *Market reaction to events surrounding the adoption of IFRS in Europe.* Working Paper No. 1937, Stanford University Graduate School of Business Research Paper Series.

Barth, M. E. (1994). Fair value accounting: Evidence from investment securities and the market valuation of banks. *The Accounting Review, 69*(1), 1–25.

Barth, M. E. (2006). Including estimates of the future in today's financial statements. *Accounting Horizons, 20*(3), 271–285.

Barth, M. E., Beaver, W. H., & Landsman, W. R. (1996). Value-relevance of banks' fair value disclosures under SFAS No. 107. *The Accounting Review, 71*(4), 513–537.

Barth, M. E., & Clinch, G. (1998). Revalued financial, tangible, and intangible assets: Associations with share prices and non-market-based value estimations. *Journal of Accounting Research, 36*(Suppl.), 199–233.

Barth, M. E., & Landsman, W. R. (1995). Fundamental issues related to using fair value accounting for financial reporting. *Accounting Horizons, 9*(4), 97–107.

Barth, M. E., Landsman, W. R., & Wahlen, J. M. (1995). Fair value accounting: Effects on banks' earnings volatility, regulatory capital, and value of contractual cash flows. *Journal of Banking and Finance, 19*, 577–605.

Beard, V., & Al-Rai, Z. (1999). Collection and transmission of accounting information across cultural borders: The case of US MNEs in Jordan. *International Journal of Accounting, 34*(1), 133–150.

Ben Hamida, N. (2007). An investigation of capital market reactions of quoted French banks to pronouncements on IAS 39. Paper presented at The British Accounting Association Annual Conference, 3–5 April, London, UK.

Benston, G. J. (2005). Accounting doesn't need much fixing (just some reinterpreting). In: D. H. Chew, Jr. & S. L. Gillan (Eds.), *Corporate governance at the crossroads: A book of readings* (pp. 492–505). Boston, MA: McGraw-Hill.

Benston, G. J. (2008). The shortcomings of fair-value accounting described in SFAS 157. *Journal of Accounting and Public Policy, 27*, 101–114.

Bernard, V. L., Merton, R. C., & Palepu, K. G. (1995). Mark-to-market accounting for banks and thrifts: Lessons from the Danish experience. *Journal of Accounting Research, 33*(1), 1–32.

Callao, S., Jarne, J. I., & Lainez, L. A. (2007). Adoption of IFRS in Spain: Effect on the comparability and relevance of financial reporting. *Journal of International Accounting, Auditing and Taxation, 16*(2), 148–178.

Carroll, T. J., Linsmeier, T. J., & Petroni, K. R. (2003). The reliability of fair value versus historical cost information: Evidence from closed-end mutual funds. *Journal of Accounting, Auditing and Finance, 18*(4), 1–23.

Daniels, J. D., Radebaugh, L. H., & Sullivan, D. P. (2011). *International business: Environments and operations* (13th ed.). Upper Saddle River, NJ: Pearson Education, Inc.

Deegan, C., & Unerman, J. (2006). *Financial accounting theory* (European ed.). Maidenhead, Berkshire: McGraw-Hill Companies, Inc.

Drever, M., Stanton, P., & McGowan, S. (2007). *Contemporary issues in accounting.* Milton Qld, Australia: John Wiley and Sons Australia, Ltd.

Eccher, E. A., Ramesh, K., & Thiagarajan, S. R. (1996). Fair value disclosures by bank holding companies. *Journal of Accounting and Economics, 22*, 79–117.

Elliott, B., & Elliott, J. (2009). *Financial accounting and reporting* (13th ed.). Harlow, Essex: Pearson Education Limited.

Evans, T. G. (2003). *Accounting theory: Contemporary accounting issues.* Thomson Learning.

Hitz, J.-M. (2007). The decision usefulness of fair value accounting – A theoretical perspective. *European Accounting Review, 16*(2), 323–362.

International Accounting Standards Board (IASB). *IAS 39: Financial instruments: Recognition and measurement.* International Accounting Standards Board.

International Federation of Accountants (IFAC). (2004). Challenges and successes in implementing international standards: Achieving convergence to IFRSs and ISAs. Availalbe at http://www.ifac.org/sites/default/files/publications/files/challenges-and-successes-in.pdf

Irvine, H. J., & Lucas, N. (2006). The globalization of accounting standards: The case of the United Arab Emirates. Faculty of Commerce papers, University of Wollongong.

Jermakowicz, E. K., & Gornik-Tomaszewski, S. (2006). Implementing IFRS from the perspective of EU publicly traded companies. *Journal of International Accounting, Auditing and Taxation, 21*, 170–196.

Joshi, P. L., Bremser, W. G., & Al-Ajmi, J. (2008). Perceptions of accounting professionals in the adoption and implementation of a single set of global accounting standards: Evidence from Bahrain. *Advances in Accounting, 24*(1), 41–48.

Khouree, N. S. (2006). Fair value and economic growth. Paper presented at the Jordanian Association of Certified Public Accountants Seventh Conference: Fair Value and Financial Reporting, 13–14 September, Amman, Jordan.

Khurana, I. K., & Kim, M. (2003). Relative value relevance of historical cost vs. fair value: Evidence from bank holding companies. *Journal of Accounting and Public Policy, 22*, 19–42.

Kumarasiri, J., & Fisher, R. (2011). Auditors' perceptions of fair-value accounting: Developing country evidence. *International Journal of Auditing, 15*(1), 66–87.

Larson, R. K., & Street, D. L. (2004). Convergence with IFRS in an expanding Europe: Progress and obstacles identified by large accounting firms' survey. *Journal of International Accounting, Auditing and Taxation, 19*, 89–119.

Laux, C., & Leuz, C. (2009a). The crisis of fair-value accounting: Making sense of the recent debate. *Accounting, Organizations and Society, 34*, 826–834.

Laux, C., & Leuz, C. (2009b). *Did fair value accounting contribute to the financial crisis?* Finance Working Paper No. 266/2009, European Corporate Governance Institute.

Lundy, F. S. (2002). Fair value accounting for commercial banks and its disclosure according to international accounting criteria: An empirical study in Jordan. *Scientific Journal of Commerce and Finance: Tanta University* (1), 121–179.

Matar, M., & Alsuwaitee, M. (2006). The effects of the uses of the fair value measurement methodology on earnings management and financial statements' fairness. Paper presented at the Jordanian Association of Certified Public Accountants Seventh Conference: Fair Value and Financial Reporting, 13–14 September, Amman, Jordan.

Nelson, K. K. (1996). Fair value accounting for commercial banks: An empirical analysis of SFAS No. 107. *The Accounting Review, 71*(2), 161–182.

Nobes, C., & Parker, R. (2010). International harmonization. In: C. Nobes & R. Parker (Eds.), *Comparative international accounting* (11th ed., pp. 79–104). Harlow, Essex: Pearson Education Limited.

Olesen, K., & Cheng, F. (2011). Convergence of accounting standards does not always lead to convergence of accounting practices: The case of China. *Asian Journal of Business and Accounting, 4*(1), 23–58.

Omet, G. (1999). The Jordanian stock exchange: Prospects and challenges. *Dirasat: Administrative Sciences, 26*(1), 132–139.

Omet, G., & Bino, A. (2000). On the assessment of risk and return in Amman Financial Market. *Dirasat: Administrative Sciences, 27*(1), 233–241.

Peng, S., & Bewley, K. (2010). Adaptability to fair value accounting in an emerging economy: The case of China's IFRS convergence. *Accounting, Auditing and Accountability Journal, 23*(8), 982–1011.

Penman, S. H. (2007). Financial reporting quality: Is fair value a plus or a minus? *Accounting and Business Research*, Special Issue: International Accounting Policy Forum, 33–44.

PricewaterhouseCoopers. (2011). Practical guide on financial instrument accounting: IFRS 9. Retrieved from https://pwcinform.pwc.com/inform2/show?action=informContent&id=1145065601124848. Accessed on 2 July 2011.

Qabajeh, M. A. (2009). *The effect of applying fair value accounting on intangible assets on content of financial statement and tax base in Jordanian public shareholding companies.* Unpublished doctoral thesis, Amman Arab University, Amman, Jordan.

Rayman, R. A. (2007). Fair value accounting and the present value fallacy: The need for an alternative conceptual framework. *British Accounting Review, 39*(3), 211–225.

Riahi-Belkaoui, A. (2004). *Accounting theory* (5th ed.). London, UK: Thomson Learning.

Ronen, J. (2008). To fair value or not to fair value: A broader perspective. *Abacus, 44*(2), 181–208.

The Hashemite Kingdom of Jordan. (2008). Regulations on accounting principles and mandatory standards related to estimating fair value and dealing with revaluation surplus for year 2007. Issued on 16 December 2007 and amended on 11 February 2008.

Yuan-yuan, Z., & Jun, D. (2009). The defects of fair value under global financial crisis. *Journal of Modern Accounting and Auditing, 5*(7), 52–55.

Zeff, S. A. (2010). Political lobbying on accounting standards – US, UK and international experience. In: C. Nobes & R. Parker (Eds.), *Comparative international accounting* (11th ed., pp. 247–278). Harlow, Essex: Pearson Education Limited.

Zikmund, W. G., Babin, B. J., Carr, J. C., & Griffin, M. (2010). *Business research methods* (8th ed.). South Western: Cengage Learning.

CORPORATE GOVERNANCE AND AUDIT REPORT TIMELINESS: EVIDENCE FROM MALAYSIA

Sherliza Puat Nelson and Siti Norwahida Shukeri

ABSTRACT

Purpose – *The purpose of this study is to examine the impact of corporate governance characteristics on audit report timeliness in Malaysia. The corporate governance characteristics examined are board independence, audit committee size, audit committee meetings and audit committee members' qualifications.*

Design/Methodology/Approach – *The sample comprises of 703 Malaysian listed companies from Bursa Malaysia, for the year 2009. It excludes companies from the finance-related sector as they operate under a highly regulated regime under supervision by the Central Bank of Malaysia. Further, regression analysis was performed to examine the audit report timeliness determinants.*

Findings – *Results show that audit report timeliness is influenced by audit committee size, auditor type, audit opinion and firm profitability. However, no association was found between board independence, audit committee meetings, audit committee members' qualifications and audit report timeliness.*

Accounting in Asia
Research in Accounting in Emerging Economies, Volume 11, 109–127
Copyright © 2011 by Emerald Group Publishing Limited
All rights of reproduction in any form reserved
ISSN: 1479-3563/doi:10.1108/S1479-3563(2011)0000011010

110   SHERLIZA PUAT NELSON AND SITI NORWAHIDA SHUKERI

Research limitations/Implications – *It is a cross-sectional study of the year 2009. Practical implications for policy makers are consideration of the minimum submission period for audit reports Regulators' support for firms to have larger audit committee sizes is also discussed.*

Originality/Value – *The study investigates the impact of corporate governance on audit timeliness in light of the recent amendments to the Malaysian Code of Corporate Governance made in 2007.*

Keywords: Audit reports; timeliness; corporate governance; audit committees; Malaysia

INTRODUCTION

Audit report timeliness is commonly measured as the number of days from the year end to the date of the audit report, and is also known as audit report lag. The audit report timeliness is found to have a great impact on financial reporting timeliness and it has become a main concern for regulators and policy makers to investigate the possible factors that may influence audit report timeliness. Strong corporate governance mechanisms may improve financial reporting quality such as the strength of the board of directors and audit committees (AC). Whereby, the audit committee is documented to be significantly associated with the quality of the financial reports as it potentially affects the auditor's risk assessments (Abbott, Parker, & Peter, 2004). Furthermore, premised on agency theory, Fama and Jensen (1983) posit that a firm's internal governance plays an important role in shaping and effectively enhancing the operations of its internal control system.

Corporate governance is an important entity-level factor that sets the tone for the overall control environment that has significant implications for auditors' risk judgments. The impact of strong corporate governance mechanisms will reduce client-related risks and subsequently reduce the timing and extent of substantive testing. Hence, auditors will perceive stronger corporate governance, and less substantive testing would be performed. This leads to better audit timeliness on the issuance of audited annual report by the independent external auditor to its client. Subsequently, this affects the issuance of corporate annual report by the organisation to their stakeholders.

The issue of timely reporting will also affect regulators and policy makers since they need to play a role in ensuring efficient financial reporting.

Given the importance of financial reporting timeliness, identifying the determinants of financial reporting delay is considered an important step to improve the financial reporting quality. Therefore, this study aims to investigate the impact of corporate governance mechanisms on audit report timeliness. We predict that strong corporate governance will reduce client-related risks and hence reduce the timing and extent of substantive testing. Further, we examine the board of directors and audit committee attributes (such as size, frequency of meetings and qualification) as explanatory independent variables. Whereby, they act as effective monitoring mechanisms that will enhance the internal controls and reduce the audit business risk, and eventually give shorter audit report timeline. The study extends current literature with evidence that shows an association between audit report timeliness and the strength of a client's corporate governance and, subsequently, this substantiates the role of corporate governance in financial reporting and the auditing process.

This study is organised as follows: in the second section, a review of audit report timeliness literature is discussed, followed by the third section on the development of hypotheses. The fourth section explains the research design, followed by a discussion on analysis of findings. The sixth section offers the conclusion.

LITERATURE REVIEW

Timeliness has long been recognised as one of the qualitative attributes of general-purpose financial reports. Timeliness of financial reporting is influenced by two specific categories: company's or client's attributes and auditor's attributes. Company's attributes comprises company size, profitability, leverage, audit risk, audit complexity and company's age. Prior studies found that financial reporting timeliness is mostly influenced by company's size (Ashton, Graul, & Newton, 1989; Payne & Jensen, 2002), auditor type (Knechel & Payne, 2001), audit risk (Sharma, Boo, & Sharma, 2007) and profitability (Ismail & Chandler, 2004). Prior literatures also documented an association between financial reporting timeliness with the auditor's attributes such as audit technology (Ashton et al., 1989), provision of non-audit services (Walker & Hay, 2007), audit qualification (Soltani, 2002), auditor size (Davies & Whittred, 1980; Jaggi & Tsui, 1999) and auditor opinion (Leventis, Weetman, & Caramanis, 2005; Soltani, 2002).

Whereby, in Ashton et al. (1989), the audit report timeliness is found to be better in a company where the auditor used a high audit technology and system and was able to complete the audit procedures and test on time. Hence, audit timeliness is one of the factors that affects financial reporting timeliness since the financial report can only be publicly announced after the independent auditor has signed and issued the audited financial report.

Further, prior literature also examined audit timeliness in relation to information intended to be released by the company. For example, Givoly and Palmon (1982) document that companies with bad news tend to delay their financial reports announcement, hence suggesting that company with bad news will tend to take more time to report than companies with good news. Part of this was because companies were hesitant to report bad news to the public and took more time to massage the numbers or resort to creative accounting techniques when they had to report bad news. This fact was supported by Ashton et al. (1989) when they examined the relationship between audit delays and timeliness of corporate reporting of 465 companies listed on Toronto Stock Exchange (TSE), and found longer audit delay was significantly associated with auditor's size, industry, extraordinary items and net income. Subsequently, Soltani (2002) documents companies that received qualified audit opinions, tend to delay in releasing their financial report, supplements prior studies that show company with bad news will tend to take more time to report than companies with good news.

Prior literature examines audit timeliness in relation to company's and auditor's attributes or characteristics with audit timeliness. Recent studies, such as Al-Ajmi (2008) and Afify (2009), extended current literature in association with company's characteristics and corporate governance characteristics. Al-Ajmi (2008) documents that company's size, profitability, industry and leverage significantly affect audit lag period, consistent with Ashton et al. (1989); Ismail and Chandler (2004); Lee, Mande and Son (2008); and Afify (2009). Consequently, Afify (2009) when examining the impact of corporate governance characteristics on audit report lag, found that corporate governance characteristics (board independence, duality of CEO and existence of audit committee) are significantly related to audit report lag. In addition, a more recent study on corporate governance characteristics shows that firms with large number of audit committee members have more frequent audit committee meetings and are more likely to produce audit reports in a timely manner (Mohd Naimi, Shafie, & Wan Nordin, 2010).

We can see that the audit timeliness literature has expanded from examining financial reporting timeliness with audit attributes (Ashton et al.,

1989; Soltani, 2002), to auditors' control environment risk (Cohen, Krishnamoorthy, & Wright, 2002; Sharma et al., 2007), dissemination of good news (Givoly & Palmon, 1982), audit lag period (Al-Ajmi, 2008) and recently on corporate governance characteristics (Afify, 2009; Mohd Naimi et al., 2010). Even though recent studies on corporate governance had been tested, and documented audit committee size and meetings are significantly associated with audit report timeliness (see Mohd Naimi et al., 2010), little can be found on other board and audit committees' characteristics, such as audit committee's qualification. Furthermore, the former study did not consider the recent MCCG changes made in October 2007; especially the changes made to board of directors and audit committees.[1]

The recent changes made in MCCG stressed on strengthening the board of directors and audit committees, and ensuring that the board of directors and audit committees discharge their roles and responsibilities effectively. In Malaysia, Bursa Malaysia views the delay of issuing audited annual reports as a serious offence and warns company's directors about their responsibility to maintain appropriate standards of corporate responsibility and account-ability. In addition, the Bursa also requires a timely financial reporting according to the provision in Chapter 9 of the Listing Requirements.[2] The Bursa had also recently issued new rules, the Bursa Malaysia Corporate Governance Guide (2009), that require the audit committee meetings to be held at least four times a year.

In light of these recent changes, there is still avenue for areas of research where corporate governance characteristics can be expanded on board's characteristics, especially the audit committees. As such, there is still a growing need to expand current literature and provide recent empirical evidence on other corporate governance characteristics that are still not widely researched in the past. Consequently, the objective of the study is to investigate the association of corporate governance characteristics such as board independence, audit committee independence and qualification, in association with audit report timeliness among Malaysian listed companies.

HYPOTHESES DEVELOPMENT

Prior literature suggests that the presence of corporate governance mechanisms will increase the monitoring of management and reduce the incidence of mismanagement or misreporting and delays in the financial reporting processes. Thus, effective corporate governance should improve internal control and reduce business risk, hence having an effect on shorter audit delay (Afify, 2009). The agency relationship between the managers and shareholders may cause the agency conflicts to occur. An efficient corporate governance mechanism is an important element to the company, especially the group of big companies, in order to ensure the credibility of internal control and monitoring of the financial reporting system (Wan Abdullah, Ismail, & Jamaluddin, 2008).

According to Safieddine (2009), for good governance to take place there should be active participation of all parties, including the board of directors, audit committee, top management team, internal auditors, external auditors and governing bodies, in fostering continuous improvements. Lack of strong corporate governance may jeopardise the performance and internal control of the organisation since all business functions are interrelated to each other ranging from issues of internal control, audits, organisational structures, board directorship and management including top management and employees.

Agency theory is relevant to this study because it explains the board of directors, directors' ownership and audit committee, each of which functions as a monitoring mechanism to reduce agency problems. Monitoring mechanisms refer to the corporate governance practices and ensure the proper management performance and financial reporting processes. The financial statement can be announced to the public in a timely manner if the organisation has less business risk, as less business risk means less audit risk, thus reducing the time taken by the auditor to complete the annual audit and subsequently, shorter audit report lag. Therefore, reducing reporting lag is also considered as another component of good corporate governance practices since it reduces the information asymmetric issues by releasing the financial information on time to public (Al-Ajmi, 2008).

There is a close association between timely corporate reporting and corporate governance mechanisms since the components of corporate governance have an important role in the corporate reporting process. Agency conflicts within the organisation lead to information asymmetry between managers and shareholders. Thus, audits serve to reduce this asymmetric information risk by attesting the reliability of published financial information among the shareholders.

The presence of corporate governance mechanisms such as board independence, executives' and nonexecutives' portion of ownership and audit committee ensure the credibility of financial information that is announced to the public. Thus, corporate governance mechanisms were used in this study to examine their effects on audit delay, whereby, it is assumed that the shorter the audit delay, the shorter the time taken by the organisation to publish its corporate report and thus bring more updated information to shareholders. Boards conduct monitoring activities (agency view) and ensure that the managerial performance of the boards will reduce the agency problems that arise in the company.

It is expected that client companies with stronger corporate governance are assessed as having lower business risk and this will increase auditors' reliance on the client's internal controls and reduce the extent of substantive tests (Sharma et al., 2007). Therefore, the corporate governance mechanisms especially relating to the board are expected to reduce the audit report lag through the ability of the board to control the company's business risk.

Thus, the hypotheses of this study were developed based on the corporate governance characteristics which include board independence, audit committee size, audit committee qualification and frequency of audit committee meetings. While examining the impact of corporate governance characteristics on audit report lag, it is important to control for possible auditor attributes that are likely to affect timeliness such as auditor type and audit opinion.

Board Independence

Fama and Jensen (1983) explained that outside board of directors could strengthen the firm value by lending experienced and monitoring services and are supposed to be guardians of the shareholders' interests via monitoring and control. Past study (O'Sullivan, 2000; Salleh, Steward, & Manson, 2006) found that the proportion of board independence had a significant positive impact on audit quality. The larger the proportion of independent directors on the board, the more effective it will be in monitoring management behaviour, and thus reduce the nature of inherent risk which at the end reduce the period of audit lag (Afify, 2009). Cohen et al. (2002) argued that in the case where a client's governance structure has effectively implemented a strong monitoring as well as strong strategic perspective, there is the potential for both a more efficient audit work which leads to less extent of tests of details and a greater assurance of the integrity of the financial statements. This could then affect the assessed level of inherent and control risks, thereby affecting the nature, timing and extent of audit work. Whereby, higher number of board independence may lead to lower ARL, as it is expected that higher independent board will give better monitoring control. Hence, less audit field work and eventually reduce the ARL. The first hypothesis will be as follows:

H1. There is a negative relationship between ARL and board independence.

Audit Committee

The effectiveness of an audit committee increases when the size of the committee increases because it has sufficient resources to address the issues faced by the company (Rahmat, Iskandar, & Saleh, 2009). In a recent work by Bédard and Gendron (2010), they indicate that the audit committee size, independence, competency and meetings have greatest impact on financial reporting quality. This is supported by Mohd Naimi et al. (2010), who document that firms with more members in the audit committee and more frequent audit committee meetings are more likely to produce audit reports in a timely manner. In addition, Abbott et al. (2004) noted that with frequent meetings, audit committee will remain informed and knowledgeable about accounting or auditing issues and can direct internal and external audit resources to address the matter in a timely fashion. Thus, strong audit committee in terms of its size, higher meeting frequency and more qualified members will ensure the internal control and procedures of the company is reduced. Therefore, it will reduce the auditor working hours and subsequently reduce the ARL. Hence, the following hypotheses are conjectured:

H2. There is a negative relationship between ARL and audit committee size.

H3. There is a negative relationship between ARL and frequency of audit committee meeting.

H4. There is a negative relationship between ARL and audit committee qualification.

Auditor's Type

Afify (2009) shows that larger audit firms have a stronger motivation to complete their audit work on time in order to maintain their reputation and name. The large audit firms normally have more efficient audit teams as they have more resources to conduct trainings for their staff and are also able to employ more powerful audit technologies which reduce the time of audit work (Owusu-Ansah & Leventis, 2006). Giroux and McLelland (2000) found that Big Four firms completed their audit work faster than the non-Big Four firms. Thus, it is expected that large audit firms (Big Four firms) will perform faster audit work as compared to the small audit firms (non-Big Four firms) as Big Four firms have more resources compared to non-Big Four firms. Given with more resources, the auditors in Big Four firms are able to complete the audit work on time and consequently reduce the ARL. Hence, the hypothesis will be as follows:

H5. There is a negative relationship between ARL and auditor type.

Audit Opinion

The company that received unqualified audit opinion is said to have proper management and internal control system, thus reducing the time of audit process and procedures (Soltani, 2002). Bamber, Bamber, and Schoderbek (1993) argued that the qualified opinions are not likely to be issued until the auditor has spent considerable time and effort in performing additional audit procedures. Moreover, companies always view audit qualified opinion as 'bad news' and might not respond to the auditor's request promptly. It is a symptom of auditor–management conflict that would also increase audit delay (Che-Ahmad & Abidin, 2008). For the company that received qualified audit opinion, the auditor may need additional time to complete the audit work and thus increase the ARL. Thus, the expected relationship for audit opinion is as follows:

H6. There is a negative relationship between ARL and audit opinion.

Firms' Performance

Prior research has found that firms that experience losses for the period would result in longer audit report lag (Ashton et al., 1989; Givoly & Palmon, 1982; Ismail & Chandler, 2004). Prior studies also reported that firms experiencing losses for the periods are expected to have a longer audit delay as compared to the ones reporting a profit. There are some underlying reasons to the expectation of firm performance with audit report lag. Firms that have bad news – the ones which have made losses – tend to delay their financial statement release because they want to avoid reporting the bad news to their shareholders and investors, and hence avoid jeopardising their firm's reputation and performance. However, for firms that experience profit, the management wants the auditor to complete their annual report in a short time because they want to report the good news to their shareholders. Moreover, the auditor may take a longer period to audit firms that incurred losses because of the associated business risk (Afify, 2009) and consequently increase the ARL. Hence, the expected relationship between firm's performance and audit report lag is as follows:

H7. There is a negative relationship between ARL and firm performance.

RESEARCH DESIGN

Sample

This study utilised secondary data as the main source of information. The information relating to the proportion of board independence, composition of audit committee size, meetings and qualification, auditor type, audit opinion and firms' profitability was collected from company annual reports for the year 2009. There were 719 companies listed in the Bursa Malaysia, but only 703 companies had available information.

The sample excluded finance-related companies, companies from Initial Public Offerings (IPO), close-end funds sectors, exchange-traded funds and Real Estate Investment Trust (REITs). Finance-related companies are excluded from the sample because these companies have significantly different requirements, rules and regulations with respect to financial reporting.[3] The sample also excluded companies under PN4[4] conditions since the companies are categorised as being unable to maintain the listing condition of the Bursa Malaysia (Rahmat et al., 2009) and do not comply with any of the specified conditions by the Bursa Malaysia.

The sample selection covers the audited annual report for the year 2009 which is considered as the latest issue of annual reports and latest available information at time of this study and it is the information after the CG revised code was implemented in 2007. In addition, the sample selection of annual report of 2009 is to complement the earlier study by Mohd Naimi et al. (2010). Almost all corporate annual reports were downloaded from the Bursa Malaysia's website and a few were hand collected.

Operationalisation of Variables

The study used multiple regression analysis by modelling ARL as a function of explanatory variables. Corporate governance characteristics are modelled as independent variables that are consistent with prior studies. Specifically, the ARL model used in this study is consistent from prior studies (Afify, 2009; Che-Ahmad & Abidin, 2008; Mohd Naimi et al., 2010).

The ARL model for this study is as follows:

$$ARL = \beta 0 + \beta 1(BIND) + \beta 2(ACSIZE) + \beta 3(ACMEET) + \beta 4(ACQUAL)$$
$$+ \beta 5(AUDTYPE) + \beta 6(AUDOPIN) + \beta 7(PERF) + \varepsilon$$

Table 1 shows the operational measures of each variable.

Table 1. Summary of Operationalisation of Variables.

Variables	Operational Measures
Dependent variable	
Audit Report Lag (ARL)	Number of days from the interval period of financial year end date to the date of annual audit report
Independent variables	
Board Independence (BIND)	The proportion of non-executive directors to the total number of directors
Audit Committee Size (ACSIZE)	Total number of audit committee members
Audit Committee Meetings (ACMEET)	The number of audit committee meetings held during the financial year
Audit Committee Qualifications (ACQUAL)	The proportion of audit committee members possessing professional accounting qualifications (ACCA etc.) or members of any professional accounting bodies (MIA, CPA etc.) to the total number of audit committee members
Auditor Type (AUDTYPE)	Assigned as 1 for Big Four firm and 0 otherwise
Audit Opinion (AUDOPIN)	Assigned as 1 for company received unqualified audit opinion and 0 otherwise
Firm Performance (PERF)	Assigned as 1 for company that incurs profit and 0 for company that incurs loss

ANALYSIS OF RESULTS AND DISCUSSIONS

Descriptive Analysis

Table 2 reports the descriptive statistics of all variables investigated in this study. The table shows the descriptive of mean, standard deviation, minimum and maximum. Using data from 703 observations of annual reports from the KLSE for a year period of 2009, it was found that the average audit report lag was 101 days with a standard deviation of 22.32 days. The analysis of the sample study also shows that only two companies were found to have audit report lag of more than 180 days and violated the Bursa Malaysia requirements on the minimum submission period of six months. However, majority of the companies in the sample complied with the reporting requirements on audit report as shown in Table 3. Hence,

Table 2.   Descriptive Statistics.

Variables ($N = 703$)	Minimum	Maximum	Mean	SD
ARL	34	239	101.09	22.32
BIND	0.17	0.83	0.44	0.12
ACSIZE	2	6	3.26	0.54
ACMEET	0	16	4.93	1.25
ACQUAL	0.00	1.00	.33	0.16

Note: ARL, number of days from the interval period of financial year end date to the date of annual audit report; BIND, the proportion of non-executive directors to the total number of directors; ACSIZE, number of AC members; ACMEET, the number of audit committee meetings held during the financial year; ACQUAL, the proportion of audit committee members possessing professional accounting qualifications (ACCA etc.) or members of any professional accounting bodies (MIA, CPA etc.) to the total number of audit committee members.

Table 3.   Descriptive Statistics.

Variables ($N = 703$)	Category	Frequency	Percentage (%)
AUDTYPE	Big Four	304	43.2
	Non-Big Four	399	56.8
AUDOPIN	Qualified audit opinion	67	9.5
	Unqualified audit Opinion	636	90.5
PERF	Loss	175	24.9
	Profit	528	75.1

Note: AUDTYPE, assigned as 1 for Big Four firm and 0 otherwise; AUDOPIN, assigned as 1 for company received unqualified audit opinion and 0 otherwise; PERF, assigned as 1 for company that incurs profit and 0 for company that incurs loss.

suggesting that firms actually adhered to the listing requirements to submit the annual audit report within the stipulated time period.

Correlation Analysis

The objective of the test is to see if there is any multi-collinearity problems among the variables and association among variables as shown in Table 4. The problem exists if independent variables are highly correlated at each other with correlation values exceeding 0.9 according to Tabachnick and Fidell (2007). However, none of the variables found to be more than 0.5. The highest correlation is between the two control variables which are audit opinion and firm performance (profitability) that is 0.306 which suggest that multi-collinearity is not a serious problem that would jeopardise the regression results (Tabachnick & Fidell, 2007). Results show that ARL are negatively and significantly correlated with audit committee size, auditor's type, audit opinion and firms' performance suggesting that as ACSIZE increases, it reduces the ARL.

Table 4. Pearson's Correlation.

	ARL	BIND	ACSIZE	ACMEET	ACQUAL	AUDTYPE	AUDOPIN	PERF
ARL	1	0.010	-0.159^*	0.070	0.014	-0.265^*	-0.214^*	-0.194^*
BIND		1	0.083^*	0.077^*	0.012	-0.080^*	-0.090^*	-0.093^*
ACSIZE			1	0.058	-0.173^*	0.145^*	0.096^*	0.105^*
ACMEET				1	-0.31	-0.022	-0.145^*	-0.047
ACQUAL					1	-0.019	0.077^*	0.029
AUDTYPE						1	0.088^*	0.181^*
AUDOPIN							1	0.306^*
PERF								1

Note: **, *, significant at 0.01 and 0.05 level (2-tailed). ARL, number of days from the interval period of financial year end date to the date of annual audit report; BIND, the proportion of non-executive directors to the total number of directors; ACSIZE, number of AC members; ACMEET, the number of audit committee meetings held during the financial year; ACQUAL, the proportion of audit committee members possessing professional accounting qualifications (ACCA etc.) or members of any professional accounting bodies (MIA, CPA etc.) to the total number of audit committee members; AUDTYPE, assigned as 1 for Big Four firm and 0 otherwise; AUDOPIN, assigned as 1 for company received unqualified audit opinion and 0 otherwise; PERF, assigned as 1 for company that incurs profit and 0 for company that incurs loss.

Multivariate Analysis

Table 5 shows the multivariate analysis. Results show that ACSIZE is negative and significantly associated with ARL. This was initially supported earlier, where ACSIZE has a negative and significant relationship with ARL and is consistent with Sharma et al. (2007). The findings support H2 (audit committee size) and provide evidence that larger audit committee size tends to ensure that the internal control of the company is strong. Consequently, it generates positive influence on the auditor's assessment of business and audit risk, planned audit hours and the level of substantive testing and good financial reporting. Therefore, reduce the audit report lag.

However, the findings find no support for H3 (audit committee meetings) and H4 (audit committee qualification). These results might be addressed in

Table 5. Multiple Regression Analysis ARL $= \beta0 + \beta1(BIND)$
$+ \beta2(ACSIZE) + \beta3(ACMEET) + \beta4(ACQUAL)$
$+ \beta5(AUDTYPE) + \beta6(AUDOPIN) + \beta7(PERF) + \varepsilon.$

Variable	Expected Sign	Coefficients	t-Value	p-Value
(Constant)		132.185	18.848	0.000
BIND	−	−0.026	−0.713	0.476
ACSIZE	−	−0.101	−2.743**	0.006
ACMEET	−	0.047	1.298	0.195
ACQUAL	−	0.009	0.238	0.812
AUDTYPE	−	−0.22	−6.051**	0.000
AUDOPIN	−	−0.152	−4.003**	0.000
PERF	−	−0.098	−2.584**	0.010
N		703		
F-value		14.73		
p-value		0.000**		
Adjusted R^2		0.12		
R^2		0.129		

Note: **,*, significant at 0.01 and 0.05 level. ARL, number of days from the interval period of financial year end date to the date of annual audit report; BIND, the proportion of non-executive directors to the total number of directors; ACSIZE, number of AC members; ACMEET, the number of audit committee meetings held during the financial year; ACQUAL, the proportion of audit committee members possessing professional accounting qualifications (ACCA etc.) or members of any professional accounting bodies (MIA, CPA etc.) to the total number of audit committee members; AUDTYPE, assigned as 1 for Big Four firm and 0 otherwise; AUDOPIN, assigned as 1 for company received unqualified audit opinion and 0 otherwise; PERF, assigned as 1 for company that incurs profit and 0 for company that incurs loss.

light of the strict adherence of listed companies on the enforcement of MCCG (2007), which requires all listed companies to have at least three members and at least one member being a financial expert. Furthermore, H1 fails to be supported, where H1 assumes a negative association between board independence and audit report lag, and finding is consistent with Mohd Naimi et al. (2010) but contradicts with Wan Abdullah et al. (2008).

The results support H5, H6 and H7, and provide evidences that auditor type, audit opinion and profitability are significantly associated with audit report lag. The results are consistent with prior studies such as Ashton et al. (1989), Jaggi and Tsui (1999), Soltani (2002), Raja Ahmad and Kamarudin (2003), Ismail and Chandler (2004), Al-Ajmi (2008), Che-Ahmad and Abidin (2008) and Afify (2009). H5 (auditor type) has a significant negative association with audit report lag and subsequently provides evidence that companies audited by the Big Four firms have a shorter audit report lag, thus report earlier to the public. Prior studies suggest that the possible reason is that Big Four firms have more resources, powerful technology, more experienced auditor which enables the audit process to be completed within a shorter period of time. Furthermore, companies that received qualified audit opinion are expected to report their financial statement early, because the auditor believed these types of companies do not have much problem which need extensive testing in providing their opinion.

H6 (audit opinion) is also supported and consistent with Soltani (2002) and Raja Ahmad and Kamarudin (2003). The findings also support H7 (firm performance) indicating that profitability is significantly associated with audit report timeliness, suggesting that companies with good news (experience profit) report faster than companies with bad news (reporting loss). The findings are consistent with Ashton et al. (1989), Afify (2009) and Ismail and Chandler (2004) that documented bad news took longer time to reach the public than good news. In addition to that, this result provides evidence that companies with higher profitability may wish to complete the audit of their accounts as early as possible in order to quickly release their audited annual reports to the public.

From the above discussion, the findings suggest that the agency conflict can be mitigated with the presence of corporate governance mechanisms. Thus, the existing effective and strong corporate governance, concomitant with proper monitoring control, leads to more efficient and effective audit work, hence reducing audit report lag. Finally, it advances towards higher financial disclosure quality.

DISCUSSION AND CONCLUSION

This study provides recent empirical evidence relating to the audit report timeliness of Malaysian listed companies in 2009. The mean audit delay is 101 days (which is still below the maximum periods of six months as stipulated by the Bursa Malaysia at that time), and an improvement by one day earlier from prior study (see Mohd Naimi et al., 2010). Nevertheless, audit committee size, auditor type, audit opinion and profitability are found to have significant relationships with audit delay. Whereby, audit delay was significant and negatively associated with audit committee size, auditor type, audit opinion and profitability of the companies.

The result suggests that larger audit committee size is associated with lower audit report lag, hence improve audit report timeliness. Therefore, this will provide more space to the external auditors to ample space for discussion with audit committee members who are more diligent to provide resources to the companies. Subsequently, they are able to give more time and effort to ensure the accuracy of financial information that is going to be disclosed to the public, and effectively improve the financial reporting quality. It is vital to identify the timeliness issues, as it is found that there are companies that exceeded the six-month period of audit report issuance. This has implication for practice. Regulators should ensure that companies comply with the minimum submission period, to avoid companies taking the advantage of the current six-month reporting period, and giving rise to issues of information asymmetry.

However, the study is not without some limitations. Since the study is based on cross-sectional study, the trend of audit delay and long-term effects of corporate governance on timeliness of audit report could not be examined. Furthermore, the exclusion of companies from the finance sector might have contributed some limitation to the study in terms of the reported overall mean of the audit delays of financial companies. Due to the different regulations for financial institutions, this research was unable to include financial institutions in the sample size and future research might consider examining the effects of corporate governance characteristics on audit report timeliness in financial companies.

Therefore it is suggested that future studies may consider other mechanisms of corporate governance such as board meetings, compensation committee and proportion of board ownership and internal audit functions in order to examine the overall influence of corporate governance on audit report timeliness. The inclusion of more variables will amplify the research and provides an in-depth explanation to examine other factors that might influence audit timeliness. For example, the inclusion of internal audit function may be considered since the study is likely to relate with investigating the effect of client's business risk on the auditor's judgment. Other than that, future research may also include companies from finance-related sectors in order to examine different qualities of financial reporting between financial and non-financial companies, and consider a longitudinal study that would compare the timeliness of audit report in two or more periods, to observe if the timeliness of audit report improves over time.

In light of the corporate governance changes and improvements over the years, the study provides prevalent implications to improve financial reporting timeliness, as well as financial reporting quality.

NOTES

1. The revised Code strives to strengthen the role of audit committees by requiring the committees to comprise fully of non-executive directors. In addition, all its members should be able to read, analyse and interpret financial statements so that they will be able to effectively discharge their functions (Securities Commission, 2007, p. 14).

2. Chapter 9, on continuing disclosure.

3. In Malaysia, financial institutions are under the supervision of the Central Bank of Malaysia besides that of the KLSE.

4. Companies that do not comply with the Bursa Malaysia requirement and experience financial difficulties.

REFERENCES

Abbott, L. J., Parker, S., & Peter, G. F. (2004). Committee characteristics and restatements. *Auditing: A Journal of Practice and Theory, 23*(1), 69–87.

Afify, H. A. E. (2009). Determinants of audit report lag does implementing corporate governance have any impact? Empirical evidence from Egypt. *Journal of Applied Accounting Research, 10*(1), 56–86.

Al-Ajmi, J. (2008). Audit and reporting delays: Evidence from an emerging market. *Advances in Accounting, 24*(1), 217–226.

Ashton, R. H., Graul, P. R., & Newton, J. D. (1989). Audit delay and the timeliness of corporate reporting. *Contemporary Accounting Research, 5*(2), 657–673.

Bamber, E. M., Bamber, L. S., & Schoderbek, M. P. (1993). Audit structure and other determinants of audit report lag: An empirical analysis. *Auditing: A Journal of Practice and Theory, 12*(1), 1–23.

Bédard, J., & Gendron, Y. (2010). Strengthening the financial reporting systems: Can audit committees deliver? *International Journal of Auditing, 14*(2), 1–37.

Bursa Malaysia. (2009). *Bursa Malaysia Corporate Governance Guide 2009*. Kuala Lumpur: Bursa Malaysia.

Che-Ahmad, A., & Abidin, S. (2008). Audit delay of listed companies: A case of Malaysia. *International Business Research*, *1*(4), 32–39.

Cohen, J., Krishnamoorthy, G., & Wright, A. M. (2002). Corporate governance and the audit process. *Contemporary Accounting Research*, *19*(4), 573–594.

Davies, B., & Whittred, G.P. (1980). The association between selected corporate attributes and timeliness in corporate reporting: Further analysis. *Abacaus*, pp. 48–60.

Fama, E. F., & Jensen, M. C. (1983). Separation of ownership and control. *Journal of Law and Economics*, *26*(2), 301–325.

Giroux, G., & McLelland, A. J. (2000). An empirical analysis of auditor report timing by large municipalities. *Journal of Accounting and Public Policy*, *19*, 263–281.

Givoly, D., & Palmon, D. (1982). Timeliness of annual earnings announcements: Some empirical evidence. *The Accounting Review*, *57*(3), 485–508.

Ismail, K. N. I., & Chandler, R. (2004). The timeliness of quarterly financial reports of companies in Malaysia. *Asian Review of Accounting*, *12*(1), 1–18.

Jaggi, B., & Tsui, J. (1999). Determinants of audit report lag: Further evidence from Hong Kong. *Accounting and Business Research*, *30*(1), 17–28.

Knechel, W. R., & Payne, J. L. (2001). Additional evidence on audit report lag. *Auditing: A Journal of Practice and Theory*, *20*(1), 137–146.

Lee, H., Mande, V., & Son, M. (2008). A comparison of reporting lags of multinational and domestic firms. *Journal of International Financial Management and Accounting*, *19*(1), 28–56.

Leventis, S., Weetman, P., & Caramanis, C. (2005). Determinants of audit report lag: Some evidence from the Athens Stock Exchange. *International Journal of Auditing*, *9*, 45–58.

MCCG. (2007). Malaysian Code on Corporate Governance, Report on Corporate Governance, Securities Commission, Kuala Lumpur.

Mohd Naimi, M. N., Shafie, R., & Wan Nordin, W. H. (2010). Corporate governance and audit report lag in Malaysia. *Asian Academy of Management Journal of Accounting and Finance*, *6*(2), 57–84.

O'Sullivan, N. (2000). The impact of board composition and ownership on audit quality; Evidence from large UK companies. *The British Accounting Review*, *32*(4), 397–414.

Owusu-Ansah, S., & Leventis, S. (2006). Timeliness of corporate annual financial reporting in Greece. *European Accounting Review*, *15*(2), 273–287.

Payne, J. L., & Jensen, K. L. (2002). An examination of municipal audit delay. *Journal of Accounting and Public Policy*, *21*, 1–29.

Rahmat, M. M., Iskandar, T. M., & Saleh, N. M. (2009). Audit committee characteristics in financially distressed and non-distressed companies. *Managerial Auditing Journal*, *24*(7), 624–638.

Raja Ahmad, R. A., & Kamarudin, K. A. (2003). *Audit delay and the timeliness of corporate reporting: Malaysian evidence*. Working Paper, MARA University of Technology, Shah Alam.

Safieddine, A. (2009). Islamic financial institutions and corporate governance: New insights for agency theory. *Corporate Governance: An International Review*, *17*(2), 142–158.

Salleh, Z., Steward, J., & Manson, S. (2006). The impact of board composition and ethnicity on audit quality: Evidence from Malaysian companies. *Malaysian Acccounting Review*, *5*(2), 61–83.

Securities Commission. (2007). Malaysian Code of Corporate Governance (Revised 2007). Kuala Lumpur.

Sharma, D. S., Boo, E., & Sharma, V.D. (2007). The impact of non-mandatory corporate governance on auditors' client acceptance, risk and planning judgments (2008). *Accounting & Business Research*, 38(2), June 2008. Retrieved from SSRN: http://ssrn.com/abstract=1113194

Soltani, B. (2002). Timeliness of corporate and audit reports: Some empirical evidence in the French context. *The International Journal of Accounting, 37*, 215–246.

Tabachnick, B. G., & Fidell, L. S. (2007). *Using multivariate statistics* (5th ed.). Pearson Education.

Walker, A., & Hay, D. (2007). *An empirical investigation of the audit report lag: The effect of non-audit services*. Working paper presented at Australian National Centre for Audit and Assurance Research Workshop. Australian National University. Retrieved from http://www.unimaas.nl/ISAR2009/02_07_Walker_Hay.pdf. Accessed October 2010.

Wan Abdullah, W. Z., Ismail, S., & Jamaluddin, N. (2008). The impact of board composition, ownership and CEO duality on audit quality: The Malaysian evidence. *Malaysian Accounting Review, 7*(2), 17–32.

THE ASSOCIATION BETWEEN CORPORATE GOVERNANCE AND AUDIT QUALITY: EVIDENCE FROM TAIWAN

Yu-Shan Chang, Wuchun Chi, Long-Jainn Hwang and Min-Jeng Shiue

ABSTRACT

Purpose – *Audit quality is traditionally defined as the joint probability that an existing problem is discovered and reported by the auditor. This study examines whether and how audit quality is associated with related-party transactions and CEO duality. The first part (i.e., the ability to discover) is related to* professional judgment, *and the second part (i.e., report truthfully) is related to* independence.

Methodology/Approach – *Regression methods was used on archival data.*

Findings – *Our results reveal that for publicly held companies in environments with stronger capital market discipline, which causes greater reputation concerns and litigation risks, a CEO who is also the board chair does not hinder auditor independence. For privately held companies, however, such a CEO hinders auditor independence due to a lack of capital market discipline. The findings on related-party financing,*

Accounting in Asia
Research in Accounting in Emerging Economies, Volume 11, 129–153
ISSN: 1479-3563/doi:10.1108/S1479-3563(2011)0000011011

on the other hand, are reversed. That is, in terms of information for an auditor, since the conflicts of interests are more severe in publicly held companies than in privately held companies, the relevance of related-party financing to a decision whether to issue a going-concern opinion is greater in publicly held companies.

Social implications – *The empirical results of publicly held companies are useful for countries with better corporate governance, while those of privately held companies are helpful for countries with relatively weak corporate governance.*

Originality/Value of paper – *Because auditors performing audit services face different litigation risks and reputation concerns, the differences in our results between the two types of clients can have implications about the suitability of these types of companies in emerging markets.*

Keywords: Corporate governance; audit quality; publicly held companies; privately held companies

INTRODUCTION

Audit quality is traditionally defined as the joint probability that an existing problem is discovered and reported by the auditor (DeAngelo, 1981). In academic studies of auditing, corporate governance is usually considered solely in its relation to auditor independence (see, e.g., Bedard, Chtourou, & Courteau, 2004; Carcello & Neal, 2000, 2003; Ruder, 2002). Following prior studies (DeFond, Raghunandan, & Subramanyam, 2002; Li, 2009; Reynolds & Francis, 2001), audit quality is measured by the probability of the auditors' issuing a going concern (GC) opinion. This study not only examines whether and how CEO duality influence auditors' reporting decisions, but also analyzes whether and how the level of related-party transactions is related to auditors' professional judgment. This is important because, according to auditing standards, auditors should collect *information* and use their professional judgment to draw fair conclusions about the companies that they are auditing, and express those conclusions in their reports. We investigate whether related-party transactions affect auditors' professional judgment.

The role of the two variables, CEO duality and the level of related-party transactions, are different in our study. GC opinions are not issued solely due to auditor independence, they depend initially on professional judgment. It is only after professional judgment indicates that a GC opinion should be issued that the question of auditor independence can arise. Professional judgment is therefore prior to the issue of independence; yet, the latter is the more commonly examined variable. We believe that a complete analysis incorporating both professional judgment and independence can offer a more realistic view of the effects of corporate governance on audit quality.

Uniquely, we include both listed and unlisted companies to address our research issues, allowing us to have a better understating whether related-party transactions and CEO duality affect the likelihood of an auditor's issuing a GC opinion. This is important because Hope and Langli (2010) indicate that unlisted companies are less likely to impose reputation risks on auditors, which implies that the negative effect of CEO duality, if any, will be more severe in *privately held* companies. We expect that the usefulness of the information of the level of related-party transactions will be greater in *publicly held* companies.

To explore the issues, we examine two corporate governance variables: whether the CEO simultaneously serves as the chairperson of the board (hereafter DUAL) and related-party financing (RPF). The variable DUAL was chosen to address the debate on whether a CEO should serve as the chair of a majority-independent board. On the one hand, a dual-role CEO enhances a firm's performance by having a focused direction for the firm's strategies and operations. On the other hand, when corporate insiders other than the CEO are absent from a majority-independent board, directors become more dependent upon their link with the CEO for inside information. As a result, critical information is often hidden from the directors or falsified (Mitchell, 2005), and the CEO may therefore unduly influence the boards on many decisions (Chang & Sun, 2010). Many studies support the perspective that the dual-role CEO is negatively related to earnings quality. For example, Anderson, Deli, and Gillan (2003) find that earnings informativeness is positively related to companies with separate CEO and chair positions. Chang and Sun (2009) also find a negative relation between dual-role CEOs and earnings informativeness after SOX in cross-listed foreign companies. Since our sample is composed of financially distressed companies, the power of the board to monitor management will be weaker when a firm has a dual-role CEO. Specifically, for auditors of companies that are financially distressed, the likelihood of their compromising independence is greater when they face a dual-role CEO than when the CEO does not chair a board with an independent majority

(Elloumi & Gueyié, 2001). Therefore, we believe that the variable DUAL is useful to examine how corporate governance affects auditor independence.

RPF is used in this study not to examine auditor independence, but instead to explore whether RPF is relevant information, other things being equal, for auditors who audit financially distressed companies. Statement on Auditing Standard No. 59 (ASB, 1988) requires auditors to assess whether there is substantial doubt as to a client's ability to continue as a GC. SAS No. 59 directs auditors to evaluate four major categories of client characteristics: negative financial trends, other financial difficulties, internal problems, and external matters. In Taiwan, the source of the data in this study, related-party transactions are one characteristic that has been identified as damaging to firm value. Yeh, Lee, and Ko (2002), for example, point out that there are many irregular related-party transactions in Taiwan, and that those transactions, conducted by insiders with private information, hinder firm value. Apparently, RPF, an important variable in emerging markets (La Porta, Lopez-de-Silanes, Shleifer, & Vishny, 1997, 1998, 1999, 2000; Peng, John Wei, & Yang, 2011), is not related to independence, but higher RPF increases the likelihood of expropriation between related companies when one or more of those companies are distressed. A large body of empirical evidence has shown that controlling shareholders may take advantage of minority shareholders through related-party transactions (Berkman, Cole, & Fu, 2009; Cheung, Rau, & Stouraitis, 2006; Johnson, La Porta, Shleifer, & Vishny, 2000).

Following prior studies (DeFond et al., 2002; Li, 2009; Reynolds & Francis, 2001), we use auditors' propensity to issue GC opinions as a proxy for auditor independence. However, GC opinions are not issued solely due to auditor independence; they depend initially on professional judgment. It is only after professional judgment indicates that a GC opinion should be issued that the question of auditor independence can arise. Professional judgment is, therefore, prior to the issue of independence, yet the latter is the more commonly examined variable. We believe that a complete analysis incorporating both professional judgment and independence can offer a more realistic view of the effects of corporate governance on audit quality.

In addition to examining both professional judgment and independence of auditors, this paper also offers a comparison of publicly held and privately held companies. We are able to do so due to a distinct feature of disclosure regulations in Taiwan: Like publicly held companies, privately held companies in Taiwan must provide audited financial statements to the public. (Details of these regulations are given in the following section.) Our evidence suggests that, in terms of the propensity of issuing GC opinions, the effects of corporate governance variables – both as information and as factors that might influence auditor independence – on privately held companies differ from their effects on publicly held companies.

The remainder of the paper is organized as follows. The second section reviews the literature. The third section describes the research design and discusses pertinent features of the Taiwanese data. The fourth section presents the data and empirical results, and the fifth section concludes.

LITERATURE REVIEW AND THEORETICAL FRAMEWORK

This section includes four subsections: (1) audit quality and GC opinions, (2) duality role of a CEO, (3) related-party financing, and (4) the theoretical framework and hypotheses development used in this study to examine the three preceding issues.

Audit Quality and GC Opinions

DeAngelo (1981) defines audit quality as the joint probability of discovering material misrepresentations and reporting them when they exist. The first part (i.e., the ability to discover) is related to *professional judgment*, and the second part (i.e., report truthfully) is related to *independence*. Therefore, neither a lack of expertise nor a lack of independence can allow high audit quality. The question of auditors' reporting decision is related not only to auditor independence but also to profession judgment. However, as we point out in the introduction, prior auditing studies which examine the relationship between corporate governance and audit quality focus exclusively on the issue of auditor independence.

Because higher audit quality represents a greater ability and/or better independence, prior studies often use the following variables as proxies for audit quality: auditor size (DeFond, 1992; Palmrose, 1988), auditor litigation (Heninger, 2001; Palmrose, 1987), industry expertise (Ferguson, Francis, & Stokes, 2003; Palmrose, 1986), earnings response coefficient (Ghosh & Moon, 2005), abnormal accruals (Chi, Hunag, Liao, & Xie, 2009; Myers, Myers, & Omer, 2003), GC opinions (Carcello & Neal, 2003; Li, 2009), and modified audit opinions (Chen, Sun, & Wu, 2010).

Empirical studies find that GC opinions cause negative market reactions (Blay & Geiger, 2001) and indicate an increased risk of business failure (Geiger, Raghunandan, & Rama, 1998). Geiger et al. (1998) point out that, when such cases occur, these companies have an incentive to change their auditors in order to "shop" for a more favorable auditor opinion. Thus, a measure of whether auditors can resist the pressure from the management team and offer a correct audit opinion is commonly used to examine auditor independence. To formulate such a measure, many auditing papers start with financially distressed companies as their research sample. Lastly, because auditors face the greatest pressure when they issue a GC opinion to their clients for the first time, DeFond et al. (2002) and Li (2009) focus on first-time GC opinions.

Auditors who issue a GC will face pressure from managers because a GC opinion causes a negative reaction in stock price (Jones, 1996) and increases the cost of capital for the firm (Firth, 1980). Therefore, Barnes (2004) suggests that the issuing of GC opinions is an excellent indicator by which auditor independence may be tested. In addition, GC provides the auditor with a processing objective that leads to the purposeful evaluation of evidence, rather than a passive evaluation of evidence in the order that it is received (Hoffman, Joe, & Moser, 2003). Logically, the pressure on an auditor will be higher if the CEO simultaneously serves as the chairperson of the board. In our study, a dual CEO/chairman role decreases the likelihood that a GC opinion will be released, and thus indicates a lower level of auditor independence.

Dual Role of a CEO

The purpose of corporate governance is to protect the providers of capital to the firm, enhance the performance of the firm, and alleviate opportunistic behaviors of members of the firm. In fact, corporate governance originates in the attempt to prevent or mitigate agency problems (Berle & Means, 1932), and therefore aims to control potential conflicts of interests due to information asymmetry.

Cohen, Krishnamoorthy, and Wright (2004) indicate that one of the most important functions that corporate governance can play is to ensure the quality of the financial reporting process. According to their framework of corporate governance and financial reporting quality, within the organization boundary there are four factors that interrelate with external auditors: the audit committee, the board of directors, management, and internal auditors. This study centers only on boards of directors and management because in Taiwan audit committees are not mandated, information on internal auditors is not publicly available, and very few companies claim that their internal control systems are weak.

Jensen (1993) believes that the CEO simultaneously serving as the chairperson of the board will lessen the monitoring function of the board. Patton and Baker (1987) find that a CEO who simultaneously serves as the chairperson of the board will sacrifice the policy of the board for his own private benefit. Based on these findings, our hypothesis is that a CEO serving such a dual role (measured by DUAL) will hinder auditor independence.

The variable DUAL has its conceptual predecessors in relevant studies of the independence of board members. Examining financially distressed companies, Carcello and Neal (2000), for example, find that the occurrence of GC is lower if the portion of nonindependent board members is higher. Carcello and Neal (2003) further point out that the dismissals of auditors who issue GCs are less frequent if the audit committee members are more independent and are financial experts. Ruder (2002) and Bedard et al. (2004) also confirm that the independence and expertise of audit committees will affect the independence of auditors.

Farber (2005) finds that fraud is correlated to a smaller portion of outside board members, a lower frequency of meetings of an audit committee, fewer financial experts in an audit committee, audits by small audit firms, and a dual-role CEO. Dey (2008) points out that the CEO's role as the chairman of the board of directors implies that the CEO has the final word in many of the decisions made by the board. Moreover, to the extent that the other members take decisions that do not antagonize the chair, the role of the CEO as the chairman of the board compromises the independence of the board. Chang and Sun (2009) explore the post-SOX associations between earnings informativeness and audit-committee independence, and find significant post-SOX – but not pre-SOX – correlation between earnings informativeness and the dual role of the CEO serving as the chair of the board. The change of magnitude in these relationships suggests that investors have lost some of their naiveté and have started to rely more on corporate-governance mechanisms to determine the quality of these companies' accounting earnings since the implementation of SOX. Chang and Sun (2010) also find a negative relation between dual-role CEOs and earnings informativeness after SOX in cross-listed foreign companies. They therefore argue that since the negative publicity of CEOs' involvement in financial scandals, investors have become suspicious that a dual-role CEO may further jeopardize the board's fiduciary duties. Accordingly, earnings informativeness is expected to be negatively related to the disclosure of a dual-role CEO. Jenkins (2002) examines the association between earnings management and audit committee effectiveness in U.S. companies and finds that an auditor in concert with an independent audit committee better monitors abnormal accruals. We expect that the effects claimed by these authors will generally be more severe among financially distressed companies.

Related-Party Financing

The variable RPF represents related-party financing, a form of related-party transaction. Research on related-party transactions typically focuses on the transfer of wealth from minority stockholders (Chang, 2003; Cheung et al., 2006) and on earnings management (Aharony, Wang, & Yuan, 2010; Beneish & Vargus, 2002; Jian & Wong, 2010). For instance, Beneish and Vargus (2002) find that greater RPF is related to lower earnings quality. Since lower earnings quality increases the likelihood of a GC opinion being released, there should be a theoretical link between RPF and the issuing of GC opinions. In other words, to an attentive auditor, a high level of RPF should be a red flag, suggesting an increased risk of bankruptcy. Hence, RPF can clearly offer relevant information to auditors, helping them formulate a better professional judgment.

However, business groups or related-party transactions may serve useful purposes, especially in less-developed countries. Some examples are transactions within a business group or between related parties, which can allow companies to avoid dysfunctional arms-length institutions and markets (Williamson, 1985), resource integration and improvement in efficiency (Guillén, 2000), better corporate resource allocation (Stein, 1997), convenience in internal financing (Hubbard & Pahlia, 1999), and risk sharing (Khanna & Yafeh, 2005). Even when considering such advantages, however, a great deal of research points out that such a business model has its own costs, such as inefficient competition among subsidiaries (Khanna & Palepu, 2000a, 2000b), increased transaction costs resulting from risk sharing (Gunduz & Tatoglu, 2003), and overinvestment (Stulz, 1990). Empirical investigations of prior researchers use Tobin's Q, return on equity, and/or return on assets to compare the performance of business-group-type companies with that of single-businesses-type companies. Some of these studies find that the former type performs better (e.g., Chang & Choi, 1988;

Khanna & Palepu, 2000a, 2000b), while some of them find that the latter type performs better (e.g., Claessens, Djankov, Fan, & Lang, 2002). In addition, some studies find that there is no statistical relation between the two types of business models and performance (e.g., Gunduz & Tatoglu, 2003; Khanna & Rivikin, 2001). In a study particularly relevant to our sample, Yeh et al. (2002) point out that there are many irregular related-party transactions in Taiwan, and that those transactions, conducted by insiders with private information, hinder firm value. Gordon, Henry, and Palia (2004) indicate that related-party transactions inherently imply earnings manipulation and tunneling, and therefore hurt the rights of outsiders. Finally, Jian and Wong (2010) find evidence that following propping of one related party through sales to another, abnormal related lending will occur in the opposite direction. Berkman et al. (2009) view related-party financing as an unambiguous and direct method of tunneling. Accordingly, auditors will consider information on related-party transactions when deciding whether or not it is necessary to issue a GC opinion.

Theoretical Framework and Hypotheses Development

The definition of audit quality implies the necessity of such a conceptual separation of professional judgment and auditor independence. Fig. 1 shows the conceptual framework of this study. Using the issuing of GC opinions on financially distressed companies as a proxy for audit quality, which is a function of professional judgment and independence, we examine both the *informational* function and the *monitoring mechanism* of corporate governance.

To explore our issues, we examine two corporate governance variables: whether the CEO simultaneously serves as the chairperson of the board (hereafter DUAL) and RPF. The variable DUAL was chosen to address the

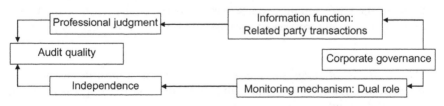

Fig. 1. Conceptual Framework.

debate on whether a CEO should serve as the chair of a majority-independent board. When corporate insiders other than the CEO are absent from a majority-independent board, directors become more dependent on their link with the CEO for inside information. As a result, critical information is often hidden from the directors or falsified (Mitchell, 2005), and the CEO may therefore unduly influence the boards on many decisions (Chang & Sun, 2010). Anderson et al. (2003) find that earnings informativeness is positively related to companies with separated CEO and chair positions. Chang and Sun (2009) also find a negative relation between dual-role CEOs and earnings informativeness after SOX in cross-listed foreign companies. Since our sample is composed of financially distressed companies, the power of the board to monitor management will be weaker when a firm has a dual-role CEO. Specifically, for auditors of companies that are financially distressed, the likelihood of their compromising independence is greater when they face a dual-role CEO than when the CEO does not chair a board with an independent majority.

RPF is used in this study not to examine auditor independence, but instead to explore whether RPF is relevant information, other things being equal, for auditors who audit financially distressed companies. This study uses the data in Taiwan. Yeh et al. (2002) point out that there are many irregular related-party transactions in Taiwan, and that those transactions, conducted by insiders with private information, hinder firm value. Accordingly, auditors will consider information on related-party transactions when deciding whether or not it is necessary to issue a GC opinion. Apparently, RPF, an important variable in emerging markets (La Porta et al., 1997, 1998, 1999, 2000; Peng et al., 2011), is not related to independence, but higher RPF increases the likelihood of expropriation between related companies when one or more of those companies are distressed.

Based on the prior literature and our conceptual framework, we developed these hypotheses:

H1. *Auditor independence approach* – There is a *negative* association between the CEO simultaneously serving as the chairperson of the board and audit partners' propensity for issuing GC opinions, ceteris paribus.

H2. *Professional judgment approach* – There is a *positive* association between the related-party financing and audit partners' propensity for issuing GC opinions, ceteris paribus.

RESEARCH METHODOLOGY AND SAMPLE SELECTION

Sample Selection

Our data includes both publicly held and privately held companies, and thus allows us to analyze whether audit quality differs for these two types of companies. The comprehensiveness of the data is due to the legal background regarding disclosure of financial statements. Until 2001, the Taiwan Company Law had mandated that all publicly held companies listed on Taiwan Stock Exchange Corporation and GreTai Securities Market and privately held companies with capital exceeding a certain threshold (NT$200 million since 1981 and NT$500 million since 2000) publicly disclose audited financial statements. Although this requirement was rescinded for privately owned companies in 2002, many privately held companies have continued to disclose their audited financial statements.[1] The *Taiwan Economic Journal* (TEJ) provides a database that collects all publicly disclosed financial statement of publicly held and privately held companies. We start our research period from 1996 because the corporate governance variables are publicly available after this year. Thus, our research period is 1996–2008. We searched the *Taiwan Economic Journal* Database for publicly held and privately held companies whose variables were actually included in the TEJ database between 1996 and 2008. Table 1 reports the selection process.

Research Design

The literature has used auditors' propensity of issuing GC opinions as an alternative proxy for auditor independence (e.g., DeFond et al., 2002; Li, 2009; Reynolds & Francis, 2001). If audit partners compromise independence because the CEO simultaneously serves as the chairperson of the board, we expect to find a *negative* association between DUAL and audit partners' propensity for issuing GC opinions.

Regarding the informational role of corporate governance, we incorporate RPF into our regression model. Beneish and Vargus (2002) argue that there is a correlation between lower earnings quality and higher levels of related-party transactions. Kahle (2000) finds that company has a high level of insider trading, with poor long-term performance being due to overvaluation. While RPF is a corporate governance variable, it plays an

Table 1.   Sample Selection Process.

Panel A: Publicly Held Companies (1996–2008)		
Original sample size		15,210
Less	Those not in financial distress	(6,741)
	Those with missing financial characteristic variables	(528)
	Those not issued a going concern opinion for the first time	(21)
	Those with missing corporate governance variables	(3,983)
Final sample size[a]		3,937
Panel B: Privately Held Companies (1996–2008)		
Original sample size		7,125
Less	Those not in financial distress	(2,859)
	Those with missing financial characteristic variables	(645)
	Those with missing audit opinion data	(1,104)
	Those not issued a going concern opinion for the first time	(35)
	Those with missing corporate governance variables	(1,923)
Final sample size[b]		559

[a]Of the 3,937 companies in our sample in panel A, 2.47% received a GC.
[b]Of the 559 companies in our sample in panel B, 3.147% received a GC.

informational role (i.e., improving professional judgment) in this study. Auditors facing financially distressed companies with poor earnings quality, other things being equal, have a greater tendency to issue a GC opinion. Therefore, we expect that, in the professional judgment of an auditor, RPF is *positively* related to GC. Our findings can support the contention that RPF plays a role in enhancing professional judgment of auditors, if, other things being equal, the auditor considers issuing a GC opinion to a financially distressed company with greater level of RPF.

In addition, to explore whether auditors' reporting decisions for publicly held companies differ from those for privately held companies, we first set up an indicator variable PRIVATE (with a value of one if the observation is a privately held company, and zero otherwise), which is then multiplied by DUAL and by RPF. Through examining the estimated coefficient of PRIVATE × DUAL and that of PRIVATE × RPF, we can compare how the listed status, public and private, affect professional judgment and independence of auditors. Likewise, we also set up an indicator variable BigN (with a value of one if the observation is audited by a large audit firm, and zero otherwise), which is then multiplied by DUAL and by RPF. The variable BigN added because Craswell, Francis, and Taylor (1995) document that the Big N auditors charge an audit fee premium over the non-Big N auditors. Studies also show that clients of the Big N auditors have lower absolute values of discretionary accruals (Becker, DeFond, Jiambalvo, & Subramanyam, 1998) and higher ERCs (Teoh & Wong, 1993). Firth and Smith (1992) find that clients of the Big N auditors incur less IPO underpricing than clients of the non-Big N auditors. In addition, by examining the estimated coefficient of BigN × DUAL and that of BigN × RPF, we can compare audit quality between large and small audit firms.

Research Model and Control variables

Regarding the control variables (LEV, SIZE, and ROA), we mainly follow four relevant papers: DeFond et al. (2002), Mutchler, Hopwood, and McKeown (1997), Altman, Haldeman, and Narayanan (1977), and McKeown, Mutchler, and Hopwood (1991). Specifically, these studies find that companies with higher leverage (LEV) increase the probability of bankruptcy and companies audited by a big audit firm (BigN) have greater likelihood to receive a GC opinion. In addition, large companies (SIZE) have more resources to avoid bankruptcy and a better ability to negotiate with audit firms, so SIZE is negatively related to GC. Finally, a more profitable company (ROA) is less likely to receive a GC opinion. The main regression model that we use, that of DeFond et al. (2002), is widely used enough to be considered a standard. Following DeFond et al. (2002), we include only financially distressed clients, which are defined as those with negative net income or negative cash flows, and focus on first-time GC opinions. We focus on companies receiving first-time GC because previous studies suggest that rendering an initial GC opinion to a client is a particularly difficult decision for the auditor (Kida, 1980; Mutchler, 1984). Auditors may hesitate to issue a GC report if management implicitly or explicitly suggests that the client will dismiss the auditor if the auditor issues a GC report. Prior research finds that clients receiving a GC report are more likely to switch auditors (Chow & Rice, 1982; Geiger et al., 1998; Mutchler, 1984). Since the pressure to auditors is the greatest for a client who is receiving its first GC report, we follow prior research (e.g., DeFond et al., 2002; Geiger & Rama, 2003; Li, 2009) and restrict our analyses to financially distressed companies and first-time recipients of GC opinions. This study runs the following logistic regression model for financially distressed clients:

The model

$$GC = b_0 + b_1 \text{ PRIVATE} + b_2 \text{ DUAL} + b_3 \text{ DUAL} \times \text{PRIVATE} + b_4 \text{ RPF}$$
$$+ b_5 \text{ RPF} \times \text{PRIVATE} + b_6 \text{ BigN} + b_7 \text{ BigN} \times \text{DUAL} + b_8 \text{ BigN} \times \text{RPF}$$
$$+ b_9 \text{ SIZE} + b_{10} \text{ LEV} + b_{11} \text{ ROA} + \gamma_i \sum \text{Year}_i + \delta_j \sum \text{Industry}_j + e \quad (1)$$

where, GC = 1, if the client receives a first-time GC opinion, and 0 otherwise; PRIVATE = 1, if the client is a privately held company, and 0 otherwise; DUAL = 1 if the CEO simultaneously serves as the chairperson of the board, and 0 otherwise; RPF = the amount of related-party financing during the year divided by end-of-year equity; SIZE = log of end-of-year total assets (thousand in NT dollars); LEV = total liabilities divided by total assets; BigN = dummy variable equal to 1 if the auditor is from a Big 4 or Big 5 audit firm, and equal to 0 otherwise; ROA = net income divided by total assets at the beginning of the year.

EMPIRICAL FINDINGS

Panels A and B of Table 1 report the sample selection process of publicly held and privately held companies, respectively. Specifically, panel A (B) shows that the original sample size is 15,210 (7,125) for the publicly held (privately held) companies. Of these, 6,741 (2,859) are not financially distressed companies and 528 (645) are missing financial characteristic variables. In addition, 1,104 observations in the private company samples are missing audit opinions. In the remaining sample of companies which are financially distressed and for which auditor opinions are available, we find that the GCs received by 21 public companies and 35 private companies are not first-time GC opinions. We finally delete those companies with missing governance variables, numbering 3,983 publicly held and 1,923 privately held companies.[2]

Descriptive Statistics

Table 2 shows univariate comparisons between the publicly held and privately held companies. GC opinions are received by 2.46% of publicly held companies and 3.04% of privately held companies. The last column of Table 2 reveals that the differences between the means (−0.006) and between

Table 2. Univariate Test.

Variables	Publicly Held Companies ($N = 3{,}937$)			Privately Held Companies ($N = 559$)			Difference	
	Mean	Median	SD	Mean	Median	SD	Mean	Median
GC	0.024	0.000	0.153	0.030	0.000	0.171	−0.006	0.000
DUAL	0.332	0.000	0.471	0.293	0.000	0.455	0.039*	0.000*
RPF	1.012	0.000	3.660	1.758	0.000	5.443	−0.746***	0.000
SIZE	6.486	6.429	0.516	6.357	6.286	0.577	0.129***	0.143***
LEV	0.474	0.480	0.177	0.616	0.620	0.237	−0.142***	−0.140***
ROA	1.826	2.160	9.403	−2.436	−0.840	11.869	4.262***	3.000***
BigN	0.780	1.000	0.414	0.726	1.000	0.446	0.054***	0.000***

Note: *, **, *** Significant at the 0.10, 0.05, and 0.01 level, respectively, based on a two-tailed *t*-statistic.
GC, a dummy variable equal to 1 if the client receives a first-time going concern opinion, and 0 otherwise; RPF, the amount of related-party financing during the year divided by end-of-year net assets; DUAL, a dummy variable equal to 1 if the CEO simultaneously serves as the chairperson of the board, and 0 otherwise; SIZE, log of end-of-year total assets (thousand in NT dollars); LEV, total liabilities divided by total assets; BigN, a dummy variable equal to 1 if the auditor is from a Big 4 or Big 5 audit firm, and equal to 0 otherwise; ROA, net income divided by total assets at the beginning of the year; PRIVATE, a dummy variable equal to 1 if the client is a privately held company, and 0 otherwise.

the medians (0.000) are insignificant for the publicly held and privately held companies in our research sample. The averages of DUAL, however, are different: that of publicly held companies (0.332) is larger than that of privately held companies (0.293). In addition, publicly held companies have a lower RPF (1.012) than privately companies (1.758).

Regarding financial characteristics variables, the average firm size (SIZE) of publicly held companies (6.486) is significantly larger than that of privately held companies (6.357). The findings for debt ratio (LEV) are reversed: The mean (median) of LEV of publicly held companies, 0.474 (0.480), is significantly smaller than the mean (median) of LEV of privately held companies, 0.616 (0.620). As for profitability, publicly held companies' average ROA (1.826) is greater than privately held companies' average ROA (−2.436). Finally, the mean BigN for the publicly held sample is 0.780, whereas that for the privately held sample is 0.726. A two-tailed *t*-statistic suggests that the difference of 0.054 is significant at the 0.01 level.

Correlation

We now turn to discussing simple Pearson correlation results in Table 3, where the upper right triangle of the correlation matrix shows the publicly held companies and the lower left triangle shows the privately held companies. GC is positively related to RPF (0.154, p-value <0.01) and DUAL (0.046, p-value <0.01) in the publicly held companies, but such relations are insignificant in the privately held companies. We hesitate to overemphasize the simple correlation analysis between the two samples, because (i) the sample size of privately held companies (559) is smaller than that of publicly held companies (3,937)[3] and (ii) the inferences on how corporate governance variables affect GC should control for financial

Table 3. Pearson Correlation Matrix.

Variables	GC	RPF	DUAL	SIZE	LEV	BigN	ROA
GC		0.154	0.046	−0.015	0.256	−0.036	−0.181
		(0.000)***	(0.003)***	(0.338)	(0.000)***	(0.022)**	(0.000)***
RPF	−0.024		0.020	−0.020	0.131	0.045	−0.177
	(0.560)		(0.191)	(0.204)	(0.000)***	(0.004)***	(0.000)***
DUAL	−0.022	0.003		−0.092	0.028	0.005	−0.014
	(0.594)	(0.937)		(0.000)***	(0.069)*	(0.741)	(0.370)
SIZE	0.044	0.040	−0.224		0.136	0.066	0.021
	(0.290)	(0.339)	(0.000)***		(0.000)***	(0.000)***	(0.183)
LEV	−0.020	0.057	−0.008	0.244		−0.069	−0.082
	(0.621)	(0.172)	(0.841)	(0.000)***		(0.000)***	(0.000)***
BigN	−0.008	0.080	0.060	0.048	−0.261		0.028
	(0.848)	(0.057)*	(0.151)	(0.249)	(0.000)***		(0.077)*
ROA	0.051	−0.048	−0.034	0.083	−0.293	0.182	
	(0.222)	(0.251)	(0.419)	(0.048)**	(0.000)***	(0.000)***	

Note:*, **, *** Significant at the 0.10, 0.05, and 0.01 level, respectively, based on a two-tailed p-value reported in parentheses.
The upper right triangle of the correlation matrix shows the publicly held companies ($N = 3,937$), and the lower left triangle shows the privately held companies ($N = 559$). GC, a dummy variable equal to 1 if the client receives a first-time going concern opinion, and 0 otherwise; RPF, the amount of related-party financing during the year divided by end-of-year net assets; DUAL, a dummy variable equal to 1 if the CEO simultaneously serves as the chairperson of the board, and 0 otherwise; SIZE, log of end-of-year total assets (thousand in NT dollars); LEV, total liabilities divided by total assets; BigN, a dummy variable equal to 1 if the auditor is from a Big 4 or Big 5 audit firm, and equal to 0 otherwise; ROA, net income divided by total assets at the beginning of the year; PRIVATE, a dummy variable equal to 1 if the client is a privately held company, and 0 otherwise.

characteristics of the companies. Therefore, we focus on the regression results. Nevertheless, in publicly held companies, we find supporting evidence that RPF has an informational role, but no evidence that DUAL hinders auditor independence.

Regression Results

Table 4 reports the empirical findings. Panel A reports the results for the full sample, and panel B provides the results for public companies and private companies separately.

Panel A shows that the estimated coefficient of PRIVATE (b_1), -0.660 (p-value $= 0.273$), is insignificant, suggesting that, in terms of their propensity to issue going concern opinions, auditors of publicly held companies are indistinguishable from auditors of private companies, other things being equal. In addition, the negative but insignificant coefficient -0.203 (p-value $= 0.711$) offers no evidence that DUAL (b_2) hinders audit independence for public companies. However, the negative sum of the estimated coefficients of DUAL and DUAL $\times$ PRIVATE ($b_2 + b_3$), -1.351, becomes *one-tailed* significant at 10% (one-tailed p-value < 0.10). Therefore, we find weak evidence (only one-tailed) to support our hypothesis that DUAL affects the audit quality. However, the dual role of a CEO does not compromise auditor independence in the public company sample.

For the informational role of RPF (b_4) in public companies, however, we find supporting evidence in the positive estimated coefficient of *RFP*, 0.083 (p-value < 0.10), but such evidence for the informational role of RPF in private companies disappears: the sum of the estimated coefficients of *RFP* and *RFP* $\times$ PRIVATE ($b_4 + b_5$), -0.021, becomes insignificant at 10% (p-value $= 0.643$).

Therefore, in public companies, consistent with our prediction, auditors have better audit quality if the publicly held companies in financial distress have more related-party financing, a finding which supports our position on the *informational* role of governance. In privately held companies, however, this role disappears. Taken together, the evidence suggests that, among financially distressed companies, it is only in those that are privately held that auditors are more likely to compromise their independence when they face a dual-role CEO than when the CEO does not chair a board with an independent majority. In addition, auditors of publicly held companies will consider RPF to be relevant information, other things being equal, for auditors who audit financially distressed companies, only if these companies

Table 4. Logistic Regression Results.

$$GC = b_0 + b_1\,\text{PRIVATE} + b_2\,\text{DUAL} + b_3\,\text{DUAL} \times \text{PRIVATE} + b_4\,\text{RPF}$$
$$+ b_5\,\text{RPF} \times \text{PRIVATE} + b_6\,\text{BigN} + b_7\,\text{BigN} \times \text{DUAL} + b_8\,\text{BigN} \times \text{RPF}$$
$$+ b_9\,\text{SIZE} + b_{10}\,\text{LEV} + b_{11}\,\text{ROA} + \gamma_i \sum \text{Year}_i + \delta_j \sum \text{Industry}_j + e \quad (1)$$

Panel A: Logistic Regression Results				
Variables		Predicted Sign	Full Model	
INTERCEPT	b_0	?	−5.289***	(0.006)
PRIVATE	b_1	?	−0.660	(0.273)
DUAL	b_2	−	−0.203	(0.711)
DUAL × PRIVATE	b_3	?	−1.148	(0.264)
RPF	b_4	+	0.063*	(0.063)
RPF × PRIVATE	b_5	?	−0.084**	(0.046)
BigN	b_6	+	−0.041	(0.923)
BigN × DUAL	b_7	+	1.009	(0.103)
BigN × RPF	b_8	+	−0.011	(0.768)
SIZE	b_9	−	−0.398	(0.185)
LEV	b_{10}	+	5.633***	(0.000)
ROA	b_{11}	−	−0.063***	(0.000)
Year Effect		?	Included	
Industry Effect		?	Included	
Number of observations			4,496	
Pseudo R^2			0.318	
Joint test			Coefficient	$\Pr(\chi^2)$
$b_2 + b_3$			−1.351	(0.157)
$b_4 + b_5$			−0.021	(0.643)

Panel B: Sensitivity Test Results for Publicly Held Companies and Privately Held Companies						
Variables		Predicted Sign	Public Firm		Private Firm	
INTERCEPT	b_0	?	−7.788***	(0.002)	−4.459*	(0.093)
DUAL	b_1	−	0.572*	(0.081)	−0.267	(0.724)
RPF	b_2	+	0.028	(0.174)	−0.045*	(0.092)
BIGN	b_4	+	0.047	(0.894)	−0.024	(0.969)
SIZE	b_5	−	−0.366	(0.348)	0.145	(0.738)
LEV	b_6	+	8.070***	(0.000)	−0.155	(0.927)
BigN	b_7	+	0.047	(0.894)	−0.024	(0.969)
ROA	b_8	−	−0.097***	(0.000)	0.033	(0.192)

Table 4. (*Continued*)

Panel B: Sensitivity Test Results for Publicly Held Companies and Privately Held Companies

Variables	Predicted Sign	Public Firm	Private Firm
Year Effect		Included	Included
Industry Effect		Included	Included
Number of observations		3,937	559
Pseudo R^2		0.441	0.102

Note: *, **, *** Significant at the 0.10, 0.05, and 0.01 level, respectively, based on a two-tailed *p*-value. Coefficients on industry and year dummies omitted for simplified exhibition. Two-tailed *p*-value based on the Huber–White standard errors clustering by firm reported in parentheses.

GC, a dummy variable equal to 1 if the client receives a first-time going concern opinion, and 0 otherwise; RPF, the amount of related party financing during the year divided by end-of-year net assets; DUAL, a dummy variable equal to 1 if the CEO simultaneously serves as the chairperson of the board, and 0 otherwise; SIZE, log of end-of-year total assets (thousand in NT dollars); LEV, total liabilities divided by total assets; BigN, a dummy variable equal to 1 if the auditor is from a Big 4 or Big 5 audit firm, and equal to 0 otherwise; ROA, net income divided by total assets at the beginning of the year; PRIVATE, a dummy variable equal to 1 if the client is a privately held company, and 0 otherwise.

are publicly held companies. These differences between our findings for publicly held companies and privately held companies can be explained by reputation concerns (Weber, Willenborg, & Zhang, 2008) and litigation risks (Krishnan & Krishnan, 1997; Shu, 2000), two mitigating factors that constrain auditors from compromising their independence for economically significant clients.

As for the effect of BigN, we find no evidence that the propensity of issuing GC is related to auditor size. In addition, the estimated coefficients of BigN × DUAL (b_7) and BigN × RPF (b_8), 1.009 and −0.001, respectively, are insignificant. Regarding the effect of our control variables on GC, the estimated coefficients of SIZE (−0.398, *p*-value = 0.185), LEV (5.633, *p*-value < 0.01), and ROA (−0.063, *p*-value < 0.00) are all consistent with the predicted sign. In sum, the greater the firm size or the more profitable the firm, the lower the probability of receiving GC opinions. The higher the debt ratio, however, the higher the probability of receiving GC opinions.

Panel B reports the results for each subsample, public and private. Although we still find no evidence that DUAL has a negative effect on GC in public companies ($b_1 = 0.572$ and *p*-value < 0.10), the weak evidence previously seen for private companies disappears in the private company column ($b_1 = -0.001$ and p-value $= 0.724$). The estimated coefficient of RPF in the public firm column ($b_2 = 0.024$ and one-tailed p-value < 0.10) offers weak evidence (only one-tailed) that auditors who audit public companies will use RPF. However, this coefficient in the private company column ($b_2 = -0.045$ and p-value < 0.10) shows that auditors who audit private companies are not more likely to issue a going concern opinion when their clients have a greater level of RPF.

Finally, the results of the effects of SIZE, LEV, and ROA in the Public Company column are qualitatively similar to those in panel A, a similarity which reveals that, for financially distressed companies, greater firm size and more profitability are linked with a lower probability of receiving GC opinions, while debt ratio is linked with a greater probability. However, none of these correspondingly estimated coefficients is significant in the Private Company column.

Sensitivity test

One question that potentially complicates the use of related-party transactions as informative for auditors is the possibility that they have positive effects as well as negative ones. Our paper avoids this issue because we limit our sample to financially distressed companies, which would tend to enjoy few if any of the potential advantages of related-party transactions. Nevertheless, we reduce such potential complications by replacing RPF with two measures. The first one is a firm's industry-medium centered value, the inclusion of which lessens the possibility that the normal RPF of a firm may be a function of its industry; the second is an indicator variable, which equals one if RPF is larger than the value of the industry medium and zero otherwise. Unabated results from rerunning our regression model with these two new variables show that our evidence is robust.

CONCLUSION

Using a unique Taiwanese dataset, we separate our sample into publicly held and privately held companies, and show that the effects of CEO duality and the level of related-party financing on audit quality vary depending on whether a company is publicly held or privately held. This data set is unique because both unlisted and listed companies are required to be audited in

Taiwan. Thus, we are able to construct comparison whether and how the two variables have different effects on the audit quality.

The importance of our paper is twofold. First, according to auditing standards, auditors should collect information and use their professional judgment to draw fair conclusions about the companies that they are auditing, and also to express those conclusions in their reports. Then, we examine how corporate governance affects auditor independence. For professional judgment, we examine whether related-party transactions affect auditors' professional judgment. This variable is important in numerous researches in financial accounting and finance; however it has not been explored in auditing research. To examine the auditor independence issue, we examine whether and how CEO duality influence audit quality.

Second, we examine the issue in publicly held and privately held companies separately. Because auditors performing audit services face different litigation risk and reputation concern, our results between the two different types of clients can provide implications for different emerging markets. The empirical results of publicly held companies are useful for the countries with better corporate governance, while those of privately held companies are helpful for the countries with poor corporate governance.

Our results reveal that for publicly held companies, with stronger capital market discipline, which causes greater reputation concerns and litigation risks, a CEO who plays a dual role does not hinder auditor independence. For privately held companies, however, such a CEO hinders auditor independence due to a lack of capital market discipline. The findings on related-party financing, on the other hand, are completely different. Interpreting party financing from the informational role, we find that since the conflicts of interests are more severe in publicly held companies than in privately held companies, the relevance of this information to enforce audit quality is greater in publicly held companies.

NOTES

1. In other words, in Taiwan, companies that are publicly traded on the stock exchanges are referred to as listed companies and companies that are not publicly traded on the stock exchanges are referred to as unlisted companies. Thus, listed companies in Taiwanese terms are the same as public companies in U.S. terms. Unlisted companies in Taiwan are similar to private companies in some European countries such as Norway (Hope & Langli, 2010).

2. The final number of observations in the publicly held sample is 3,937, while that in the privately held sample is 559. In the final research sample, 97 (3,937 of 2.46%) companies out of 3,937 publicly held companies and 17 (559 of 3.04%) companies out

of 559 privately held companies have received a GC opinion. Since the requirements for privately held companies to file financial statements changed in 2002, data is not available for all private companies throughout the entire research period; for consistency between the data on public and private companies, we have included only those private companies that continued to provide financial statements after 2002.

3. The sample size itself makes it more difficult to draw significant findings from the correlation analysis for the privately held companies than for the publicly held companies.

REFERENCES

Aharony, J., Wang, J., & Yuan, H. (2010). Tunneling as an incentive for earnings management during the IPO process in China. *Journal of Accounting and Public Policy*, 29(1), 1–26.

Altman, E. I., Haldeman, R. G., & Narayanan, P. (1977). Zeta analysis: A new model to identify bankruptcy risk of corporations. *Journal of Banking and Finance*, 1(1), 29–54.

Anderson, K. L., Deli, D. N., & Gillan, S. L. (2003). *Board directors, audit committees, and the information content of earnings*. Weinberg Center for Corporate Governance Working Paper No. 2003-04. Georgetown University, Washington DC; Arizona State University, Tempe, AZ; and University of Delaware, Newark, DE.

Auditing Standards Board (ASB). (1988). The auditors consideration of an entity's ability to continue as a going concern. Statement on Auditing Standard No. 59. New York, NY: ASB.

Barnes, P. (2004). The auditor's going concern decision and Types I and II errors: The Coase Theorem, transaction costs, bargaining power and attempts to mislead. *Journal of Accounting and Public Policy*, 23(6), 415–440.

Becker, C., DeFond, M., Jiambalvo, J., & Subramanyam, K. R. (1998). The effect of audit quality on earnings management. *Contemporary Accounting Research*, 15(1), 1–24.

Bedard, J., Chtourou, S. M., & Courteau, L. (2004). The effect of audit committee expertise, independence, and actively on aggressive earnings management. *Auditing: A Journal of Practice and Theory*, 23(2), 13–35.

Beneish, M. D., & Vargus, M. E. (2002). Insider trading, earning quality, and accrual mispricing. *The Accounting Review*, 77(4), 755–791.

Berkman, H., Cole, R. A., & Fu, L. J. (2009). Expropriation through loan guarantees to related parties: Evidence from China. *Journal of Banking and Finance*, 33, 141–156.

Berle, A., & Means, G. (1932). *The modern corporation and private property*. New York, NY: Macmillan.

Blay, A. D., & Geiger, M. (2001). Market expectations for first-time going-concern recipients. *Journal of Accounting, Auditing and Finance*, 16(3), 209–226.

Carcello, J. V., & Neal, T. L. (2000). Audit committee composition and auditor reporting. *The Accounting Review*, 75(4), 453–467.

Carcello, J. V., & Neal, T. L. (2003). Audit committee characteristics and auditor dismissals following "New" going-concern reports. *The Accounting Review*, 78(1), 95–117.

Chang, J. C., & Sun, H. L. (2009). Crossed-listed foreign companies' earnings informativeness, earnings management and disclosures of corporate governance information under SOX. *The International Journal of Accounting*, 44(1), 1–32.

Chang, J. C., & Sun, H. L. (2010). Does the disclosure of corporate governance structures affect companies' earnings quality? *Review of Accounting and Finance*, 9(3), 212–243.

Chang, S. J. (2003). Ownership structure, expropriation, and performance of group-affiliated companies in Korea. *Academy of Management Journal, 46*(2), 238–253.

Chang, S. J., & Choi, U. (1988). Strategy, structure and performance of Korean business groups: A transaction cost approach. *The Journal of Industrial Economics, 37*(2), 141–159.

Chen, S., Sun, S. Y. J., & Wu, D. (2010). Client importance, institutional improvements, and audit quality in China: An office and individual auditor level analysis. *The Accounting Review, 85*(1), 127–158.

Cheung, Y. L., Rau, P. R., & Stouraitis, A. (2006). Tunneling, propping, and expropriation: Evidence from connected party transactions in Hong Kong. *Journal of Financial Economics, 82*(2), 343–386.

Chi, W., Hunag, Y., Liao, H., & Xie, H. (2009). Mandatory audit partner rotation, audit quality, and market perception: Evidence from Taiwan. *Contemporary Accounting Research, 26*(2), 359–391.

Chow, C. W., & Rice, S. J. (1982). Qualified audit opinions and auditor switching. *The Accounting Review, 57*(2), 326–335.

Claessens, S., Djankov, S. J., Fan, O. H., & Lang, L. H. (2002). Disentangling the incentive and entrenchment effects of large shareholdings. *The Journal of Finance, 57*(6), 2741–2771.

Cohen, J., Krishnamoorthy, G., & Wright, A. (2004). The corporate governance mosaic and financial reporting quality. *Journal of Accounting Literature, 23*, 87–152.

Craswell, A., Francis, J., & Taylor, S. (1995). Auditor brand name reputations and industry specializations. *Journal of Accounting and Economics, 20*(3), 297–322.

DeAngelo, L. (1981). Auditor size and audit quality. *Journal of Accounting and Economics, 3*(3), 183–199.

DeFond, M. (1992). The association between changes in client firm agency costs and auditor switching. *Auditing: A Journal of Practice and Theory, 11*(1), 16–31.

DeFond, M. L., Raghunandan, K., & Subramanyam, K. R. (2002). Do non-audit service fees impair auditor independence? Evidence from going concern audit opinions. *Journal of Accounting Research, 40*(4), 1247–1274.

Dey, A. (2008). Corporate governance and agency conflicts. *Journal of Accounting Research, 46*(5), 1143–1181.

Elloumi, F., & Gueyié, J. P. (2001). Financially distress and corporate governance: An empirical analysis. *Corporate Governance, 1*(1), 15–23.

Farber, D. B. (2005). Restoring trust after fraud: Does corporate governance? *The Accounting Review, 80*(2), 539–561.

Ferguson, A., Francis, J. R., & Stokes, D. J. (2003). The effects of firm-wide and office-level industry expertise on audit pricing. *The Accounting Review, 78*(2), 429–448.

Firth, M. (1980). A note on the impact of audit qualifications on lending and credit decisions. *Journal of Banking and Finance, 4*(3), 257–267.

Firth, M., & Smith, A. (1992). Selection of auditor companies by companies in the new issue market. *Applied Economics, 24*(2), 247–255.

Geiger, M. A., Raghunandan, K., & Rama, D. V. (1998). Costs associated with going concern modified audit opinions: An analysis of auditor changes, subsequent opinions, and client failures. *Advances in Accounting, 16*, 117–139.

Geiger, M. A., & Rama, D. V. (2003). Audit fees, nonaudit fees, and auditor reporting on stressed companies. *Auditing: A Journal of Practice & Theory, 22*(2), 53–69.

Ghosh, A., & Moon, D. (2005). Auditor tenure and perceptions of audit quality. *The Accounting Review, 80*(2), 585–612.

Gordon, E. A., Henry, E., & Palia, D. (2004). Related party transactions and corporate governance. *Advances in Financial Economics*, *9*, 1–27.

Guillén, M. F. (2000). Business groups in emerging economics: A resource-based view. *Academy of Management Journal*, *43*(3), 362–380.

Gunduz, L., & Tatoglu, E. (2003). A comparison of the financial characteristics of group affiliated and independent companies in Turkey. *European Business Review*, *15*(1), 48–54.

Heninger, W. G. (2001). The association between auditor litigation and abnormal accruals. *The Accounting Review*, *76*(1), 111–126.

Hoffman, V. B., Joe, J. R., & Moser, D. V. (2003). The effect of constrained processing on auditors' judgments. *Accounting, Organizations & Society*, *28*(7/8), 699–714.

Hope, O.-K., & Langli, J. C. (2010). Auditor independence in a private firm and low litigation risk setting. *The Accounting Review*, *85*(2), 573–605.

Hubbard, R. D., & Pahlia, J. D. (1999). A reexamination of the conglomerate merger wave in the 1960s: An internal capital markets view. *The Journal of Finance*, *54*(3), 1131–1152.

Jenkins, N. T. (2002). *Auditor independence, audit committee effectiveness and earnings management*. Ph.D. dissertation proposal. Henry B. Tippie College of Business, The University of Iowa.

Jensen, M. C. (1993). The modern industrial revolution, exit, and the failure of internal control systems. *Journal of Finance*, *48*(3), 831–880.

Jian, M., & Wong, T. J. (2010). Propping through related party transactions. *Review of Accounting Studies*, *15*(1), 70–105.

Johnson, S., La Porta, F., Shleifer, A., & Vishny, R. (2000). Tunneling. *American Economic Review*, *90*, 22–27.

Jones, F. L. (1996). The information content of the auditor's going concern evaluation. *Journal of Accounting and Public Policy*, *15*(1), 1–27.

Kahle, K. M. (2000). Insider trading and the long-run performance of new security issues. *Journal of Corporate Finance*, *6*(1), 25–53.

Khanna, T., & Palepu, K. (2000a). Is group affiliation profitable in emerging markets? An analysis of diversified Indian business groups. *The Journal of Finance*, *55*(2), 867–891.

Khanna, T., & Palepu, K. (2000b). The future of business groups in emerging markets: Long run evidence from Chile. *Academy of Management Journal*, *43*(3), 268–285.

Khanna, T., & Rivikin, J. W. (2001). Estimating the performance effects of business groups in emerging markets. *Strategic Management Journal*, *22*(1), 45–74.

Khanna, T., & Yafeh, Y. (2005). Business groups and risk sharing around the world. *Journal of Business*, *78*(1), 301–340.

Kida, T. (1980). An investigation into auditors' continuity and related qualification judgments. *Journal of Accounting Research*, *18*(2), 506–523.

Krishnan, J., & Krishnan, J. (1997). Litigation risk and auditor resignations. *The Accounting Review*, *72*(4), 539–560.

La Porta, R., Lopez-de-Silanes, F., Shleifer, A., & Vishny, R. (1999). The quality of government. *Journal of Law, Economics and Organization*, *15*(1), 222–279.

La Porta, R., Lopez-de-Silanes, F., Shleifer, A., & Vishny, R. (1997). Legal determinants of external finance. *Journal of Finance*, *52*(July), 1131–1150.

La Porta, R., Lopez-de-Silanes, F., Shleifer, A., & Vishny, R. (1998). Law and finance. *Journal of Political Economy*, *106*, 1113–1155.

La Porta, R., Lopez-de-Silanes, F., Shleifer, A., & Vishny, R. (2000). Investor protection and corporate governance. *Journal of financial Economics*, *58*(1–2), 3–27.

Li, C. (2009). Does client importance affect auditor independence at the office level? Empirical evidence from going-concern opinions. *Contemporary Accounting Research*, 26(1), 201–230.

McKeown, J. C., Mutchler, J. F., & Hopwood, W. (1991). Towards an explanation of auditor failure to modify the audit opinions of bankrupt companies. *Auditing: A Journal of Practice & Theory*, 10(Suppl.), 1–13.

Mitchell, L. (2005). Structural holes, CEOs, and the missing link in corporate governance. *Brooklyn Law Review*, 70, 1313–1368.

Mutchler, J. F. (1984). Auditors' perceptions of the going-concern opinion decision. *Auditing: A Journal of Practice & Theory*, 3(2), 17–30.

Mutchler, J. F., Hopwood, W., & McKeown, J. M. (1997). The influence of contrary information and mitigating factors on audit opinion decisions on bankrupt companies. *Journal of Accounting Research*, 35(2), 295–310.

Myers, J., Myers, L., & Omer, T. (2003). Exploring the term of the auditor-client relationship and the quality of earnings: A case for mandatory auditor rotation? *The Accounting Review*, 78(3), 779–799.

Palmrose, Z. V. (1986). Audit fees and auditor size: Further evidence. *Journal of Accounting Research*, 24(1), 97–110.

Palmrose, Z. V. (1987). Litigation and independent auditors: The role of business failures and management fraud. *Auditing: A Journal of Practice and Theory*, 6(1), 90–103.

Palmrose, Z. V. (1988). An analysis of auditor litigation and audit service quality. *The Accounting Review*, 63(1), 55–73.

Patton, A., & Baker, J. C. (1987). Why do not directors rock the boat? *Harvard Business Review*, 65, 10–18.

Peng, W. Q., John Wei, K. C., & Yang, Z. (2011). Tunneling or propping: Evidence from connected transactions in China. *Journal of Corporate Finance*, 17(2), 306–325.

Reynolds, J. K., & Francis, J. R. (2001). Does size matter? The influence of large clients on office-level auditor reporting decisions. *Journal of Accounting and Economics*, 30(3), 375–400.

Ruder, D. S. (2002). Oversight hearing on accounting and investor protection issues raised by Enron and other public companies. Senate Committee on Banking, Housing, and Urban Affairs. 107th Cong., 2nd sess., 12 February. Retrieved from http://www.senate. gov/-banking/02-02hrg/021202/ruder.htm

Shu, S. Z. (2000). Auditor resignations: Clientele effects and legal liability. *Journal of Accounting and Economics*, 29(2), 173–205.

Stein, J. C. (1997). Internal capital markets and the competition for corporate resources. *The Journal of Finance*, 52(1), 111–133.

Stulz, R. (1990). Managerial discretion and optimal financing policies. *Journal of Financial Economics*, 26(1), 3–27.

Teoh, S. H., & Wong, T. J. (1993). Perceived auditor quality and the earnings response coefficient. *The Accounting Review*, 68(2), 346–366.

Weber, J., Willenborg, M., & Zhang, J. (2008). Does auditor reputation matter? The case of KPMG Germany and ComROAD AG. *Journal of Accounting Research*, 46(4), 941–972.

Williamson, O. E. (1985). *The economic institution of capitalism*. New York, NY: The Free Press.

Yeh, Y. H., Lee, T. S., & Ko, C. E. (2002). Corporate governance and rating system. Taipei: Sunbright Publishing Co. (in Chinese).

THE EFFICIENT MANAGEMENT OF SHAREHOLDER VALUE AND STAKEHOLDER THEORY: AN ANALYSIS OF EMERGING MARKET ECONOMIES

Orhan Akisik

ABSTRACT

Purpose – *The aim of this paper is to examine the relationship of the efficient management of shareholder value as the main objective of corporate governance systems with stakeholder theory.*

Design/Methodology – *The study uses data from 29 emerging market economies from 1997 to 2006. In order to control possible endogeneity issue, generalized two-stage least squares (G2SLS) and generalized method of moments (GMM) estimation techniques were conducted using country-level panel data.*

Findings – *The results provide evidence that the efficient management of shareholder value is strongly associated with managers' credibility, social responsibility, employment, and customer satisfaction, suggesting that emerging market economies should consider the interests of stakeholders for the efficient management of shareholder value.*

Accounting in Asia
Research in Accounting in Emerging Economies, Volume 11, 155–182
Copyright © 2011 by Emerald Group Publishing Limited
All rights of reproduction in any form reserved
ISSN: 1479-3563/doi:10.1108/S1479-3563(2011)0000011012

Originality/Value – *This is the first study of its kind that attempts to explore the association of the efficient management of shareholder value with country-level determinants of stakeholder theory.*

Research Limitations/Implications – *The lack of sufficient data is a major problem in international studies. This study also has some limitations in this respect as some emerging economies have not been included in the sample.*

Keywords: Efficient management of shareholder value; managers' credibility; social responsibility; employment; customer satisfaction

INTRODUCTION

This study aims to examine the relationship of the efficient management of shareholder value with stakeholder theory in 29 emerging countries over the period from 1997 to 2006.[1] Efficient management of shareholder value may be defined on the basis of efficiency concept. In this case, efficiency is synonymous with productivity, and is measured by the ratio of output quantities to input quantities (Sudit, 1996). To put it differently, an increase in production or income in relation to resources or investments increases efficiency. Shareholders are interested in achieving the maximum possible return on their investments. An effective corporate governance system, which is designed to motivate managers to efficiently manage shareholder value, leads to an increase in return on shareholders investments. There are three primary motives that drive management of companies to increase the shareholder value. Creating shareholder value enables management to make better decisions, to earn higher salaries and bonuses, and to deliver better performance to shareholders and other stakeholders. It is argued that managers, who continually fail to maximize shareholder value, may be replaced by those who can better serve to achieve this goal (Morin & Jarrell, 2001, p. 7).

Although corporate governance has been extensively examined in many interdisciplinary studies in the last three decades (Gugler, Mueller, & Yurtoglu, 2004), there has been a renewed interest among academics and members of the business world on corporate governance issues over the past few years. This has been triggered partly by the Asian financial crisis and financial reporting scandals, which caused investors to lose their confidence in capital markets, and partly by the increase in foreign investments as a result of globalization (Claessens & Fan, 2002; Corporate Governance – A Survey of OECD Countries, 2004, p. 18; Gibson, 2003; Johnston, 2003, p. 371; Mallin, 2011, p. 153; Singh, 2003). At the core of this interest lies a major controversy about the fundamental goal of a firm (Wallace, 2003). Many scholars stress the maximization of shareholder value as the ultimate objective of corporate governance systems (Denis, 2001; La Porta, Lopez-de-Silanes, Shleifer, & Vishny, 2000; Shleifer & Vishny, 1997). In the past decade, this view has exerted a tremendous pressure on corporate executives to increase their stock prices and shareholder values at the expense of long-term gains. The main challenge to this approach is the stakeholder theory of corporate governance, which argues that firms should benefit major constituencies, such as employees, customers, suppliers, government, and local community in addition to shareholders because the success of firms in terms of the shareholder value maximization depends not only on resolving the agency problem with their shareholders, but also on the good cooperation with those who have a stake in firms (Freeman, 2008, p. 78; Langtry, 1994; Wallace, 2003). This view suggests that firms that put their stakeholders first will inevitably achieve greater growth in shareholder value than those firms that focus primarily on boosting their stock prices at the expense of other constituencies (George, 2003).

Using the broad definition of corporate governance, this study argues that the reconciliation of competing interests of stakeholders is important for the efficient management of shareholder value in emerging market countries. This argument is based on the idea that, in contrast to Anglo-Saxon countries, the maximization of shareholder value is not regarded as the single goal of firms in European and Asian countries. Managers in these countries focus on balancing the conflicting claims, allowing for labor participation in company management (Shaw, 2000, p. 45).

In this study, Generalized Two-Stage Least Squares (G2SLS) and generalized method of moments (GMM) estimation techniques are used to examine the relationships of the efficient management of shareholder value with the countrywide components of stakeholder governance.

The paper contributes to the corporate governance literature in several ways. First, this is the first country-level study of its kind that examines the relationship of the efficient management of shareholder value with several aspects of stakeholder theory in emerging market economies. Second, the results of analyses indicate that the efficient management of shareholder value is positively associated with major aspects of stakeholder governance, such as corporate social responsibility, employment, and customer satisfaction.

This suggests that firms that are both socially responsible and emphasize customer satisfaction also contribute to the shareholder value efficiently. These are important findings, in particular, for emerging market countries that need to increase their shares of foreign investment. The conclusions that have been obtained are important for a number of groups such as investors, employees, customers, financial market regulators, government agencies, and firms, suggesting that a good cooperation with stakeholders would have a positive impact on the creation of shareholder value in emerging market countries.

The paper is designed as follows: the second section consists of two parts. The first part presents the theoretical background by discussing attributes and types of stakeholders, and responsibilities of firms to their stakeholders in the literature. The second part is about the development of hypotheses underlying the empirical analyses. The third section is also divided into two parts, with the first part presenting the econometric model and the second part discussing the data. The fourth section presents the results of empirical analyses. The results provide evidence of a strong relationship between the components of stakeholder governance and the efficient management of shareholder value. In the fifth section concluding remarks are given.

THEORETICAL BACKGROUND AND HYPOTHESES DEVELOPMENT

Theoretical Background

Stakeholder theory is based on the view that firms are the nexus of relationships among stakeholders who consist of owners, customers, employees, suppliers, creditors, government, and the local community. Stakeholders play a vital role in the success of firms by interacting with each other to create value in the long run (Freeman, 1984, p. 25; Freeman, Harrison, Wicks, Parmar, & De Colle, 2010, p. 24; Ingley & Karout, 2011, p. 137; Sternberg, 2000, p. 49). The stakeholder theory is compatible with a broad definition of corporate governance, according to which corporate governance is a set of relationships between and among a company's board of directors, its management, and stakeholders (Colley, Doyle, Logan, & Stettinius, 2005; Dallago, 2007, p. 16; Gillan & Starks, 2003; La Porta et al., 2000; Roche, 2005, p. 4; White Paper on Corporate Governance in Asia, 2003, p. 12). This broad definition of corporate governance focuses on the reconciliation of the stakeholders' interests. According to the proponents of stakeholder theory, the main purpose of a firm is to create value for its stakeholders, that is, those who have a stake or an interest in the firm (Freeman, 1984, pp. 31–32; Miller, 1998, p. 5; Shelton, 2001, p. 12; Youngmo, 2001, p. 217).[2] Shaw (2000, p. 37) argues that

> A business will only be able to deliver sustained and sustainable shareholder value through continuous improvement and innovation by what is being increasingly referred to a 'stakeholder symbiosis.' Stakeholder symbiosis is the belief in the interdependence of financial performance, customer loyalty, employee motivation and good corporate practice.

In European countries, in particular, building better relations with major stakeholders, such as employees, customers, suppliers, and government agencies is likely to affect financial returns positively by helping firms develop intangible, but valuable assets, which can be sources of competitive advantage. Firms that invest in stakeholder relations may not only gain customer loyalty and societal prestige, but may also reduce the turnover of employees, which in turn has a positive effect on shareholder value (Hillman & Keim, 2001). Firms of this kind are considered good in French Company Law because they aim to reconcile the interests of society and different stakeholders (Halpern, 2000, p. 5). A bulk of evidence indicates that, in Europe and the United States, companies that have good reputations in terms of product and service quality, and responsibility to community and environment are likely to outperform stock market averages. Kodama (2008, p. 118) notes that

> Corporations need to place strategic importance on building win-win relationships among customers, employees, and partners, including shareholders. Along with providing new value to customers, corporations need to focus efforts on creating business models and profit structures that have competitive advantage for both corporations and partner companies. It is then just a matter of course that this philosophy and behavior on the part of corporations will also result in profits for shareholders. Management that pursues only short-term profits for the sake of shareholder value has no substance.

This suggests that the maximization of shareholder value is closely related to meeting the needs and expectations of other constituencies (Willetts, 1997, p. 23; Young & O'Byrne, 2001, p. 13). Colley et al. (2005, p. 4) support this view, indicating that the primary goal of corporations in today's global economic environment is to better serve their customers because achieving this goal will increase the profitability and shareholder value. This view is more comprehensive than the shareholder value approach to corporate governance that focuses solely on maximizing the value of firms to their owners (Denis & McConnell, 2003).

Mitchell, Agle, and Wood (1997) offered a theory of stakeholder identification and salience by defining three attributes of stakeholders, namely, legitimacy, power, and urgency.[3] Stakeholders may possess one, two, or three of these attributes. Mitchell et al. (1997) argue that stakeholder salience is positively related to the cumulative number of attributes. Stakeholders who possess any one of these attributes are called latent stakeholders. Moderately salient stakeholders are those who possess any two of these three attributes, such as power–urgency, or legitimacy–urgency, or power–legitimacy. Stakeholders who fall into this category are called expectant because they expect something. Finally, stakeholders who possess all these three attributes are called highly salient. To put it differently, stakeholders become salient to firms' managers to the extent that managers consider them as possessing legitimacy, power, and urgency (Friedman & Miles, 2002). Agle, Mitchell, and Sonnenfeld (1999) tested the theory of stakeholder identification and salience by Mitchell et al. (1997) using the data provided by the CEOs of large U.S. firms. They find strong support for the attribute-salience relationship and some significant relationships among CEO values, salience, and corporate social performance.

Stakeholders have also been categorized as either primary or secondary. Primary stakeholders, who are directly engaged in transactions with firms, consist of employees, customers, suppliers, shareholders, community, and government. On the other hand, secondary stakeholders, who influence, or are influenced by businesses, are not engaged in direct business transactions, and therefore are not essential for a firms' survival (Clarkson, 1995). The media and special interest groups are considered as secondary stakeholders. However, the importance of secondary stakeholders should not be underestimated as they may have a significant impact on the firm through their interactions with primary stakeholders (Polonsky, 1995).

Firms have fiscal, social, and legal responsibilities to their primary stakeholders. The question is what group of primary stakeholders is the most important for firms to achieve success in the long run? Although Miller (1998, p. 6) defines firms' responsibility to shareholders only as fiscal, it may be argued that firms are also legally responsible to shareholders since the latter are legal owners of the firms. As a result, shareholders expect a certain level of financial performance (Polonsky, 1995). The board of directors should protect the interests of shareholders against managers by overseeing and evaluating the performance of managers (Alkhafaji, 1998, p. 4). Meeting the needs of their other stakeholders depends on firms' abilities to first meet the needs of their shareholders. In other words, fiscal responsibility is considered as a prerequisite. (Miller, 1998, p. 10). At this point, fiscal responsibility coincides with the social responsibility defined by Friedman (1970). He argues that firms have a social responsibility only to shareholders as the owners of firms for making as much money as possible. However, this is not sufficient because firms are also socially responsible to other stakeholders such as employees, customers, suppliers, and the local community. For example, firms try to keep workers not only based on contracts, but also on social responsibility by providing them training and personal development opportunities. One of the most important contributions that firms can make with respect to their social responsibility is to deliver high-quality and eco-friendly products whose production and consumption do not damage the environment (Wales, Gorman, & Hope, 2010, p. 104). As an extension of the social responsibility to customers and the local community, firms must also refrain from increasing prices of their products in order to prevent inflation, which is considered at the same time as a social problem. The social responsibility to their suppliers and trading partners requires firms to organize themselves around an ethical supply chain management system that would diminish, if not entirely eliminate, unfair labor practices, unhealthy working conditions, and environmental degradation within their industry or sector. For example, they could make trade agreements that protect producers and workers in emerging market countries by guaranteeing minimum prices, and better and safe working conditions (Crane & Matten, 2004, p. 333; Sison, 2008, p. 90).

Although firms have three different responsibilities – fiscal, social, and legal – to stakeholders, only the fiscal responsibility to shareholders is fiduciary in the sense that managers hold assets of shareholders in trust and run firms in the interests of shareholders.[4] Goodpaster (1991) and Sternberg (1997, 1998, p. 107) argue that it is impossible for firms to treat all stakeholders equally, which may be defined as a multifiduciary approach (Boatright, 1994). To put it differently, firms cannot be held equally accountable to all their stakeholders. However, this does not mean that they do not need to pay attention to stakeholders' interests and concerns. In contrast to this argument, some authors expand the view of social responsibility, suggesting a multifiduciary approach that includes all primary stakeholders, in addition to shareholders. This implies that there is a conflict of interests between and among stakeholders since their objectives are often very different and compete with each other. Moreover, primary stakeholders are listed in order of importance as customers, employees, local community, and firms (see, for example, Martin, 2010;

Preble, 2005; Preston & Sapienza, 1990). The success of businesses in the long run depends upon the ability of managers to equally consider the expectations and interests of primary stakeholders and to create sufficient value, wealth, and satisfaction for them. For example, shareholders are interested in maximizing the return on their investments while employees expect safe working conditions, decent compensation, and benefits in return for services they provide. Customers want firms to deliver high-quality products that satisfy their complex needs and wants (Freeman et al., 2010, p. 25; Polonsky, 1995; Spence & Rinaldi, 2010, p. 54). According to this view, profit is a by-product of success in meeting responsibly the legitimate needs and expectations of primary stakeholders (Clarkson, 1995; Preston & Sapienza, 1990).[5] Shareholders would benefit if managers focused on protecting the interests of customers, employees, and community.

Hypotheses Development

Stock Market Development and the Efficient Management of Shareholder Value

When economies grow and incomes rise, firms increase their profits. During an economic expansion, publicly owned companies create more value for their owners, leading to the development of stock markets. To put it differently, creating shareholder value is crucial for public companies to attract more equity investments. It is argued that the stock market boom in the United States in the 1990s has resulted from the increase in shareholder value (Corporate Governance, 1998, p. 18; Lazonick & O'Sullivan, 2004, pp. 298–299). In contrast to this view, Young & O'Byrne (2001, p. 6) contend that the shareholder value results largely from the development of capital markets that is stimulated by advances in information technology and by removing capital and exchange controls. In light of these conflicting views, it may be argued that there could be a two-way relationship between the shareholder value and the stock market development. Hence, the efficient management of shareholder value not only affects, but also is affected by the development of stock market. It is, therefore, hypothesized in the alternative form that

Hypothesis 1. There is a positive and two-way relationship between stock market development and the efficient management of shareholder value.

Social Responsibility and the Efficient Management of Shareholder Value
The success of firms in terms of increasing profitability and market share depends on a variety of factors. In market economies, corporations are run by their managements to primarily serve the interests of their owners who are interested in increasing the return on their investments. However, every decision made by management to create value for shareholders has either positive or negative consequences for other stakeholders such as customers, employees, and the general public. In other words, it is not possible in today's economies to create shareholder value without affecting other stakeholders (Roche, 2005, p. 157). Company policies that focus solely on creating shareholder value without taking into account the possible negative effects on other groups would fail to achieve the long-term economic and reputational values (Principles of Corporate Governance, 2002). Therefore, modern managements, apart from serving the interests of their owners, also need to be concerned with the interests of general public, which is known as corporate social responsibility. Those corporations in emerging economies that are socially responsible would not only gain prestige, but also sustain their profitability and market shares in the long run by providing social justice as economic, social, and cultural chaos are prevalent in these economies (Abrams, 2008, p. 30; Nuevo, Ruohtula, & Schwalbach, 2001, p. 21; Rashid & Islam, 2008, p. 21).[6] It is, therefore, hypothesized in the alternative form that

Hypothesis 2. There is a positive relationship between the social responsibility and the efficient management of shareholder value.

Customer Satisfaction and the Efficient Management of Shareholder Value
Prior research provides evidence that product safety/quality directly affects financial performance and firm performance (Berman, Wicks, Kotha, & Jones, 1999; Logsdon, 2004). It is argued that goods and services that satisfy needs and wants of customers effectively lead to an increase in share prices and profits, which in turn increases the shareholder value (Anderson, Fornell, & Mazvancheryl, 2004). Today it is difficult for firms to remain competitive unless they produce high-quality products that conform to changing needs and wants of their customers. Basically, there are three channels through which customer satisfaction affects shareholder value. First, loyal and satisfied customers provide a ready market for new add-on products and services. This leads to a market penetration and, in turn, to larger cash flows (Anderson et al., 2004; Srivastava, Tasadduq, & Liam, 1999). Second, greater customer satisfaction enables firms to charge higher

prices without experiencing any strong resistance from their customers (Anderson, 1996; Narayandas, 1998). Third, satisfied customers might positively influence the shareholder value by enhancing the bargaining power of firms with respect to their suppliers and partners (Anderson et al., 2004). Based on these arguments, it is hypothesized that customer satisfaction leads to the efficient management of shareholder value.

Hypothesis 3. There is a positive relationship between the customer satisfaction and the efficient management of shareholder value.

ECONOMETRIC MODEL AND DATA

Econometric Model

This study examines the relationship of the efficient management of shareholder value with country-specific determinants of stakeholder governance, using a panel data that cover 29 emerging market economies over the period from 1997 to 2006. As previously mentioned, the main objective of firms, in particular of publicly owned ones, is to create as much value as possible for their owners. The maximization of shareholder value is under the responsibility of managers. In order to attain this objective, management should produce and evaluate business strategies, and put them into practice (Morin & Jarrell, 2001, p. 4). However, this is not an easy task because firms operate in a complex setting that is shaped by rules and regulations, as well as social norms and cultural traditions, which to some extent may impose restrictions on their operations. For example, laws and regulations about employment, environmental protection, health, and public safety form the formal environment in which corporations operate (Corporate Governance, 1998, p. 17). Shareholders are residual claimants; that is, they are entitled to whatever remains after all revenues are collected and all debts, expenses, and contractual obligations are paid (Fox & Heller, 2006, p. 6; Rappaport, 1998, p. 33; Rubach, 1999, p. 9). In the literature, shareholder value is defined as the sum of future expected cash flows, discounted using an appropriate interest rate, and it is created when return on capital exceeds the cost of capital (Morin & Jarrell, 2001, p. 5). It will increase as long as firms generate income over and above the cost of capital (Wasmer, 2003). Future expected cash flows result largely from new investment opportunities that should be exploited by management. Wallace and Zinkin (2005) argue that shareholder value is driven by the ability of companies' managements to (1) allocate capital between projects efficiently, (2) increase the company's efficiency by reducing costs, (3) achieve innovations that are critical to maintaining future streams of income, and (4) turn great ideas into profitable business operations.

In this study, in order to control the probable endogeneity issue, G2SLS and GMM estimation techniques are used to examine the relationship between the efficient management of shareholder value and country-specific determinants of stakeholder governance (Denis, 2001; Renders & Gaeremynck, 2006). Econometric model is as follows:

First-Stage Estimation:

$$\text{MRKTCAP}_{it} = \beta_0 + \beta_1 \text{LEGALREG}_{it} + \beta_2 \text{GDPPC}_{it} + \beta_3 \text{SHOLDV\_L}_{i,t-1} + \varepsilon_{it}$$

Two-Stage Estimation:

$$\text{SHOLDV}_{it} = \alpha_0 + \alpha_1 \text{SOCRESP}_{it} + \alpha_2 \text{CREDMGMT}_{it} + \alpha_3 \text{CUSTOMER}_{it} + \alpha_4 \text{EMPLY}_{it} + \alpha_5 \text{INFL}_{it} + \alpha_6 \text{MRKTCAP}_{it} + \varepsilon_{it}$$

Where i refers to the country and t refers to the time period. In first-stage estimation, stock market development (MRKTCAP$_{it}$), which is measured by market capitalization in US\$ billion, is related to the legal regulation (LEGALREG$_{it}$), meaning that an effective legal system is crucial for financial development (La Porta, Lopez-de-Silanes, Shleifer, & Vishny, 1998, 2000), per capita GDP in US\$ at purchasing power parity (GDPPC$_{it}$), and shareholder value in the previous period (SHOLDV_L$_{i,t-1}$). In the two-stage estimation, SHOLDV$_{it}$ refers to the efficient management of shareholder value index, which measures how efficiently the shareholder value is managed in the society. SHOLDV$_{it}$ is measured by a country-specific index, and is based on executive opinion surveys conducted every year by the International Institute for Management Development (IMD). SOCRESP$_{it}$ is the social responsibility index that measures whether social responsibility of business leaders is high or low. As previously noted, firms have social responsibility to primary stakeholders, such as shareholders, suppliers, customers, and the local community. CREDMGMT$_{it}$ is managers' credibility index that measures whether managers' credibility is high or low. Both CEOs and senior managers are expected to run firms with due care, diligence, and integrity. They should never put their interests before those of stakeholders. Managers' credibility increases to the extent that managers act in good faith in the best interest of firms and avoid conflict of interests with other stakeholders (Wallace & Zinkin, 2005, pp. 263–264). CUSTOMER$_{it}$ refers to customer satisfaction index, which measures whether customer satisfaction is emphasized or not. EMPLY$_{it}$ is the employment rate as a percentage of population. Sison (2008, p. 91) argues that among different stakeholders, employees are the ones who are most closely identified and integrated with firms. Perhaps, they are the most important factor of production because they represent company toward other stakeholders. INFL$_{it}$ is the inflation rate, measured as an annual percentage change in GDP$_{it}$ deflator.

Data

The entire data set for this study has been obtained from the website of the IMD. In addition to economic data, the IMD has been publishing comprehensive country-specific indexes concerning social, managerial, governmental, and legal issues since 1989. The IMD World Competitiveness Yearbook team gathers quantitative and qualitative information separately. Hard data, which represent two-thirds of the overall weight in the final rankings, are statistics from international, national, and regional organizations, such as the World Bank, IMF, OECD, UNESCO, United Nations, WTO, and Partner Institutes worldwide. On the other hand, Soft data representing one-third of the overall weight, are compiled from annual Executive Opinion Survey. While hard data analyze competitiveness as it can be measured, survey data analyze competitiveness as it is perceived. The survey is designed to quantify issues that are not directly and easily measured. Responses to survey questions reflect present and future perceptions of competitiveness by executives who are working in international business environment. The Executive Opinion Survey is sent to senior and middle management. The respondents assess the competitiveness issues by answering the questions on a scale of 1–6. Later, an average value for each country is computed and converted into a 0–10 scale. A panel of 4,000 executives completes the survey. The survey respondents form a representative cross-section of the business community in each country analyzed. They are from the country itself because it would be impossible to find so many people, worldwide, who have relevant expertise in all of the countries analyzed. However, in order to be as objective as possible, the IMD surveys local and foreign firms operating in a given country, and nationals as well as expatriates. The distribution reflects a breakdown of economic sectors:

primary/extractive, manufacturing, and services/finance. In order to be statistically representative, a sample size that is proportional to the GDP of each country is selected (World Competitiveness Yearbook, 2008, pp. 472–478).

RESULTS OF EMPIRICAL ANALYSES

Tables 1–3 present descriptive statistics – number of observations, mean, minimum and maximum values, and standard deviations for the entire variables of country groups. Table 1 displays descriptive statistics for all available observations. SHOLDV has a mean value of 4.55 out of 10. It reaches a maximum value of 7.56 in Chile in 2006. Main variables of interest for the stakeholder governance – SOCRESP and CUSTOMER – have mean values of 4.28 and 5.90, respectively. Among emerging market economies included in the sample, Hong Kong has the maximum value of 7.83 for CUSTOMER in 2005. On the other hand, South Africa takes the maximum value of 6.98 for SOCRESP. The mean value for EMPLY is 39.00, meaning that the share of employment in population is 39%. EMPLY takes a

Table 1. Descriptive Statistics.

	All Available Observations 1997–2006				
	N	Mean	SD	Min.	Max.
Dependent variable					
SHOLDV	243	4.55	2.13	0	7.56
Independent variables					
SOCRESP	243	4.28	2.04	0	6.98
CREDMGMT	261	4.85	2.20	0	7.93
EMPLY	290	39.00	11.41	0	58.12
CUSTOMER	223	5.90	1.00	3.29	7.83
INFL	290	5.06	1.40	2.41	12.82
MRKTCAP	289	1.46e + 11	2.54e + 11	2000000	2.43e + 12
LEGALREG	223	4.53	1.57	0	8.57
GDPPC	271	10987	6402	2314	37655

Note: Emerging and transitional economies included in the sample are as follows: Argentina, Brazil, Bulgaria, Chile, China, Colombia, Czech Republic, Estonia, Greece, Hong Kong, Hungary, India, Indonesia, Korean Republic, Lithuania, Malaysia, Mexico, Philippines, Poland, Romania, Russia, Slovakia, Slovenia, South Africa, Taiwan, Thailand, Turkey, Ukraine, and Venezuela.

maximum value of 58.12% in China in 2006. China has the highest share of employment in population among emerging countries.

MRKTCAP has the mean of US$146 billion, ranging from US$2 million to US$2,43 trillion. GDPPC, a variable that measures per capita GDP at purchasing power parity in US$, has 2,314 minimum and 37,655 maximum values. The mean of GDPPC is US$10,987.

Tables 2 and 3 present descriptive statistics for two different periods. Period 1 covers the years from 1997 through 1999 while period 2 includes the years from 2000 through 2006. Descriptive statistics presented in two different groups may enable the reader to capture the effects of the Asian financial crisis on the variables. According to some authors, the Asian financial crisis of 1997 resulted from the ineffective corporate governance practices (Johnson, Boone, Breach, & Friedman, 2000; Shleifer & Vishny, 1997). When comparing the mean values of main variables of interest in these two different periods, it is observed that SHOLDV, SOCRESP, EMPLY, and CUSTOMER have considerably improved after 1999. In addition, there is also an increase in the mean of GDPPC from US$8,859 to US$11,779. In terms of countries that take minimum and maximum for

Table 2.   Descriptive Statistics.

		Year < 1999			
	N	Mean	SD	Min.	Max.
Dependent variable					
SHOLDV	27	4.30	2.71	0	7.21
Independent variables					
SOCRESP	27	3.68	2.30	0	6.00
CREDMGMT	29	4.24	2.55	0	7.05
EMPLY	58	35.89	15.36	0	56.62
CUSTOMER	22	5.44	0.82	4.00	7.24
INFL	58	4.71	1.22	2.41	10.71
MRKTCAP	58	$7.46e+10$	$9.67e+10$	2000000	$4.13e+11$
LEGALREG	22	4.94	1.29	2.49	7.79
GDPPC	52	8859	4823	2341	23049

Note: Emerging and transitional economies included in the sample are as follows: Argentina, Brazil, Bulgaria, Chile, China, Colombia, Czech Republic, Estonia, Greece, Hong Kong, Hungary, India, Indonesia, Korean Republic, Lithuania, Malaysia, Mexico, Philippines, Poland, Romania, Russia, Slovakia, Slovenia, South Africa, Taiwan, Thailand, Turkey, Ukraine, and Venezuela.

Table 3. Descriptive Statistics.

			Year > 1999		
	N	Mean	SD	Min.	*Max.*
Dependent variable					
SHOLDV	189	4.66	2.00	0	7.56
Independent variables					
SOCRESP	189	4.40	1.95	0	6.98
CREDMGMT	203	4.99	2.08	0	7.93
EMPLY	203	40.40	8.98	0	58.12
CUSTOMER	178	5.98	0.98	3.79	7.83
INFL	203	5.18	1.44	3.61	12.82
MRKTCAP	202	1.71e + 11	2.90e + 11	5.05e + 08	2.43e + 12
LEGALREG	178	4.45	1.60	0	8.57
GDPPC	193	11779	6758	2415	37655

Note: Emerging and transitional economies included in the sample are as follows: Argentina, Brazil, Bulgaria, Chile, China, Colombia, Czech Republic, Estonia, Greece, Hong Kong, Hungary, India, Indonesia, Korean Republic, Lithuania, Malaysia, Mexico, Philippines, Poland, Romania, Russia, Slovakia, Slovenia, South Africa, Taiwan, Thailand, Turkey, Ukraine, and Venezuela.

GDPPC in these two periods, there is no change. India has the lowest GDPPC while Hong Kong has the highest.

Table 4 presents the Pearson correlation matrix among dependent and independent variables in the data set. All of the independent variables with the exception of INFL and EMPLY are strongly correlated with SHOLDV at a 5% significance level. In particular, there exists a strong positive correlation of SHOLDV with SOCRESP, CREDMGMT, and CUSTOMER ($\rho = 0.6673$, 0.6956, and 0.5565, respectively) as expected, suggesting that SHOLDV is positively affected by an improvement in SOCRESP, CREDMGMT, and CUSTOMER. MRKTCAP is also significantly correlated with SHOLDV. However, its impact is not so strong ($\rho = 0.1927$). Although INFL is negatively correlated with SHOLDV, it is not significant at 5% level. There is a negative correlation between SHOLDV and EMPLY. However, it is neither significant nor strong ($\rho = -0.0023$).[7]

Note that a strong positive correlation exists between SHOLDV and GDPPC ($\rho = 0.3081$), suggesting that economic growth leads to an increase in the shareholder value by increasing profits. GDPPC is negatively significantly correlated with INFL ($\rho = -0.1368$). Accordingly, it may be

Table 4. Pearson Correlation Matrix.

1997–2006

	SHOLDV	SOCRESP	CREDMGMT	EMPLY	INFL	CUSTOMER	MRKTCAP	LEGALREG	GDPPC	SHOLDV_L
SHOLDV	1.0000									
SOCRESP	0.6673*	1.0000								
CREDMGMT	0.6956*	0.7328*	1.0000							
EMPLY	−0.0023	−0.0552	−0.0874	1.0000						
INFL	−0.0970	0.0918	0.1448*	−0.3556*	1.0000					
CUSTOMER	0.5565*	0.6149*	0.5509*	0.3561*	0.0483	1.0000				
MRKTCAP	0.1927*	0.1953*	0.3389*	0.0341	0.1463*	0.3345*	1.0000			
LEGALREG	0.4891*	0.4581*	0.4751*	0.1446*	−0.1552*	0.4733*	0.2542*	1.0000		
GDPPC	0.3081*	0.1177	−0.0166	0.0775	−0.1368*	0.3551*	0.0937	0.2135*	1.0000	
SHOLDV_L	0.8292*	0.6447*	0.6565*	−0.0377	−0.1110	0.4983*	0.0988	0.4861*	0.2236*	1.0000

*5% level of significance.

argued that, in emerging market economies, economic growth is adversely affected by high inflation.

On the other hand, although there exists a positive correlation between GDPPC and EMPLY as expected, it is not significant ($\rho = 0.0775$). There is a strong positive correlation between two major aspects of stakeholder governance, namely, SOCRESP and CUSTOMER ($\rho = 0.6149$), which indicates that socially responsible firms are likely to influence customer satisfaction positively. A strong positive correlation between CREDMGMT and SOCRESP ($\rho = 0.7328$) might imply that as firms become more socially responsible, managers' credibility in society increases. In other words, they gain prestige in the society.[8] Finally, the positive and significant correlation of CUSTOMER with EMPLY needs to be emphasized ($\rho = 0.3561$). This is important for two reasons for stakeholder governance. First, better customer satisfaction leads to an increase in employment through its impact on profits. Second, there is not a conflict of interest between workers and customers. To put it differently, firms that take into account the interests of customers also contribute to the well-being of workers in emerging market economies.

Table 5 presents the results of analyses of the determinants of SHOLDV, using G2SLS with fixed effects.[9] In all estimations for the entire set of emerging market countries, all of the variables are highly significant with the exception of CREDMGMT, CUSTOMER, and INFL. These results are consistent with the hypotheses that SHOLDV is positively related to MRKTCAP, SOCRESP, and EMPLY. In particular, two main variables of interest, SOCRESP and EMPLY, are positively and strongly associated with SHOLDV, indicating that firms that are socially responsible, and promote employment manage the shareholder value efficiently. In contrast to arguments by some authors that company policies that aim to enhance SHOLDV would negatively affect labor market (Lazonick & O'Sullivan, 2004, p. 293), a strong positive relationship has been found between EMPLY and SHOLDV. This suggests that macro- and microeconomic policies that emphasize long-term job tenure affect SHOLDV positively in emerging market economies. Although INFL is positively associated with SHOLDV, it is not significant. In estimations for Asian group of emerging countries, CREDMGMT, EMPLY, INFL, and CUSTOMER turn out to be very significant.

In Asian countries, firms that emphasize customer satisfaction achieve higher shareholder value. The positive relationship of inflation with the shareholder value means that although Asian emerging market countries have experienced high inflation, firms could enhance the shareholder value by increasing their earnings more than the rate of inflation. In untabulated

Table 5. G2SLS Regression Results.

	(1)	(2)	(3)	(4)	(5)	(6)
	Overall	Asian	Overall	Asian	Overall	Asian
	FE	FE	FE	FE	FE	FE
MRTKCAP	0.120***	0.117***	0.110***	0.0705**	0.0929***	0.0402
	(0.015)	(0.028)	(0.017)	(0.028)	(0.020)	(0.030)
SOCRESP	0.277***	0.288*	0.295***	0.319**	0.206**	0.289**
	(0.070)	(0.16)	(0.070)	(0.13)	(0.082)	(0.12)
CREDMGMT	0.155*	0.405***	0.170*	0.513***	0.143*	0.389***
	(0.089)	(0.15)	(0.088)	(0.13)	(0.084)	(0.12)
EMPLY	0.687***	1.213**	0.649***	1.128***	0.617***	1.089***
	(0.21)	(0.50)	(0.21)	(0.43)	(0.20)	(0.37)
INFL			0.0369	0.255***	0.0176	0.204***
			(0.029)	(0.079)	(0.029)	(0.069)
CUSTOMER					0.196*	0.337***
					(0.10)	(0.12)
Constant	−4.576***	−7.122***	−4.436***	−7.126***	−3.952***	−6.292***
	(0.70)	(1.53)	(0.69)	(1.29)	(0.72)	(1.16)
Observations	175	63	175	63	175	63
R^2 – overall	0.152	0.404	0.143	0.614	0.178	0.549
R^2 – within	0.542	0.749	0.563	0.824	0.600	0.866
R^2 – between	0.0800	0.333	0.0681	0.545	0.0945	0.451
Wald test	93178	42941	97175	60161	105391	77301

Note: Dependent variables are SHOLDV and MRTKCAP in two-stage and first stage estimations, respectively. All of the variables are in natural logarithms. FE refers to fixed effect estimations. Standard errors are robust with the correction of heteroskedasticity. Instrumented variable is MRKTCAP. Excluded instruments are LEGALREG, GDPPC, and SHOLDV_L. Emerging economies included in the sample are as follows: Argentina, Brazil, Bulgaria, Chile, China, Colombia, Czech Republic, Estonia, Greece, Hong Kong, Hungary, India, Indonesia, Korean Republic, Lithuania, Malaysia, Mexico, Philippines, Poland, Romania, Russia, Slovakia, Slovenia, South Africa, Taiwan, Thailand, Turkey, Ukraine, and Venezuela. Standard errors in parentheses.
***$p < 0.01$, **$p < 0.05$, *$p < 0.1$.

results of first-stage estimations, LEGALREG, GDPPC, and SHOLDV_L turn out to be highly significant and are positively associated with MRKTCAP. The overall model explains a significant portion of the variation in SHOLDV.

Finally, Table 6 reports the results of GMM robust estimation technique that is used to control heteroskedasticity. As in G2SLS method, all of the main variables are again highly significant with the exception of INFL. In

Table 6. GMM Regression Results.

	(1)	(2)	(3)	(4)	(5)	(6)
	Overall	Asian	Overall	Asian	Overall	Asian
	FE	FE	FE	FE	FE	FE
MRTKCAP	0.116***	0.105***	0.105***	0.0708***	0.0916***	0.0400*
	(0.016)	(0.027)	(0.017)	(0.023)	(0.020)	(0.022)
SOCRESP	0.274***	0.310**	0.297***	0.316***	0.216**	0.293***
	(0.081)	(0.12)	(0.081)	(0.097)	(0.092)	(0.082)
CREDMGMT	0.166*	0.408***	0.188**	0.515***	0.156*	0.395***
	(0.095)	(0.12)	(0.094)	(0.13)	(0.093)	(0.13)
EMPLY	0.745***	1.262***	0.715***	1.128***	0.684***	1.062***
	(0.21)	(0.44)	(0.20)	(0.40)	(0.20)	(0.36)
INFL			0.0377	0.261**	0.0156	0.214**
			(0.026)	(0.12)	(0.026)	(0.100)
CUSTOMER					0.191	0.336***
					(0.12)	(0.10)
Observations	175	63	175	63	175	63
R^2	0.55	0.76	0.57	0.82	0.60	0.87
R^2 Adj.	0.462	0.703	0.484	0.779	0.519	0.828
Kleibergen Paap stat	41.08	14.06	40.12	19.14	34.88	13.60
p-value	6.28e-09	0.0028	0.0000	0.0003	0.000	0.0035
Hansen-J stat	2.196	1.080	3.110	0.556	2.994	0.0236
p-value	0.334	0.5829	0.211	0.757	0.224	0.988
Endogeneity test stat	11.75	2.780	8.994	3.015	7.249	2.177
p-value	0.0006	0.0955	0.0027	0.0825	0.0070	0.140

Note: Dependent variables are SHOLDV and MRTKCAP in two-stage and first-stage estimations, respectively. All of the variables are in natural logarithms. FE refers to fixed effect estimations. Standard errors are robust with the correction of heteroskedasticity. Instrumented variable is MRTKCAP. Excluded instruments are LEGALREG, GDPPC, and SHOLDV_L. Emerging economies included in the sample are as follows: Argentina, Brazil, Bulgaria, Chile, China, Colombia, Czech Republic, Estonia, Greece, Hong Kong, Hungary, India, Indonesia, Korean Republic, Lithuania, Malaysia, Mexico, Philippines, Poland, Romania, Russia, Slovakia, Slovenia, South Africa, Taiwan, Thailand, Turkey, Ukraine, and Venezuela. Robust standard errors in parentheses.
***$p<0.01$, **$p<0.05$, *$p<0.1$.

particular, three main variables of stakeholder theory – MRTKCAP, SOCRESP, and EMPLY – are strongly associated with SHOLDV in all estimations. CREDMGMT, INFL, and CUSTOMER are strongly related to SHOLDV in Asian countries. Also, both R^2 and adjusted R^2 explain a significant portion of the variation in response variable in all regressions.

This estimation technique basically tests the validity of the selected instruments based on the values of three statistics. All of these statistics are significant and indicate that the model is a suitable one. Kleibergen Paap statistic is a test of underidentification, which determines whether the excluded instruments are correlated with the endogenous variable. The null hypothesis that the equation is underidentified is rejected. This means that the selected instruments are relevant. Hansen J statistic is a test of over-identification. Test results suggest that the joint hypothesis that the instruments are relevant, that is, uncorrelated with the error term, and that the excluded instruments are correctly excluded from the estimation equation is accepted. Finally, endogeneity test statistic suggests that the null hypothesis that the instrumented variable is exogenous should be rejected in all estimations. Accordingly, MRKTCAP turns out an endogenous variable.

Overall, regression results are consistent with the hypotheses that the SHOLDV is strongly related to SOCRESP, CREDMGMT, CUSTOMER, EMPLY, and MRKTCAP, suggesting that good stakeholder governance contributes to SHOLDV positively.

CONCLUSIONS

This study examines the relationship of the efficient management of shareholder value as the main objective of Anglo-Saxon corporate governance system with stakeholder theory in 29 emerging market economies over the period from 1997 to 2006. Corporate governance does not have an agreed-upon definition; it has been defined in different ways by authors. According to a broad definition, corporate governance is a system that regulates relationships of firms' managers with their stakeholders. In addition to shareholders, stakeholders include employees, customers, suppliers, creditors, government agencies, and the local community.

Considering the endogeneity issue in studies on corporate governance, the relationship between the efficient management of shareholder value and stakeholder governance has been examined using G2SLS and GMM estimation techniques with panel data. The results of empirical analyses indicate that there is a strong relationship between the efficient management of shareholder value and country-specific components of stakeholder governance. Stock market development, employment, managers' credibility, social responsibility, and customer satisfaction have been found to positively affect the shareholder value. In particular, the strong positive association between the efficient management of shareholder value and employment implies that corporate governance policies that support long-term job tenure would have a positive impact on the shareholder value in emerging market countries. Conclusions are important for a variety of groups, such as investors, managers, employees, government agencies, and local communities in which firms operate.

The study has a few limitations. One of these limitations results from insufficient data in international studies. Therefore, the study does not cover all of the emerging market economies. In addition, some variables do not have the entire data set for the period of 1997–2006. A future study that would examine the impact of "good" stakeholder governance on the shareholder value between emerging and developed economies might yield interesting results.

NOTES

1. There is no generally accepted definition of emerging market economies. They are differently classified by different organizations such as S&P, Morgan Stanley International, Dow Jones, and *The Economist*. Emerging market economies account for nearly 80% of world population. One major characteristic of these countries is that they are in a transitional phase, moving from developing to developed economies (Bond, 1970; Hoskisson, Eden, Lau, & Wright, 2000).

2. Gospel and Pendleton (2005, p. 3) define corporate governance as a system that regulates relationships among shareholders, managers, and the labor. According to them, the justification for identifying these three parties is based on the idea that each of these has some stakes in the form of either financial or human capital.

3. Legitimacy can be defined as a claim on a business entity based upon a legal or contractual obligation, or a moral right. A major characteristic of stakeholders is that they have formal, official, and contractual relationships with the firm (Polonsky, 1995). In addition to shareholders, customers, employees, suppliers, and government also have a legal claim on firms, which is based on a contractual agreement. For example, customers receive goods and services in exchange for payment. Firms make promises to their customers through advertising that products conform to certain specifications. If they do not, firms have to compensate the loss of their customers in accordance with their legal responsibility. Similarly, employees and suppliers will get paid when they provide services and deliver products to firms based on a contractual and legal obligation (Bender & Ward, 2009; Friedman & Miles, 2002). Power is the ability of stakeholders to affect firms' activities whether stakeholders have a legitimate claim. Urgency is the degree to which stakeholders' claims call for immediate attention (Mitchell et al., 1997; Preble, 2005).

4. The reason why the traditional view of corporate governance emphasizes fiscal responsibility, while considering the social responsibility in a very restricted sense, is trust and agency laws. "In trust law and agency law, a principal party gives a 'fiduciary' (trusted person) the power to control the principal's property. The fiduciary lacks ownership interest in the property and is obligated to use his control for the benefit of the principal (or a third party)" (Joo, 2010, p. 160).

5. In 1950, General Robert E. Wood, CEO of Sears', mentioned four groups to any business entity in order of their importance as customers, employees, community, and stockholders. He argued that if the first three groups are properly taken care of, the stockholders will benefit in the long run as shareholder value is maximized (Preston & Sapienza, 1990).

6. There are two conflicting views about the role of corporate social responsibility on profitability of firms (McGuire, Sundrgren, & Schneeweis, 1988). According to one view, a trade-off exists between social responsibility and financial performance. Socially responsible behavior puts firms in an economic disadvantage compared to other, less responsible firms (Aupperle, Carroll, & Hatfield, 1985; Ullmann, 1985; Vance, 1975). On the other hand, proponents of corporate social responsibility argue that socially responsible actions might improve productivity and employee morale, leading to an increase in profitability (Moskowitz, 1972).

7. This negative correlation between SHOLDV and EMPLY may be strong for developed countries with shareholder governance that emphasizes the maximization of SHOLDV. For example, Fligstein and Shin (2004, pp. 402–403) are of opinion that the increasing importance of shareholder value has made US labor market insecure, especially for low-skilled employees. Some businesses closed their plants, moved them offshore, leading to massive layoffs during the recessions of the early 1980s and 1990s. Moreover, they argue that the shareholder value gained importance over stakeholder rights in 1980s as a result of the change in management philosophy that favors profits rather than growth and size. With this change, employees are not seen partners any more.

8. Some correlations turn out to be high. However, they are less than ± 0.80. So there is no serious threat of multicollinearity (Farrar & Glauber, 1967; Judge, Griffiths, & Hill, 1985). Kennedy (2003, p. 210) argues that if t-statistics are all greater than 2, there is no need to worry about multicollinearity.

9. G2SLS and GMM are used if there is an endogeneity issue in which dependent variable is correlated with the error term. In order to detect whether there is endogeneity, Hausman test has been conducted. The test result suggests that MRKTCAP is endogenous (χ^2 [4] = 123.93; prob. $> \chi^2 = 0.0000$).

ACKNOWLEDGMENT

The author thanks Ozgur Arslan, Christopher F. Baum, Ben Branch, Graham Gal, and Suleyman Ozmucur for their insightful comments and suggestions.

REFERENCES

Abrams, F. W. (2008). Management's responsibility in a complex world. In: A. J. Zakhem, D. E. Palmer & M. L. Stoll (Eds.), *Stakeholder theory – Essential readings in ethical leadership and management* (pp. 26–31). Amherst, NY: Prometheus Books.

Agle, B. R., Mitchell, R. K., & Sonnenfeld, J. A. (1999). Who matters to CEOs? An investigation of stakeholder attributes and salience, corporate performance, and CEO values. *Academy of Management Journal, 42*, 507–525.

Alkhafaji, A. F. (1998). *A stakeholder approach to corporate governance: Managing in a dynamic environment*. New York, NY: Quroum Books.

Anderson, E. W. (1996). Customer satisfaction and price tolerance. *Marketing Letters, 7*(July), 19–30.

Anderson, E. W., Fornell, C., & Mazvancheryl, S. K. (2004). Customer satisfaction and shareholder value. *Journal of Marketing, 68*(October), 172–185.

Aupperle, K. E., Carroll, A. B., & Hatfield, J. D. (1985). An empirical examination of the relationship between corporate social responsibility and profitability. *Academy of Management Journal, 28*(2), 446–463.

Bender, R., & Ward, K. (2009). *Corporate financial strategy*. Hungary: Elsevier.

Berman, S. L., Wicks, A. C., Kotha, S., & Jones, T. M. (1999). Does stakeholder orientation matter? The relationship between stakeholder management models and firm financial performance. *Academy of Management Journal, 42*, 488–506.

Boatright, J. R. (1994). What's so special about shareholders? *Business Ethics Quarterly, 4*(4), 393–408.

Bond, R. R. (1970). Emerging nations and emerging institutions. *The International Journal of Accounting Education and Research, 6*(1), 83–90.

Claessens, S., & Fan, J. P. H. (2002). Corporate governance in Asia: A survey. *International Review of Finance, 3*(2), 77–103.

Clarkson, M. B. E. (1995). A stakeholder framework for analyzing and evaluating corporate social performance. *Academy of Management Review, 20*, 92–117.

Colley, J. L., Doyle, J. L., Logan, G. W., & Stettinius, W. (2005). *What is corporate Governance?* USA: McGraw-Hill.

Crane, A., & Matten, D. (2004). *Business ethics: Environmental responsibility*. New York, NY: McGraw-Hill.

Dallago, B. (2007). Corporate governance in transformation economies: A comparative perspective. In B. Dallago, & I. Iwasaki (Eds.), *Corporate restructuring and governance in transition economies* (pp. 15–39). Studies in Economic Transition. UK: Palgrave Macmillan.

Denis, D. K. (2001). Twenty-five years of corporate governance research ... counting. *Review of Financial Economics, 10*, 191–212.

Denis, D. K., & McConnell, J. J. (2003). International corporate governance. *Journal of Financial and Quantitative Analysis, 38*(1), 1–36.

Farrar, D., & Glauber, R. (1967). Multicollinearity in regression analysis: A problem revisited. *Review of Economics and Statistics, 49*(1), 92–107.

Fligstein, N., & Shin, T. J. (2004). The shareholder value society: A review of the changes in working conditions and inequality in the United States, 1976 to 2000. In: K. M. Neckerman (Ed.), *Social inequality* (pp. 401–432). New York, NY: Russell Sage Foundation.

Fox, M. B., & Heller, M. A. (2006). What is good corporate governance? In: M. B. Fox & M. Heller (Eds.), *Corporate governance lessons from transition economy reforms* (pp. 3–31). USA: Princeton University Press.

Freeman, E. R. (1984). *Strategic management – A stakeholder approach.* Boston: Pitman.

Freeman, E. R. (2008). Managing for stakeholders. In: A. J. Zakhem, D. E. Palmer & M. L. Stoll (Eds.), *Stakeholder theory – Essential readings in ethical leadership and management* (pp. 71–88). Amherst, NY: Prometheus Books.

Freeman, E. R., Harrison, J. S., Wicks, A. C., Parmar, B. L., & De Colle, S. (2010). *Stakeholder theory – The state of the art.* New York: Cambridge University Press.

Friedman, A. L., & Miles, S. (2002). Developing stakeholder theory. *Journal of Management Studies, 39*(1), 1–21.

Friedman, M. (1970). The social responsibility of business is to increase its profits. *The New York Times,* September 13.

Frooman, J. (1997). Socially irresponsible and illegal behavior and shareholder wealth: A meta-analysis of event studies. *Business & Society, 36,* 221–249.

George, B. (2003). Managing stakeholders vs responding to shareholders. *Strategy & Leadership, 31*(6), 36–40.

Gibson, M. S. (2003). Is corporate governance ineffective in emerging markets? *Journal of Financial and Quantitative Analysis, 38*(1), 231–250.

Gillan, S. L., & Starks, L. T. (2003). *Corporate governance, corporate ownership, and the role of institutional investors: A global perspective.* Working Paper Series 2003-01, John Weinberg Center for Corporate Governance, University of Delaware, DL. Retrieved from http://www.lerner.udel.edu/ccg/

Goodpaster, K. E. (1991). Business ethics and stakeholder analysis. *Business Ethics Quarterly, 1,* 53–73.

Gospel, H., & Pendleton, A. (2005). Corporate governance and labour management: An international comparison. In: H. Gospel & A. Pendleton (Eds.), *Corporate governance and labour management – An international comparison* (pp. 1–32). New York: Oxford University Press.

Gugler, K., Mueller, D. C., & Yurtoglu, B. B. (2004). Corporate governance and globalization. *Oxford Review of Economic Policy, 20*(1), 129–156.

Halpern, P. J. N. (2000). Systemic perspectives on corporate governance systems. In: S. S. Cohen & G. Boyd (Eds.), *Corporate governance and globalization – Long range planning issues* (pp. 1–58). Cheltenham, UK: Edward Elgar.

Hillman, A. J., & Keim, G. D. (2001). Shareholder value, stakeholder management, and social issues: What's the bottom line? *Strategic Management Journal, 22,* 125–139.

Hoskisson, R. E., Eden, L., Lau, C. M., & Wright, M. (2000). Strategy in emerging economies. *Academy of Management Journal, 43*(3), 249–267.

Ingley, C., & Karout, L. (2011). Corporate governance and the smaller firm. In: A. Tourani-Rad & C. Ingley (Eds.), *Handbook on emerging issues in corporate governance* (pp. 129–154). Singapore: World Scientific.

Johnson, S., Boone, P., Breach, A., & Friedman, E. (2000). Corporate governance in the Asian financial crisis. *Journal of Financial Economics, 58,* 141–186.

Johnston, M. J. (2003). Portfolio investment in emerging markets: An investor's perspective. In: P. K. Cornelius & B. Kogut (Eds.), *Corporate governance and capital flows in a global economy* (pp. 371–382). New York, NY: Oxford University Press.

Joo, T. W. (2010). Theories and models of corporate governance. In H. K. Baker, & R. Anderson (Eds.), *Corporate governance – A synthesis of theory, research, and practice* (pp. 157–174). The Robert W. Kolb Series in Finance. Hoboken, NJ: Wiley.

Judge, G. G., Griffiths, W. E., & Hill, R. C. (1985). *The theory and practice of econometrics* (2nd ed.). New York, NY: Wiley.

Kennedy, P. (2003). *A guide to econometrics* (5th ed.). USA: The MIT Press.

Kodama, M. (2008). Challenge to innovation through new governance. In: K. V. Lowery (Ed.), *Corporate governance in the 21st century* (pp. 3–12). New York, NY: Nova Science Publishers, Inc.

La Porta, R., Lopez-de-Silanes, F., Shleifer, A., & Vishny, R. (1998). Law and finance. *Journal of Political Economy, 106*(6), 1113–1155.

La Porta, R., Lopez-de-Silanes, F., Shleifer, A., & Vishny, R. (2000). Investor protection and corporate governance. *Journal of Financial Economics, 58*, 3–27.

Langtry, B. (1994). Stakeholders and the moral responsibilities of business. *Business Ethics Quarterly, 4*(4), 431–443.

Lazonick, W., & O'Sullivan, M. (2004). Maximizing shareholder value: A new ideology for corporate governance. In: T. Clarke (Ed.), *Theories of corporate governance – The philosophical foundations of corporate governance* (pp. 290–303). London: Routledge.

Logsdon, J. M. (2004). Global business citizenship: Applications to environmental issues. *Business and Society Review, 109*, 67–87.

Mallin, C. (2011). Corporate governance developments in the UK and the evolving role of institutional investors. In: A. Tourani-Rad & C. Ingley (Eds.), *Handbook on emerging issues in corporate governance* (pp. 155–168). Singapore: World Scientific.

Martin, R. (2010). The age of customer capitalism. *Harvard Business Review, January–February*, 58–65.

McGuire, J. B., Sundrgren, A., & Schneeweis, T. (1988). Corporate social responsibility and firm financial performance. *Academy of Management Journal, 31*(4), 854–872.

Miller, A. (1998). *Strategic management* (3rd ed.). USA: McGraw-Hill.

Mitchell, R. K., Agle, B. R., & Wood, D. J. (1997). Toward a theory of stakeholder identification and salience: Defining the principle of who and what really counts. *Academy of Management Journal, 22*(4), 853–886.

Morin, R. A., & Jarrell, S. L. (2001). *Driving shareholder value – Value-building techniques for creating shareholder wealth.* New York, NY: McGraw-Hill.

Moskowitz, M. (1972). Choosing socially responsible stocks. *Business and Society Review, 1*, 71–75.

Narayandas, D. (1998). Measuring and managing the benefits of customer retention: An empirical investigation. *Journal of Service Research, 1*(2), 1–10.

Nuevo, J., Ruohtula, S., & Schwalbach, J. (2001). Governance of a company in a fast changing business and technology environment. In: J. Schwalbach (Ed.), *Corporate governance – Essays in honor of Horst Albach* (pp. 14–24). Germany: Springer-Verlag.

OECD. (1998, April). Corporate governance – Improving competitiveness and access to capital in global markets – A report to the OECD by the business sector advisory group on corporate governance. Paris: OECD.

OECD. (2003). White Paper on Corporate Governance in Asia. Paris: OECD.

OECD. (2004). Corporate Governance – A survey of OECD countries. Paris: OECD.

OECD. (2004). Principles of Corporate Governance. Paris: OECD.

Polonsky, M. J. (1995). A Stakeholder theory approach to designing environmental marketing strategy. *Journal of Business & Industrial Marketing, 10*, 29–47.

Preble, J. F. (2005). Toward a comprehensive model of stakeholder management. *Business and Society Review, 110*(4), 407–431.

Preston, L. E., & Sapienza, H. J. (1990). Stakeholder management and corporate performance. *Journal of Behavioral Economics, 19*(4), 361–375.

Rappaport, A. (1998). *Creating shareholder value – A guide for managers and investors*. New York: The Free Press.

Rashid, K., & Islam, S. M. N. (2008). Corporate governance and firm value: Econometric modelling and analysis of emerging and developed financial markets. International Business Management, 23. Bingley, UK: Emerald.

Renders, A., & Gaeremynck, A. (2006). *Corporate governance and performance: Controlling for sample selection bias and endogeneity*. Working Paper, Katholieke Universiteit Leuven, Department of Accountancy, Finance and Insurance (AFI). Retrieved from http://www.econkuleuven.be/eng/tew/academic/afi/pdfs/AFI0606.pdf

Roche, J. (2005). *Corporate governance in Asia*. London: Routledge.

Rubach, M. J. (1999). Institutional shareholder activism – The changing face of corporate ownership. In: S. Bruchey (Ed.), *Garland studies on the financial sector of the American economy* (pp. 26–42). New York, NY: Garland.

Shaw, R. (2000). Shareholder value or stakeholder value? That is the question. In: L. Schuster (Ed.), *Shareholder value management in banks,* (pp. 36–52). New York: Palgrave Macmillan Press.

Shelton, J. R. (2001). Introduction. In *Corporate governance in Asia – A comparative perspective*. Paris: OECD.

Shleifer, A., & Vishny, R. W. (1997). A survey of corporate governance. *The Journal of Finance, 52*(2), 737–783.

Singh, A. (2003). Corporate governance, corporate finance and stock markets in emerging countries. *Journal of Corporate Law Studies, 41*(April), 41–72.

Sison, A. J. G. (2008). *Corporate governance and ethics – An Aristotelian perspective (new horizons in leadership studies)*. Cheltenham, UK: Edward Elgar.

Spence, L. J., & Rinaldi, L. (2010). Sainsbury's: Embedding sustainability within the supermarket supply chain. In: A. Hopwood, J. Unerman & J. Fries (Eds.), *Accounting for sustainability* (pp. 47–71). London: Eartscan.

Srivastava, R. K., Tasadduq, A. S., & Liam, F. (1999). Marketing, business processes, and shareholder value: An organizational embedded view of marketing activities and the discipline of marketing. *Journal of Marketing, 63*(Special Issue), 168–179.

Sternberg, E. (1997). The defects of stakeholder theory. *Corporate Governance – An International Review, 5*(1), 3–10.

Sternberg, E. (1998). *Corporate governance: Accountability in the marketplace*. The Institute of Economic Affairs. Great Britain: Hartington Fine Arts Limited.

Sternberg, E. (2000). *Just business – Business ethics in action* (2nd ed.). New York: Oxford University Press.

Sudit, E. F. (1996). *Effectiveness, quality, and efficiency: A management oriented approach*. Boston, MA: Kluwer Academic Publishers.

Ullmann, A. A. (1985). Data in search of a theory: A critical examination of the relationships among social performance, social disclosure, and economic performance of U.S. firms. *Academy of Management Review, 10*(3), 540–557.

Vance, S. C. (1975). Are socially responsible corporations good investment risks? *Management Review, 64*(8), 19–24.

Wales, A., Gorman, M., & Hope, D. (2010). *Big business, big responsibilities – From villains to visionaries: How companies are tackling the world's greatest challenges.* Great Britain: Palgrave Macmillan.

Wallace, J. S. (2003). Value maximization and stakeholder theory: Compatible or not? *Journal of Applied Corporate Finance, 15*(3), 120–127.

Wallace, P., & Zinkin, J. (2005). *Mastering business in Asia – Corporate governance.* Singapore; Hoboken, NJ: John Wiley & Sons (Asia) Pte Ltd.

Wasmer, K. J. (2003). *Increasing shareholder value.* Retrieved from http://www.wasmer.com/consulting_shareholder.asp

Willetts, D. (1997). The poverty of stakeholding. In: G. Kelly, D. Kelly & A. Gamble (Eds.), *Stakeholder capitalism* (pp. 20–28). New York: St. Martin's Press, Inc.

World Competitiveness Yearbook. (2008). *International Institute for Management Development,* Geneva.

Young, S. D., & O'Byrne, S. F. (2001). *EVA and value-based management – A practical guide to implementation.* USA: McGraw-Hill.

Youngmo, Y. (2001). Chaebol reform: The missing agenda. In *Corporate governance in Asia – A comparative perspective.* Paris: OECD.

APPENDIX

		List of Variables			
Variable	Description of variable	Measure	Source	Expected sign	Actual sign
SHOLDV	Shareholder value index	Shareholder value is efficiently managed	IMD[a]		
CREDMGMT	Managers' credibility index	Managers' credibility in society is strong	IMD	+	+
SOCRESP	Social responsibility index	Social responsibility of business leaders is high	IMD	+	+
CUSTOMER	Customer satisfaction index	Customer satisfaction is emphasized	IMD	+	+
INFL	Inflation rate	Annual percentage change in GDP deflator	The World Bank	+/−	+
LEGALREG	Legal regulation index	Legal regulation encourages the competitiveness of enterprises	IMD	+	+
GDPPC	Economic growth	Per capita GDP in US$ at Purchasing Power Parity	The World Bank	+	+
MRKTCAP	Financial development	Stock market Capitalization US$ billion	IMD	+	+
EMPLY	Employment	Employment rate as a percentage of population	IMD	+	+

[a]International Institute for Management Development.